UNDOING DRUGS

UNDOING DRUGS

Beyond Legalization

DANIEL K. BENJAMIN
ROGER LEROY MILLER

BasicBooks
A Division of HarperCollins*Publishers*

To our children,
with gratitude

Library of Congress Cataloging-in-Publication Data
Benjamin, Daniel K.
   Undoing drugs : beyond legalization / Daniel K. Benjamin,
Roger LeRoy Miller.
    p. cm.
   Includes bibliographical references and index.
   ISBN 0–465–08853–8
   1. Narcotics, Control of—United States. 2. Drug abuse—
United States. 3. Drug legalization—United States. I.
Miller, Roger LeRoy. II. Title.
   HV5825.B45 1991   91–70407
   363.4'5'0973—dc20   CIP

CONTENTS

CONTENTS

PREFACE

President Richard Nixon declared victory in the war on drugs in 1973. More recently, President George Bush has opined that at least we are making progress. Despite the optimism of our leaders, the war on drugs grinds on—as it has for most of the twentieth century.

The federal government's open warfare on drugs—and often on its own citizens—has produced little in the way of tangible benefits. Recognizing this, some observers, including elected public officials, judges, and former prosecuting attorneys, have argued that we should simply give up the fight, by legalizing drugs nationwide. Such proposals have been met with expressions of dismay and fierce opposition, even by knowledgeable individuals who are well aware of the failings of current policy. The result is a policy mired in compromise, in which the American people are forced to bear the personal, social, and economic costs of the war against drugs, even as they must continue to bear the costs of widespread drug use.

Today's policies are not working, yet the prospects of nationwide drug legalization seem too fearful to contemplate. And so we offer a path that leads beyond. We do not have the audacity to suggest that we have found a "solution" to drugs, for there is no silver bullet. Yet our extensive research on drugs and drug policy has suggested to us an alternative that will enable the American people to forge ahead with solutions.

In the course of our research we have benefited from discussions with numerous law-enforcement officials, including U.S. Customs and Coast Guard officials and drug-enforcement agents, federal and state judges, prosecuting attorneys, drug treatment specialists, physicians, and other participants in the war on drugs. In some measure, what you are about to read is the result of the countless hours they spent discussing with us their views, problems, and experiences. We owe them a great debt of thanks, and we hope that they can see the results of their efforts in the pages that follow.

We have also benefited from numerous discussions with our professional colleagues in economics departments, law schools, and public policy centers across the country. We extend our gratitude to them, as well as to Richard Hinson, who provided us with expert legal research, to Robbie Benjamin, who critically reviewed and proofread the manuscript at every stage of our work, and to Sue Jasin, who typed more drafts than she cares to remember. Additional proofreading was carried out by Marie-Christine Loiseau and W. Eric Hollowell.

Crossfire

The average American is caught in a crossfire. The combatants are drug dealers who prowl our neighborhoods, drug addicts who steal to support their habits, and drug-enforcement agents waging warfare upon dealers, addicts, and innocent citizens alike. You can try to protect yourself by digging a deeper hole, keeping your head low, and hoping for the best. Or you can place yourself on a higher level, from which you can look down and understand what is happening to America. When you do, you will discover that we have found the enemy, and it is us. We, the people of America, have let the dealers and addicts and drug agents take control, and only we—not the bureaucrats and politicians in Washington—can retake America.

If you are the average informed citizen, you already know a lot about the war on drugs. Bear with us, though, and take a moment to test your knowledge.

DRUG TEST

1. What percentage of illegal drugs in the United States is being consumed by blacks in the inner cities?

2. What is the most addictive drug yet discovered?

3. About a million drug arrests occur each year in America. How many of those million involve drug traffickers?

4. How much of the cocaine used in the United States is consumed by casual users?

5. What percentage of South American land suitable for growing coca leaves (the raw ingredient for cocaine) is actually being utilized?

6. Suppose the federal government decides to spend an additional $2 billion this year on its efforts to reduce cocaine imports. Based on our experiences with current and past federal efforts, what will be the resulting impact on the retail price of cocaine in the United States?

ANSWERS TO DRUG TEST

1. Inner-city blacks consume, at most, 20 percent of all illicit psychoactives. The amount is probably closer to 10 percent. Most of the $100 billion per year worth of illicit drugs are consumed by white, middle-class Americans.[1]

2. To date, the most addictive drug known is nicotine. Studies show that 80 percent of people who try smoking cigarettes for any length of time become addicted. This number, surprisingly, is much lower for crack cocaine.[2]

3. No more than 25 percent of Americans arrested for drugs are involved in "trafficking," and almost all of those are petty, small-time dealers. The remaining 75 percent of the arrests are for simple possession, often for marijuana.[3]

4. Casual users are responsible for at most 20 percent of total cocaine consumption; the rest is consumed by abusers and addicts. (And, incidentally, the same figures are true for alcohol.)[4]

5. There are 2.5 million square miles in South America alone that are suitable for coca production; only about 1,000 square miles, or 4/100ths of 1 percent, are now being used for coca production. Coca shrubs can be grown virtually anywhere between the Tropic of Cancer and the Tropic of Capricorn, so current production is actually an infinitesimally small percentage of potential worldwide production.[5]

6. The result will be a 2 to 4 percent increase in the street price of cocaine. The resulting decrease in cocaine consumption will be imperceptible (less than 1 percent).[6]

If you answered all six questions correctly, you have passed your drug test—which is more than we can say for any of the so-called experts who have taken this test before. For example, when we asked a group of legal experts what percentage of South American land suitable for coca production was actually being used, most of them guessed 30 percent or more. When we asked the same panel of experts where most of the consumption of illicit drugs is currently taking place, without fail they believed it was in the inner cities of America. It is such fundamental misunderstandings of the facts and analyses concerning America's war on drugs that have locked us into a war that cannot be won using today's policies. All Americans do, nonetheless, have to form a rational drug policy. There is a way to do so. There is a way to undo drugs and thereby retake America.

Most Americans know all too well that the current war on drugs isn't working. Drugs have taken over the streets of America. Drug lords flaunt our laws and imperil our safety. Drug-enforcement agents wage gun battles with drug dealers 365 days and nights a year. Addicts flood our emergency rooms and threaten the public health. Our judicial system is clogged with over a million drug cases each year, and our jails are overflowing with convicted drug users and dealers.

It is possible to retake America, but only if we truly understand the causes of the drug crisis and the costs of the current attempts to solve it. Most Americans seem to think that there are only two possible ways to handle America's drug problem: escalate the current war on drugs, or have the national government legalize all drugs. But there is a third alternative—one that is reasonable, practical, and perfectly legal. It is called the Constitutional Alternative. It is based on the unassailable foundations of our federal system of governing, which were established by the framers of the Constitution. The Constitutional Alternative carries with it over two centuries of evidence that it works. In the pages that follow you will see that the Constitutional Alternative is the only viable solution to America's war on drugs.

Nationwide legalization won't work. It is not politically possible, because there is no national consensus supporting it. A congressional act or a Supreme Court decision that legalizes all drugs everywhere in the United States would remove the fundamental right of individuals to be governed the way they want to be governed. Public opinion polls reveal that a majority of Americans want to live in communities in which drugs such as cocaine and heroin are illegal, and in which the penalties for their consumption and trafficking are severe. Under full-scale nationwide legalization, those individuals will have no-where to turn. Moreover, full-scale nationwide legalization of drugs will fail to protect our children from drugs, just as current drug policy fails to protect them, for neither our current policy nor blanket legalization offers any effective incentives *not* to sell drugs to children.

The alternative—a true national get-tough policy—won't work either. The fourteen-year Great Experiment from 1920 to 1933 certainly proved that point. No matter how much the national government spent on enforcement of Prohibition, the production, trafficking, and consumption of alcoholic beverages continued to rise. Similarly, government spending on the war on drugs has escalated every year for more than a decade; while casual use of certain drugs, such as cocaine, does seem no longer to be growing, the total use of illegal psychoactives continues to climb. The crime associated with that industry has mushroomed to staggering proportions. Parents are now buying their children bulletproof clothing in case they get caught in the crossfire on their way to and from school.

The current war on drugs is a perfect illustration of the *balloon principle:* Push on one part of the balloon and it simply spreads out in another direction. Get tough with one geographical area where drugs are being sold, and they show up elsewhere. Wipe out one field of marijuana and another is put into production. Destroy ten fields of coca plants in Bolivia or Peru and twenty others will show up somewhere else, maybe in Guatemala, maybe even in the United States. (Yes, they grow it here, too.) Force Turkey to stop its production of opium poppy plants and more are grown in Mexico. Force Mexico to shut its poppy production down and more comes in from Southeast Asia. Stop the flow of opiates from Asia and, lo and behold, opium poppy plants start growing in the United States. (Don't laugh; they do already.)

Stop the importation of marijuana from Mexico and Asia, and homegrown varieties that are even more powerful take over. (America produces the highest-potency, finest-quality marijuana in the world today—much of it in our national parks). Send in the National Guard to eradicate outdoor crops and the growers simply move their operations inside.

Effectively eliminate the importation of cocaine and heroin, suppress the raw-material production in the United States completely, and synthetic cocaine, synthetic heroin, and worse will be sold on the streets of America. Synthetic heroin roughly 100 times more powerful than natural heroin already exists, as does synthetic cocaine. The only reason they are not very popular is because they are too expensive—right now, that is.

Our prison population is at record levels and our jails are literally overflowing, yet those who seek a tougher drug-enforcement policy want us to arrest and jail more citizens. As you found out in the answers to the drug test, the majority of arrests are for simple possession of illicit drugs. What we do with those users who we incarcerate is equivalent to sending them on for advanced training in drugs and crime. When we put a pot smoker in jail he ends up in an environment in which every illicit drug known to humans is available. There probably isn't a prison in America where a prisoner can't, at the right price, get an illegal psychoactive. While in jail, the pot smokers can also get a full-fledged education in any imaginable aspect of criminal activity. Incarcerate a casual drug user and what you get in return is a well-schooled criminal who has been able to experiment with much more powerful drugs.

It is clear that something must be done, but it certainly isn't an escalation in the current war on drugs using current federal policy. By the time you finish reading this book you will have recognized the only viable alternative. The crux of the current failure in the war on drugs lies in the fact that we have a policy of uniformity imposed upon a nation of diversity. America is comprised of an incredibly heterogeneous set of individuals who have radically different attitudes toward the best policies for dealing with drugs. Indeed, the spectrum of opinions held by American voters and taxpayers ranges from the view that drug users should be subject to the death penalty to the opinion that all drugs, no matter how harmful, should be legally available. Yet drug strategy in America is fundamentally a policy of the federal government. It is a monopoly policy driven by decisions made in Washington, D.C., rather than in the states and cities and neighborhoods in which we live. As such, drug policy in America goes too far for many of us and not far enough for the rest of us. Forged by the forces of compromise at the national level, it is an ungainly and ineffective strategy that imposes tremendous costs on all Americans, while accomplishing almost none of the goals we seek.

Our proposal, the Constitutional Alternative, necessitates only one simple change in current federal drug law: an elevated legal status and power for state and local jurisdictions in the war on drugs. This move will eliminate the federal monopoly on drug policy, at the same time that it will force state and local governments to undertake new initiatives that match the preferences and circumstances of their citizens. We currently employ such a system with respect to a wide variety of social, legal, political, and economic issues: when, where, and by whom alcoholic beverages may be sold; the rules of the road; health requirements in restaurants; the legal circumstances of marriage and divorce and the methods of certifying and recording births and deaths; the conditions for sale of prescription pharmaceuticals; and the legal minimum age for purchasing cigarettes. And despite the simplicity of the legal aspects of the change, the substantive, real-life effects will be profoundly beneficial. The Constitutional Alternative will offer Americans the opportunity to *choose* among government drug policies rather than having a single policy—too harsh for some, too weak for others—imposed upon them. It will also enable Americans to develop government strategies that conform to their wishes and the wishes of their families, friends, and neighbors, rather than having a single policy imposed upon them by political forces over which they have no control. And finally, the Constitutional Alternative will enable the American people to do what they do best—find innovative solutions to seemingly intractable problems, by utilizing the strengths of collective action, at the same time that they protect their long-cherished individual freedoms.

Our proposed course of action isn't perfect, but then no alternative is. Indeed, one of the major mistakes of policy analysis involves "the grass is always greener" syndrome. We must compare the real with the real, not the real with the ideal. It does no good to think in terms of a world in which drug use is nonexistent. That would be the same thing as hypothesizing a world in which there were never any car accidents, people never overate, or disease was nonexistent. A valid comparison contrasts current drug policy—which most agree is a disaster—with the feasible alternatives, each of which will carry certain costs and certain benefits. Only through the analysis of those costs and benefits can we ever hope to come up with the best alternative for America right now.

As you will see, the Constitutional Alternative will lead to innovation, experimentation, and improvement. As a result of the Constitutional Alternative:

- The backbone of the organized drug gangs will be crushed.
- The possibility of widespread armed intervention by the U.S. military in South and Central America will be sharply reduced.
- Crime rates will diminish across the land.
- Innovation and improvement in drug-treatment programs will accelerate.
- Corruption among our law-enforcement officials will drop precipitously.
- Life in the inner cities will be transformed almost overnight.
- Our children will begin to be truly protected from the scourge of drugs.

Now settle back and take a ride with us, first through a bit of eye-opening history and then through a revealing assessment of what has happened to this once-rational, once-great nation of ours. Then you will see and agree that the Constitutional Alternative is the only way out of America's dilemma.

The time is now. We can undo drugs and retake America.

PART ONE

THE LIMITS OF CONTROL

CHAPTER I

······························

Roots

IN SEPTEMBER 1899, AMERICAN NEWSPAPERS AND MAGAZINES ADVER-
tised a variety of invigorating "tonics" guaranteed to relieve fatigue,
as well as a miraculous new cough suppressant only recently introduced to the American market. The tonics contained cocaine, the
cough remedy was heroin-based, and the ads were placed by some
of the day's leading suppliers of these drugs, including both the Parke-
Davis pharmaceutical company and the Bayer chemical company.

In September 1990, American magazines and newspapers carried
"advertisements" of a different sort regarding cocaine and heroin—
news reports that schoolchildren in New York City had recently
begun wearing $450 bulletproof vests to school.[1] Parents had pur-
chased the vests in an attempt to protect their children from stray
bullets. The bullets were being fired by some of the day's leading
suppliers of cocaine and heroin—Jamaican posses and Chinese
tongs—and by their chief adversaries, the police.

Over the past century, American society has been transformed from
one in which drugs such as heroin, cocaine, and marijuana were
among the principal remedies for pain, depression, and despair to
one in which these same drugs are now among the principal causes
of anguish, fear, pessimism—and death. Neither the basic nature of
drugs nor that of the American people has changed in the intervening
years; yet as we approach the end of the twentieth century, there is
no doubt that the relationship between drugs and the American people is fundamentally, agonizingly different.

A century ago, Americans used drugs for a variety of reasons. Some
drugs were believed to be of medicinal value, others produced plea-

sure, and still others had the salubrious capacity both to do good and to make one feel good. Today, Americans choose to consume drugs for exactly the same reasons, but we are now forced to take into account a factor largely absent from the considerations of our grandparents and great-grandparents.

Our ancestors chose to consume drugs (or refrained from consuming them) based upon what they perceived to be the beneficial consequences and adverse effects of those drugs. Often they consulted with their physicians, pharmacists, or trusted friends and relatives; sometimes they heeded the advice of the firms that sold the drugs; or perhaps they even listened to the opinions of public officials. But the decisions they made were fundamentally their decisions, and so long as the decisions did not adversely affect the welfare of other individuals, they felt justified in exercising that freedom.

The prerogatives of our grandparents are gone. We still make choices about drugs, but these choices are no longer solely ours, for we are constrained by the prior choices that government—most notably the federal government—has made about drugs. More importantly, our choices about a host of matters *other* than drugs are also constrained by the decisions that government has made about drugs, for those decisions can deprive us of the choice of where to live, how to live, and, indeed, even whether we shall live—a point surely not lost on flak jacket–clad children on their way to school.

PRELIMINARIES

Psychoactives are chemicals that affect the brain, yielding changes in emotions, perceptions, and behavior. The most widely used psychoactives—caffeine, nicotine, and alcohol—are such an ingrained part of American life that referring to them as "psychoactives" may seem grandiose. Yet all three are chemicals that affect the brain and produce effects that most of us associate with "drugs." Just as crack cocaine and methamphetamine are potent stimulants, so too are caffeine and nicotine. The power of alcohol as a depressant is equaled only by barbiturates, opiates (including heroin), and modern tranquilizers. The best-known hallucinogens are LSD, PCP, and mescaline, but nicotine can produce comparable effects when ingested in sufficiently massive doses. We have all heard of cocaine-induced heart seizures and lethal overdoses of heroin or sleeping pills; yet nicotine, caffeine, and alcohol are all potentially deadly.[2]

The ability of psychoactives to alter our emotions, perceptions, and behavior has made their use popular among humans since fermentation was first discovered some 10,000 years ago. Over the ensuing millennia, humans have experimented with every psychoactive they have encountered—or concocted. These experiences have taught us that psychoactives can have both beneficial and adverse effects, and that sensible decisions about using them require a sense of balance. When the results of consuming particular psychoactives have been pleasurable or productive, their use has spread. When the outcomes have been destructive or deadly, the human instinct for survival has mitigated—albeit not eliminated—the damage.*

Until recently, decisions about the use of psychoactives have largely been left up to the individual or family group. To the extent that government has become involved, it has chiefly been to levy taxes on drug use, or to control usage so as to minimize adverse effects on innocent parties. While every principal psychoactive, including caffeine, nicotine, and alcohol, has been prohibited somewhere at some time, outright bans have been sporadic and largely ad hoc, and usually have been discarded in short order.

During the past century, however, governments concerned about the potential adverse effects of psychoactives have increasingly attempted to eliminate (rather than control) their use by imposing sweeping, nationwide prohibitions on them. Although many nations have turned to this approach, it has been the United States government, above all others, that has championed the outright elimination of use as the principal means of dealing with psychoactives. It has been the U.S. government that has pressed for the strongest international drug treaties over the years. It was the U.S. government that took the lead in banning opiates, cocaine, and marijuana. And it has been the U.S. government that has coerced so many nations throughout the Far East, the Middle East, and South and Central America to alter their domestic policies and drug laws to suit the prohibitionist desires of the U.S. government. Ultimately, then, it has been the federal government of the United States that has been pivotal in the creation of what we now call the "war on drugs."

*There is a more detailed discussion of the history of psychoactives in Appendix A.

LESSONS OF HISTORY

All psychoactives—ranging from nicotine and alcohol to cocaine and heroin—share this feature: Their consumption brings together a willing seller with a willing buyer, resulting in an act of "mutually beneficial exchange" (at least in the view of the parties involved). Partly because of this fact, sweeping nationwide attempts to prohibit the consumption of these goods are singularly costly to society. The costs of today's drug wars in America include not merely the $20 billion or $30 billion we are now spending each year in our efforts to interdict drug suppliers and users. The costs of the drug wars also include rising violent crime; the paralysis of our legal system; corruption; adverse health consequences of epidemic proportions in our nation's inner cities; and the erosion of our civil liberties.

Even the most ardent drug warriors acknowledge the existence of such costs. But they argue that many of these costs arise chiefly because matters are not yet quite "under control." Thus, it is said, once we convince the drug-runners that society is serious about "saying no" to drugs, the adverse effects of today's drug wars will fade. Alternatively, but no less frequently, the drug warriors maintain that the violence, disease, corruption, and disillusion that accompany today's drug wars are somehow unique, occasioned only by the latest breed of drug smugglers, or the new drugs currently in vogue. Thus, it is argued, if we merely eradicate this drug cartel or that drug, we shall be able to rid ourselves of the scourge.

In fact, the costly consequences of today's war on drugs will not go away, whatever the rectitude with which the war is fought, and regardless of how many resources are poured into the battle. Today's strategies are the strategies of the past, and history has proven them futile. The philosopher George Santayana remarked that "Those who cannot remember the past are condemned to repeat it." The lesson of history is simple: The consequences of today's drug policies are unique neither to our nation nor to our time, and thus they cannot simply be avoided by well-intentioned, progressive, and committed policy makers. The consequences are inherent in both the nature of psychoactives and the nature of the misguided national policies being pursued. Psychoactives are a fact of life; their use and abuse are costly, as are society's attempts to control them. The issue is not whether these costs must be borne but how high they will be. And today's policies guarantee that the costs will be far higher than necessary.

We begin by sketching the fundamental features of the process of enforcement and response—using three historical episodes to illustrate that whenever and wherever sweeping, nationwide prohibition is attempted, the consequences are likely to be the same.

1. Prior to World War I, cocaine and opiates were generally legal in this country, readily available over the counter or even by mail order. Both classes of drugs were outlawed with the passage of the Harrison Narcotics Act in 1914. This act, which transformed American society from one in which these drugs were legal to one in which they are not, helped send us down the path toward today's drug wars.[3]

2. The enactment of the Eighteenth Amendment in 1920 began the era known as Prohibition, whose parallels to the present are simply too compelling to ignore. America's decision to prohibit the use or sale of alcoholic beverages, the experiences of the ensuing fourteen years, and the decision to repeal Prohibition in 1933 vividly reveal the fatal flaws that are also found in today's drug policies.[4]

3. In 1985, Soviet premier Mikhail Gorbachev decided to restrain drastically and forcibly the consumption of alcohol by Russians. Although alcohol was not prohibited per se, its (legal) production was curtailed so sharply that the distinction became close to irrelevant. The responses by thirsty Soviet citizens and ingenious Communist entrepreneurs again illustrate the universal consequences of government stepping too intrusively between citizens and their psychoactives of choice.[5]

SUPPLY-SIDE ENFORCEMENT

The consumption of most psychoactives is normally preceded by the act of voluntary exchange: A willing seller provides a willing buyer with the drug of choice. Preventing such exchanges is thus necessary to prevent consumption. When the government tries to prohibit voluntary exchange, officials must consider whether to target the seller or the buyer. In most cases, and certainly when psychoactives are involved, the government cracks down most heavily on sellers, because this creates the most impact for the enforcement dollar. Manufacturers or importers of most goods usually supply a host of wholesalers, each servicing many retailers, who in turn each supply numerous consumers. By targeting suppliers, the government can prevent several—or even several thousand—transactions from taking place down the line, making this approach much more cost-effective than going after the buyers one by one. This is not to say that the authorities ignore the consumers of illegal goods; indeed, "sting" operations, in which the police pose as illicit sellers, often make the headlines. Nevertheless, most enforcement efforts focus on the supply side, and so too shall we.

When the Harrison Act was passed in 1914, it sharply limited the distribution of cocaine and opiates, with an eye toward radically curtailing their consumption to "therapeutic" uses only. To accomplish this goal, the law focused on manufacturers, importers, and distributors of the drugs, requiring them to register their activities with the federal government, pay special taxes, and sharply limit distribution. Suppliers who did not comply were threatened with substantial legal penalties.

The initial enforcement of Prohibition similarly focused on the supply side. Most domestic distillers, vintners, brewers, and importers of alcoholic beverages were large, easily identifiable firms. The federal government told the firms to cease operations or face substantial legal penalties, including fines and imprisonment.

Most direct of all was the 1985 Soviet effort to curtail the use of alcoholic beverages. Since the manufacture and distribution of alcohol (predominantly vodka) were conducted by government-owned firms, the central government simply directed that production be cut sharply, and prices hiked 15 to 25 percent. In addition, the government closed many of its sales outlets, and allowed the remainder to sell spirits only between 2:00 P.M. and 7:00 P.M.

Ultimately, the objective of supply-oriented measures is to reduce the consumption of psychoactives by making them more difficult to obtain and available only at higher prices. When suppliers are large, reputable, easily identifiable firms, the impact is usually quite direct: Such firms simply can't afford the bad publicity and risks to their legitimate activities that would occur if they tried to sell illegal goods. They usually just obey the law, employing their commercial skills elsewhere.

Less visible suppliers are often tempted to remain in business, especially since the departure of their larger rivals increases sales opportunities for them. Even so, the illegal nature of the business hampers their endeavors to supply customers, because the risk of fines, jail sentences, and possibly even violence all become added costs of doing business. Firms unwilling or unable to incur these costs simply leave the business, turning their talents to other activities; those who remain must resort to clandestine (and costly) means to hide their operations from the authorities. Moreover, sellers typically must restrict the circle of buyers with whom they are willing to deal, so as to minimize the chances that a customer is a cop. At every turn, customers find the illegal substance more difficult to obtain, and more expensive as well.

In the case of Gorbachev's efforts to curtail Russian drinking, reducing the supply of booze was fairly simple: The state monopoly cut its operations and hiked its prices. In the United States, many of the manufacturers and importers of cocaine and opiates in 1914, and alcohol in 1920, were sufficiently large and well known that ignoring government orders to halt or curtail operations was not an option. They simply obeyed. Smaller firms that felt they could escape detection by the authorities opted to remain in business—discreetly, of course. Even here, the law took its toll, as it does in today's drug wars: Government enforcement efforts pushed up suppliers' operating costs across the board, and at any given price, less of the product was available. This resulted in higher prices for the psychoactives, coupled with a rise in the difficulty of finding someone willing to supply them.

The rise in the monetary and nonmonetary costs of obtaining the illegal goods is exactly what enforcement officials are after, for the consumers of psychoactives behave according to what economists call the Law of Demand: The higher the cost of a good, the smaller the amount consumed. The immediate impact of enforcement efforts directed at sellers is thus to reduce the consumption of the illegal good by buyers. In America, the consumption of alcoholic beverages fell more than 70 percent during the first year of Prohibition. In Russia, consumption of vodka dropped 40 percent during the first eighteen months of Gorbachev's program, and overall consumption of state-supplied alcoholic beverages fell 56 percent. The decline in cocaine and opiate use following the passage of the Harrison Act was less pronounced, because the law initially did not prohibit the drugs outright, but simply made them inordinately difficult to obtain. Nevertheless, the law's impact on supplies and thus consumption was quickly evident: Doctors reported a sharp increase in the number of patients seeking relief from addiction, and long lines formed at public clinics where morphine and heroin could still legally be obtained.

If this were the end of the process, the story of prohibiting the use of psychoactives would be short and sweet. The requisite laws are passed, a modest investment in law enforcement is made, and consumption declines accordingly. Given the capacity of the psychoactives for producing physical and psychological damage, stringent government controls on their use, and possibly even prohibition of them, would seem to be the obvious public policy approach. As it turns out, however, psychoactives provide plenty of opportunities for the proverbial slip 'twixt cup and lip.

HARD LIQUOR, HIGH STAKES

The exodus of suppliers that initially accompanies alcohol or drug prohibition not only creates problems for consumers but also offers profit opportunities to a new breed of supplier. Legal commodities are generally supplied by firms and individuals that are relatively proficient at legal means of competition. In the ordinary course of business, customers are attracted by low prices and high-quality products, convenient locations and hours of operation, cheerful, helpful salespeople, and so forth. Firms that are efficient at providing these features thrive in the supply of legal commodities, but are the first ones driven from the market when a commodity is made illegal. Their departure reduces competition, driving the price of the newly illegal good still higher.

The high prices and lack of competition that initially follow prohibition attract new suppliers who tend to differ in character from the distributors they replace. Quite simply, since the good in question is now illegal, people who are good at conducting illegal activities will be drawn to the business of supplying the good. Some may have an existing criminal record and be relatively unconcerned about adding to it. Others may have developed skills in evading detection and prosecution while engaged in other criminal activities. Some may simply look at the illegal activity as another means of thumbing their nose at society. The general point is that *when an activity is made illegal, people who are good at being criminals are attracted to that activity.*

For a variety of reasons, the people attracted to the trade in illegal psychoactives are also likely to be adept at violence, and are given incentives to employ their talents in this dimension. Whenever exchange occurs (legally or otherwise) one of the parties may find it advantageous to renege on the deal; the seller may deliver a product that fails to match the quantity or quality promised, or the buyer may fail to pay. For legal goods, the risk of such cheating can sometimes be avoided by establishing a regular, long-term buyer-seller relationship. The value of such a continuing relationship exceeds what either party could gain from cheating on any one transaction, and so the individual transactions become effectively self-enforcing. Another way to avoid the risk of being cheated on a transaction is to deal with parties who have established reputations in their dealings with others. Reputable buyers and sellers will avoid cheating even new customers, because to do so would damage their credibility with other traders once word got out. Finally, even if measures such as these fail and cheating results, the damaged party may be able to appeal to the legal authorities for redress.

For the buyers and sellers of illegal goods, all of these means of preventing cheating are frustrated. Attempts to establish long-term trading relationships are often disrupted by the police, who are so inconsiderate as to haul one or both of the parties off to jail. Reputations are more difficult to establish, partly because advertising is likely to attract more cops than customers. Moreover, buyers and sellers actually have incentives to *hide* their identities from each other, so that if one is subsequently arrested, he or she cannot reveal the identity of the other to police. Finally, of course, in the event that one party to an illegal transaction cheats, the other party will hardly wish to appeal to the legal authorities for assistance. Illegal contracts are not enforceable at law, and besides, few bootleggers or drug dealers would be so foolish as to complain to the police that their buyer walked off without paying.

Similar considerations make legal means of competition more costly in the illegal drug trade. Advertising and establishing convenient, regular times and places of business increase the chances of detection and prosecution. Price cutting becomes a less effective means of competition, because information about the existence of lower prices is so difficult to disseminate. The high cost of legal means of competition and contract enforcement induces buyers and sellers of illegal drugs to turn to illegal means, the ultimate and most effective form of which is violence. Thus, not only do people who are attracted to the industry tend to be skilled in committing violence, but they are given added incentives to use those skills.

The association of violence with the prohibition of psychoactives is heightened by another factor. The illegal status of drugs today (or alcohol sixty years ago) produces a peculiar cost structure, as the criminal prosecution "tax" levied on suppliers ends up being applied unevenly. Some sellers are caught, while others are not. Those who are detected and prosecuted are big losers. On average, market prices of psychoactives will rise to the point where profit margins compensate suppliers for the risk of punishment. But this means that those who happen to be lucky enough or skillful enough to avoid prosecution end up earning enormous profits. During Prohibition, for example, a bottle of gin that sold for about $1 in Ontario, Canada, was worth $6 if successfully marketed across the river in Detroit. A gallon of beer that could be brewed legally in Canada at a cost of about 25 cents sold for $3.20 when smuggled across the U.S. border. Profit margins like these turned what had been a staid business into vicious, high-stakes warfare.

Consider a Prohibition-era bootlegger running truckloads of booze across the border from Canada. His raw material, which consisted of 500 cases of scotch whiskey legally imported from Britain into Canada, cost about $50,000 per load, measured in terms of today's dollars. Smuggled across the border into Detroit and sold by the bottle at retail, the whiskey was worth approximately $500,000. Trucked to New York or Chicago and sold by the drink in any of hundreds of speakeasies, the whiskey would fetch over $1 million in today's dollars.

Profits like these naturally attracted attention, from police and competitors alike. At the local level, the police often proved the less troublesome of the two; a wad of well-placed cash often could ensure cooperation. It has been estimated that at the height of Prohibition, between one-third and one-half of the entire Chicago police force was "on the take"; nationwide, perhaps as many as one out of ten policemen in major cities received payments from bootleggers or speakeasy operators. After all, Eliot Ness's famous Untouchables did not receive their nickname because they were social outcasts or inflicted with some unspeakable disease. The name's origin lay in the fact that they, unlike many local police, resisted the "touch" of bootleggers' bribes.

With so many police on the take, competitors posed the major obstacles to illicit success. Every truckload delivered by a rival meant less profits for one's own organization. Bloody hijackings of booze-laden trucks became sufficiently common that bootleggers began moving liquor across the border only in heavily armed convoys, often via back roads on which cooperative local police were stationed to ensure safe passage. Drive-by shootings, popular among cocaine dealers today, originated during Prohibition. In New York City alone, the period saw more than 1,000 gangland murders, most of them believed to be related to bootleg liquor. Even the infamous 1929 St. Valentine's Day Massacre, in which Al Capone's men machine-gunned six members of the Bugs Moran gang, was simply part of Capone's efforts to consolidate control over the Chicago market.

Nationwide, the murder rate hit record levels during Prohibition, rising to a level 25 percent above the years preceding 1920.[6] When Prohibition was finally repealed, the murder rate declined for eleven consecutive years. Assaults with firearms followed a similar pattern, rising sharply with the onset of Prohibition and falling abruptly with its repeal. In 1933, the last year of Prohibition, there were more than 12,000 homicides nationwide and nearly 8,000 assaults with firearms; within eight years after Repeal, both figures had declined by more than one-third. No one doubted the source of this mayhem. As the police commissioner of Chicago put it in 1929, "Prohibition is the root of these gang killings, and despite the most vigorous efforts that can be employed to stop them, they probably will continue as long as [it] is a law." The Thompson submachine gun—Capone's favorite— reigned supreme. It took the repeal of Prohibition to dethrone it.

BLIND DRUNK

Law officers' attempts to drive sellers of illegal goods out of business have other potent effects. At recent wholesale prices, $50,000 worth of cocaine weighs about 5 pounds; $50,000 worth of imported marijuana weighs almost 150 pounds.* As any drug smuggler worth his salt can tell you, hiding 5 pounds of contraband is a lot easier than hiding 150 pounds. The same fact is true at all levels of distribution. Thus, to avoid detection and prosecution, suppliers of illegal goods direct their efforts toward the more valuable versions of their product, which in the case of psychoactives means the more potent varieties. Bootleggers during Prohibition concentrated on hard liquor, rather than beer and wine. Even today, illegal "moonshine" typically has

---

*The same dollar amount of the more potent (and thus more valuable) domestic marijuana weighs only about thirty-five pounds, which is one of the attractions of dealing in domestic rather than imported pot.

an alcohol content one-third to one-half higher than that of legal hard liquor. After narcotics became illegal in this country eighty years ago, importers switched from opium to its more valuable and more potent derivative, heroin.

The move to more potent versions of illegal commodities is enhanced by enforcement activities directed against users. Not only do users, like suppliers, find it easier to hide the more potent versions, but the structure of user penalties also encourages the use of more potent psychoactives. The penalties for possessing a given physical amount of an illegal psychoactive are commonly the same regardless of potency. During Prohibition, for example, a bottle of wine and a bottle of more potent hard liquor were equally illegal. Today, the possession of one gram of, say, 90 percent pure cocaine brings the same penalty as the possession of one gram of 10 percent pure cocaine. Given the physical quantities, there is a fixed cost (the legal penalty) associated with being caught, regardless of the potency of the substance. Hence, the structure of legal penalties raises the relative cost of less potent versions, encouraging users to use more potent versions: heroin instead of opium, hard liquor instead of beer.

The impact of the change in relative costs during Prohibition was striking. Overall, Prohibition managed to reduce per capita alcohol consumption by about 30 percent.[7] Across the different categories of alcohol, however, the impact was singularly uneven. Consumption of beer, for example, initially dropped more than 90 percent, and recovered only modestly during the remaining years of Prohibition. Few bootleggers or drinkers were willing to assume the legal risks of bothering with beer. Wine consumption also dropped sharply when Prohibition was instituted. The higher alcohol content of wine, however, made it a more appealing product for both suppliers and consumers. Thus, consumption soon began to rise again, and by the time of Repeal it was greater than it had been before Prohibition. The pattern for distilled spirits (hard liquor) was even more pronounced: The passage of Prohibition caused an initial decline in consumption, but by the mid-1920s consumption of hard liquor had risen to levels above those observed before 1920. Indeed, it is estimated that during the last five years of Prohibition, per capita consumption of hard liquor was higher than at any time during the sixty years before or since! Suppliers and consumers alike treated the adage "hang for a penny, hang for a pound" as though it had been written with them in mind.

Penalties against users also encourage a change in the *nature* of usage. Prior to 1914, cocaine was legal in this country and used openly as a mild stimulant, much as people use caffeine today. Cocaine was even an ingredient in the original formulation of Coca-Cola.[8] This "extensive" type of usage—small, regular doses spaced over long intervals—becomes more expensive when a substance is made illegal. Such usage is more likely to be detected by the authorities than is "intensive" usage (a large dose consumed at once), because the drug is possessed longer and must be accessed more frequently. Thus, when a substance is made illegal there is an incentive for consumers to switch toward usage that is more intensive. In the case of cocaine, rather than ingesting it orally in a highly diluted liquid solution, as was done before 1914, people switched to snorting or even injecting it after the passage of the Harrison Act. During Prohibition, people dispensed with cocktails before dinner each night; instead, on the less frequent occasions when they drank, they more often drank to get drunk. The same phenomenon is observed today among teenagers who (illegally) consume alcohol: People under the age of twenty-one use alcoholic beverages less frequently than do people over the age of twenty-one, but when they do drink, they are more likely to drink to get drunk. Even Communists seem to respond to incentives. During the first two years of Gorbachev's war on vodka, the number of cases of drunkenness on the job more than doubled.

DEAD DRUNK

Not surprisingly, the suppliers of illegal commodities are reluctant to advertise their wares openly. The police are every bit as capable of reading billboards and watching TV as are potential customers. Suppliers are also reluctant to establish easily recognizable identities and regular places and hours of business, because to do so increases the chances of being caught by the police. In effect, information about prices and qualities of the products being sold goes underground, often with unfortunate effects for consumers.

In choosing legal goods, consumers have several sources of information: friends, advertisements, and personal experience. Legal goods can be trademarked, so that the courts will protect them from being copied. Easily identified brands let consumers be made aware of the quality and price of each product, via advertisements and the recommendations of friends. If experience does not jibe with anticipation, they can assure themselves of no further encounter with the unsatisfactory product by never buying that brand again.

When a general class of products becomes illegal, there are fewer ways of obtaining information. Brand names are no longer protected by law, so counterfeiting of well-known names ensues. When products do not meet expectations, it is more difficult for consumers to punish suppliers. Commonly, the result of these forces is degradation of product quality, and a rise in uncertainty about the nature of that quality. The consequences for consumers of the illegal goods are often unpleasant, sometimes fatally so.

Today, alcoholic beverages are heavily advertised to establish their brand names, and are manufactured and distributed by reputable firms. Customers can readily punish suppliers for any deviation from what is expected in terms of potency or quality by withdrawing their business, telling their friends, or even bringing a lawsuit. Similar circumstances prevailed before Prohibition and, prior to 1914, also governed the sale of many products containing opium and cocaine.

When a good is made illegal, it becomes much more difficult for consumers to punish suppliers who behave irresponsibly or maliciously. The consequences are often tragic. During Prohibition, consumers of alcohol often did not know exactly what they were buying, or where to find the supplier the next day if they were dissatisfied. Fly-by-night operators sometimes adulterated liquor with methyl alcohol—the kind used in portable cooking stoves. In extremely small concentrations, the addition gave watered-down booze more "kick"; in only slightly higher concentrations, methyl alcohol could blind or even kill the unsuspecting consumer. Even in "reputable" speakeasies (those likely to be in business at the same location the next day), bottles bearing the labels of high-priced foreign whiskeys were refilled repeatedly with either locally (and illegally) produced "rotgut" or cheap bootleg imports until, ultimately, their labels wore off.

We noted earlier that legal penalties for the users of illegal goods encourage them to use more potent forms and to use them more intensively. Adding to these facts the uncertain quality and potency of the illegal products creates a deadly combination. During Prohibition, the death rate from acute alcohol poisoning (overdose) was more than thirty times higher than it is today. During 1927 alone, 12,000 people died from acute alcohol poisoning, and many thousands more were blinded or killed by contaminated booze.[9]

Similar tragedies befell Soviet consumers after Gorbachev began his crackdown on drinking. Unable to get legal booze, consumers turned to an incredible array of "surrogate" substances, some of them used to increase the kick of home-brewed liquor, others consumed straight in place of hard-to-get vodka. The list of surrogates is staggering: after-shave lotion, antifreeze, brake fluid, cough medicine, disinfectant, glue, hair tonic, insecticide, and nail polish. Industrial-grade alcohol, methanol, and other toxic spirits were stolen and consumed. Perfume sales in the Soviet Union soared 40 percent between 1985 and 1987, due not to a rise in romance but to the fact that perfumes are alcohol-based. Hospitals even experienced shortages of isopropyl (rubbing) alcohol, which was stolen for use in home brewing.

The results were lethal. In 1987 alone, 40,000 Russians were poisoned by drinking surrogate-based concoctions; 11,000 of them died. In one episode, a farm mechanic and a school principal died after drinking black-market booze that was subsequently shown to contain industrial-grade alcohol. The 100 guests at the funeral unsuspectingly drank the same brew, and many of them died as well. Clearly, *caveat emptor* (let the buyer beware) is a warning to be taken seriously if one is consuming an illegal product.

LEGALLY DRUNK

The effects of prohibiting psychoactives—violence, corruption, intoxication, overdose, death by adulteration, and the like—can occur, of course, only if the police spend a fair amount of their time actually enforcing the prohibition. Both the extent and the nature of these law-enforcement activities turn out to have some peculiar consequences of their own.

Since the police, the prosecutors, and the courts are busy making sure that people are imbibing Shirley Temples instead of Bloody Marys, they don't have much time left to enforce the other laws of the land. This creates problems even in a police state such as the Soviet Union. When Premier Gorbachev shortened the hours of state liquor stores during his crackdown on booze, long lines (and short tempers) formed at the stores during the five hours a day they remained open (the Moscow News reported that by 1988 the average man was spending between seventy and ninety hours a year standing in line for liquor).[10] Between 1985 and 1988 the number of police needed to quell "hooliganism" in Moscow liquor store lines doubled. And since there wasn't enough time to serve all the customers coming in the front door, enterprising liquor store clerks began an active backdoor, black-market trade in vodka. Ultimately, policemen were deployed at every liquor store in the country in a (futile) effort to quash these backdoor deals. On one front or another, the police spent so much time fighting the vodka wars that few resources were left for other law enforcement. As a result, crimes of all types, including larcenies, assaults, and homicides, soared. Not until Gorbachev scrapped his temperance efforts in 1988 was order on the streets restored.

Diligent enforcement of prohibition also creates crime where none was present before. Consider the opiates—opium, morphine, and heroin. These drugs were legal in America before 1914 and were consumed by casual users as well as some 250,000 to 300,000 addicts.[11] Opiates were readily available and cheap, enabling even addicts discreetly and peaceably to accommodate their habits within their regular budgets. The Harrison Act eliminated the peaceful coexistence between addicts and other citizens by driving the price of opiates up to record heights. Unable or unwilling to give up their drugs, many addicts could afford their suddenly expensive habits only by supplementing (or replacing) their regular income with the proceeds of criminal activity, such as shoplifting, pocket picking, burglary, larceny, prostitution, and anything else that would generate quick cash. A population of addicts that had been largely ignored or pitied suddenly became enemies of society, not because they had undergone personality changes but because the Harrison Act had driven up the cost of their comfort.

The enforcement of alcohol and drug prohibition also fundamentally changes the organizational structure of criminal activities. We noted earlier that both reputation (brand names) and the existence of regular, ongoing business relationships are important ingredients in ensuring the quality (and safety) of all goods. This is particularly true for psychoactives, where a lack of quality assurance can kill. For all the addict knows, the white powder in that plastic bag could be confectioner's sugar, or even rat poison, as easily as the hoped-for heroin. Only the pusher knows for sure—until, perhaps, it is too late. When psychoactives are illegal, quality and safety become hard for suppliers to assure. Thus, sellers who are able to offer that assurance gain an enormous advantage over their competitors. And this assurance is often most effectively established through the creation of organized crime gangs (or "families"), whose membership is sharply delimited by racial or ethnic factors.

Gangs whose members were of Italian, Irish, or German extraction dominated the large-scale distribution of booze during Prohibition. The Mafia largely controlled the distribution of heroin in this country until the 1970s; since then, the heroin market has been dominated by Chinese gangs called "tongs."* And today, some 40 percent of the American crack cocaine market is controlled by Jamaican gangs known as "posses."

The ethnic or racial basis for the gangs makes the identification of "outsiders" (cops and informants) much easier. In addition, the existence of a common cultural background facilitates an organizational code of conduct that emphasizes the importance of a one-for-all-and-all-for-one attitude by gang members toward each other. The chances are thus reduced that an arrested member will reveal the identities of fellow gang members who serve as his suppliers or distributors. Members of the organization are also less likely to cheat on their dealings with each other or with customers.

These features have long made organized gangs potent factors in the markets for illegal psychoactives. Indeed, the "successes" racked up by the enforcement agencies most often come at the expense of fringe suppliers who are unprotected by a gang organization. In effect, the enforcement efforts of the drug and alcohol warriors act like a tax on unorganized competitors, strengthening the competitive position of the gangs. Thus, today as in the past, laws prohibiting psychoactives have helped create and maintain the economic viability of organized crime in America.

STILL DRUNK

The fact that government makes choices about drugs is not undesirable in and of itself, even when the government thereby limits the

---

*The end of the Mafia domination of this market in the 1970s was largely the result of the Justice Department's success in infiltrating the Mafia and then prosecuting its leadership. This created a vacuum in the heroin market, one quickly filled by Chinese immigrants who were members of tongs. At least partly because so few drug-enforcement agents are of Chinese extraction, the government has had almost no success in penetrating the tong organizations.[12]

choices we may make as individuals. For example, even in the "land of the free," we may not freely choose to operate a motor vehicle while under the influence of intoxicating substances. Despite the diminution in our personal freedom, important benefits result, principally because this same constraint is placed on other vehicle operators. In this example and many others, there are clear and compelling reasons why the constraints placed on us by government may be both reasonable and beneficial.

There is another side to the story. The mere fact that the government makes decisions about drugs does not in itself mean that those decisions confer more benefits than harm upon us. No government is omniscient. And when government errs—particularly a national government—its power produces results that can be singularly damaging.

So what have the psychoactive prohibitions of this century actually delivered? In America and the U.S.S.R., seventy years ago and today, the answer is, sadly, not much. At best, fourteen years of waging war on booze during Prohibition managed to reduce total liquor consumption by about 30 percent; but by the last years of Prohibition, people were drinking as much as ever. Gorbachev had no more success in his three-year attempt to reduce liquor consumption in the U.S.S.R. Indeed, some Soviet observers argue that the production of home-brewed liquor increased so much between 1985 and 1988 that the reduction in state-produced booze was almost completely offset. And what of America's experience under the Harrison Act? Prior to the act, when opiates were legal, cheap, and readily available, the rate of opiate addiction varied between 2.5 and 3.5 persons per thousand. By the mid-1970s, after sixty years of heroin wars, the opiate addiction rate was at best 20 to 30 percent less.

We have all heard the adage "you get what you pay for." The sad history of the booze and opiate wars reveals a far less appealing moral: When national governments try to impose sweeping prohibitions on the use of psychoactives, we all too often end up paying for more than we get. As we turn to the costs of today's drug wars, it is a message well worth keeping in mind.

CHAPTER 2

··

Scourge

THE EFFORTS OF AMERICA'S FEDERAL DRUG WARRIORS BEGIN WITH THE attempt to stop illegal drugs from reaching our shores. Punitive actions against producers and traffickers, including vessel seizures on the high seas and high-speed boat chases, make the most news and cost the most money. Behind the scenes, foreign governments are offered financial incentives to enlist their aid in halting the cultivation and processing of drugs. The drug warriors have even tried crop-substitution programs, and crop-eradication schemes patterned after those used in Vietnam. Despite the headlines produced by these efforts, their substantive impact on the flow of drugs to America has been minimal. Here we examine why this is so and why so little can be done to change this fact.

Much of the earth's surface is suitable for growing and processing psychoactive plants, the raw materials for drugs such as marijuana, cocaine, and heroin. Only a trivial fraction of this area is needed to produce the flood of drugs now coming into America. Even if we could wipe out all of today's sources of supply, a virtually inexhaustible set of alternative suppliers would remain. Many of the people who inhabit the primary producing areas, including South America and Asia, face starvation if they spurn the drug trade, and death at the hands of traffickers if they try to stop the trade. No credible threat or inducement will convince foreign growers and processors to give up their livelihood. Once produced, the drugs can enter America by any number of methods, across any of thousands of miles of open borders, and our efforts to stop smugglers serve chiefly to drive up the profits of those who succeed. Short of employing our entire armed services as a domestic drug militia, there is no feasible way to prevent drugs from entering the country. Even here in America, in locations ranging from national forests to bedroom "grow closets" and basement laboratories, psychoactives can be grown or concocted in quantities sufficient to satisfy the most demanding drug appetites. Thus, even if we somehow stopped the flood of foreign drugs, domestic producers stand ready, willing, and able to jump into the breach.

The bottom line is short and simple. In attempting to eliminate the world supply of drugs, the federal government has been building sand castles against the incoming tide. Despite occasional fleeting satisfactions, in the long run there is no realistic chance of success. If we are to undo drugs, we shall have to look elsewhere.

GUERRILLA AGRICULTURE

Marijuana plants, coca bushes, and opium poppies don't grow everywhere, but they come close. The coca bush (*Erythroxylon coca*), whose leaves form the raw material for cocaine, is averse to freezing temperatures, but can otherwise flourish in any climate that gets between 40 and 240 inches of rain per year. Much of the 2,500-mile-wide band from the Tropic of Cancer to the Tropic of Capricorn, girdling Central and South America, Africa, India, Southeast Asia, and even northern Australia and southern Florida, is thus suitable.[1] Cultivation of the coca bush can be performed with rudimentary hand tools, and requires no specialized training or care. The leaves of the bush, harvested three to four times a year, are sturdy enough to be transported to market in burlap sacks on the backs of burros or men.

The opium poppy (*Papaver somniferum*) is a bit more demanding than coca, requiring mild, sunny, and somewhat drier conditions. Historically, the poppy's preferred habitat has included India, Iran, Turkey, China, and the Balkan peninsula. In recent decades, however, the "Golden Triangle" area of Southeast Asia (incorporating portions of Myanmar, Laos, and Thailand) has become the major supply nexus, and Central America is rapidly emerging as an important source of supply.[2] Although harvesting the poppy's sap (the raw material for heroin) requires more time and care than does harvesting coca leaves, heroin's extraordinary street value—more than $100,000 per ounce in pure form—makes the extra effort worthwhile.

The marijuana plant (*Cannabis sativa*) is one of nature's ultimate survivors. Quite literally, it grows like a weed, flourishing in the wild on every continent except Antarctica. Left untended, the plant reaches a height of up to fifteen feet within a few months, at which point its crop of leaves and buds is worth $500. Pruned, watered, and fertilized regularly, a single pampered plant can fetch $2,500. Marijuana will grow high on mountainsides, on open plains, and in dense forests. It thrives in pots hung from and hidden among the branches of trees, or can be trained to grow close to the ground in the midst of other, legal crops. Moreover, with less than $100 worth of equipment, an individual can produce a thriving crop year after year in his or her own closet or basement.

Roughly 75 percent of the marijuana consumed by Americans is imported, chiefly from Central and South America, although domestic production is expanding rapidly.[3] The leading producer states are California, Oregon, Kentucky, and Hawaii, but the legal authorities have confiscated plants from Alaska to Florida, and from Maine to Arizona. Cannabis is a plant for all seasons and every locale.

Despite the diversity of conditions under which the principal psychoactive crops will grow, remarkably little arable land is presently devoted to their cultivation. The U.S. Department of Agriculture has estimated that more than 2.5 million square miles in South America alone are suitable for growing coca, yet less than 1,000 square miles (less than 0.04 percent) is currently used for that purpose.[4] Elsewhere in the world, the combined land area suitable for coca exceeds the amount available in South America, and yet almost none of it is now under commercial coca cultivation. If coca eradication attempts had any appreciable success in causing supply disruptions, vast tracts of land could rapidly be cultivated as a source of supply.

Most of the 4,000 metric tons of marijuana produced in the United States each year is grown in only a dozen or so counties scattered across the principal producing states, and total U.S. production represents a trivial fraction of worldwide marijuana output.[5] And since marijuana cultivation is eminently suitable for commercial cultivation indoors as well as outdoors, one must realistically view the entire surface of the earth as a potential source of supply.

Far less land is suitable for opium poppy production, yet many experts believe that total world production of the flower takes place on less than one-thousandth of the acreage on which poppy production is feasible under current market conditions.[6] If growers were left undisturbed by government officials, the poppy crop required for

America's entire annual consumption of heroin could be grown on twenty-five square miles of land.[7] Of course, government officials have not been this cooperative, but it hasn't made much difference. Largely as a result of prodding from U.S. officials, the government of Turkey has been trying for three decades to curtail opium poppy production in that nation without appreciable success. For every field plowed under, another arises in its place. In Thailand, growers risk death at the hands of competitors hoping to steal their crops and soldiers seeking to destroy them; despite this, Thailand's opium poppies form the basis for much of the world's highest-quality heroin.

The overall picture is clear: An immense portion of the world's surface area is eminently suitable for the cultivation of psychoactive plants; much of this land area is lightly populated and poorly suited for other uses; and the current flood of drugs on the world market is the product of a minuscule fraction of this land. Even if every square inch of land currently devoted to raising psychoactive plants could somehow be rendered sterile, cultivation could quickly and easily be shifted to other land. Within a short period of time, we would again be awash in drugs.

Even this bleak picture fails to capture the immensity of the problem facing those who would try to prevent the cultivation of psychoactive plants. Consider marijuana. During the late 1970s, U.S. efforts to interdict imports of the drug began to have some modest success. Irritated by the disruption to their supplies, users and dealers expanded cultivation of the plant at home, thereby avoiding the risks of smuggling the drug past customs agents.[8]

American growers quickly learned that although a suitable crop could be produced by simply tossing a few seeds into their backyard gardens, there were two drawbacks to this method. First, untended plants were inclined to grow straight up, reaching heights of fifteen feet or more. This made it relatively easy for law-enforcement officials to spot the marijuana, even when the plants were interspersed with other crops, such as corn. So the growers began pruning the plants, inducing them to produce denser arrays of leaves and buds on shorter stalks. The result was a compact bush that was almost indistinguishable from surrounding vegetation except upon close inspection.

Even so, growing the plants on one's own property had a remaining disadvantage: In the unlikely event that the cultivation was discovered, ownership was readily established, and a prison sentence or stiff fine was the likely outcome. Hence, serious growers began using public lands to raise their crops. They soon discovered that state and national forests were ideal. Typically, no one lived there. Access to remote areas was difficult. And the lush indigenous vegetation shielded the marijuana plants from the eyes of both visitors and forest rangers. Most importantly, even if the plants happened to be discovered, ownership was almost impossible to prove, leaving the growers free to plant a replacement crop.[9]

Naturally, since growers were taking extra efforts with their plants, they sought to improve them so as to increase the financial returns. They soon found that the application of bone meal and a few other nutrients not only enhanced the growth of the plants but raised their potency by increasing the plant's production of THC, the active ingredient in marijuana. Growers also learned that when they separated the female plants from the male plants, the isolated females would produce enormous THC-loaded buds in their futile efforts to become inseminated. Because of its high THC content, the resulting sinsemilla (seedless) marijuana carried a punch ten to twenty times greater than that of the imported marijuana it replaced.[10]

The ultimate outcome of early success against marijuana imports was thus singularly perverse. Not only was domestic production encouraged, but the resulting development of guerrilla agriculture techniques in the United States yielded a product that was, from the perspective of its consumers, vastly improved. Marijuana supplies in the United States soon became more plentiful, more potent, and less expensive than ever before.

The ability of psychoactive plants to flourish under a wide variety of conditions has produced another twist: Suppliers have been able to select growing locations that make the interdiction efforts of authorities unlikely to succeed.[11] The coca plant, for example, has been grown for centuries in the Andes Mountains, where residents chew the leaves to stave off hunger and to increase work endurance. The efforts of South American governments to eradicate coca have led peasants simply to move their fields farther up the mountains and away from road systems. As a result, modest (but well-publicized) early successes in eradicating crops quickly became futile searches for the fields planted to replace them. Government attempts to eradicate marijuana fields in Mexico and Thailand, or poppy fields in Turkey and Myanmar (formerly Burma), have met with similar responses by growers in those nations: Operations are simply moved to less accessible areas. Guerrilla armies have long known that difficult terrain is an ally against numerically superior opponents. Guerrilla farmers have found the same ally in their battles with government forces seeking to put them out of business.

PROSPER OR PERISH

The nations where most of the world's psychoactive plants are grown share an overriding characteristic: They are poor, horribly poor by the standards of the United States and Western Europe.[12] Mexico, an important source of marijuana, is the most prosperous of the major supplier nations, with an average per capita income of about $2,000 a year. In Colombia, where most cocaine is processed, average income is less than $1,500 per year, and in Bolivia, the biggest supplier of coca leaves, annual income is under $800 per person. In the Golden Triangle of Southeast Asia, an important source of both marijuana and heroin, a person who earns the equivalent of $10 per week is considered modestly prosperous.

The crushing poverty of these nations creates powerful forces that make suppression of their drug trade most unlikely. These forces are well illustrated in the nations that supply cocaine. Almost all of the world's cocaine derives from the leaves of coca bushes cultivated in South America. Peru and Bolivia grow about 80 percent of the South American crop, with Colombia accounting for the remaining plants.[13] Processing of the coca leaves into the final product, cocaine hydrochloride powder, takes place chiefly in Colombia, which also serves as the principal point of export to the United States and Europe.[14]

The cocaine supply chain begins with the peasants of these countries, whose existence depends on agriculture. The typical plot of land cultivated by a peasant family covers about 2.5 acres. A family using the land to raise livestock can hope to earn at most $100 per year; a crop such as maize can bring in $300 more. But if the land is suitable and the family is willing, earnings of $1,200 to $1,500 per year are assured if the crop is coca.[15]

In recent years, U.S. government officials have repeatedly proposed halting the cocaine trade by inducing South American peasants to give up growing coca in favor of "alternative agriculture," such as livestock husbandry or the cultivation of other crops. As the numbers above make clear, such a notion is patently absurd, for it would require peasant families to voluntarily give up 70 percent or more of their income. Asking such families to rely on "alternative agriculture" is akin to asking them to court death by starvation.[16]

In these poverty-stricken settings of South America, bribes and intimidation become the order of the day. A mid-level law-enforcement official in Colombia earns at best $200 per month from his job; in Bolivia, the figure is 50 percent lower.[17] By turning his back on a single drug deal, the official can double his income. A senior policeman who regularly cooperates with smugglers can easily raise his annual income to ten times the national average. For the police and many other government officials in Colombia, Bolivia, and Peru, simply ignoring drug transactions can make the difference between a life of bare subsistence and one of prosperity.[18]

If the carrot won't work, there is always the stick. As in most nations where the difference between life and death routinely turns on no more than this year's harvest, the financial cost of assassination is low. In Medellín, Colombia, a routine murder (a *trabajito*, or "little job") can easily be arranged for $100.[19] A more complicated task, such as the execution of a government cabinet minister, might cost as much as $20,000 (about ten minutes' worth of profits for the Medellín cocaine cartel). Partly as a result of the ample supply of would-be assassins, the per capita homicide rate in Medellín is five times higher than in New York City. As one commentator has put it, the choice facing politicians, judges, policemen, and editors in the drug-supplying nations is quite simple: "Turn a blind eye and you get $10,000; take notice and your son gets killed."[20]

Quite apart from the survival value of cooperating with (or at least ignoring) the drug cartels, the political obstacles facing antidrug campaigns in nations such as Mexico, Colombia, and Peru are enormous. Largely as a result of the drug appetites of American consumers, the richest in the world, drugs now constitute a significant part of the economies of supplying nations. The export of coca leaves earns Bolivia perhaps $600 million per year, enough money to support 30 to 40 percent of its population.[21] Roughly one-third of all illegal drugs and perhaps 70 percent of the cocaine now entering the United States is estimated to enter the country by way of Mexico, much of it transshipped from Southeast Asia or South America.[22] Simply moving the drugs through the country and across the border provides employment for tens of thousands of Mexicans. Cocaine, along with coffee and cut flowers, is one of Colombia's three most important sources of export earnings.[23] Indeed, cocaine is more important to the Colombian economy than the automobile industry is to the U.S. economy. It is little wonder then that government leaders in these nations balk at American demands that they cripple their nations' economies to solve the America drug problem.

NEEDLES AND HAYSTACKS

At current street prices, high-quality sinsemilla marijuana is more expensive than fine Beluga caviar, cocaine is more valuable than pure gold, and gram for gram, heroin is worth more than $1,000 bills. Yet an ounce of pharmaceutical grade (pure) cocaine can be manufactured in this country for about $50. Cut to a street-level purity of, say, 60 percent, and sold on the streets of Los Angeles, that ounce has a value of about $2,500. Even under the difficult conditions faced by cocaine processors in Colombia, where necessary chemicals must be smuggled into the country and the final product smuggled out, the cost of manufacturing cocaine is less than 5 percent of its street value in America. Similarly, marijuana that sells for $100 in the United States can be grown and harvested in Mexico for about $1. And a quantity of heroin that sells for $1,000 in America can be manufactured for less than $10 in Thailand.

The enormous difference between the foreign export price of psychoactive drugs and their street value in the United States can be accounted for in part by the standard distribution costs associated with all goods, but the difference is primarily due to the high risks associated with dealing in illegal substances. In any event, the relatively low value of psychoactives at their point of origin yields a simple but striking conclusion: Even spectacular successes in driving up the costs of growing and processing psychoactives are unlikely to have much impact on their street price, and thus unlikely to have much impact on total consumption.

Consider the following example. Under current market conditions, cocaine with a street value of $100 in the United States can be manufactured in Colombia for about $4, an amount that includes the cost of the coca leaves and all of the chemicals, labor, and equipment used to convert the leaves into cocaine hydrochloride powder. Suppose that a massive new interdiction effort causes manufacturing costs to triple to $12 from $4. Naturally, this $8 increase in costs will cause the price in the United States to rise from its original level of $100;

but as a first approximation, the United States price will change by only about 8 percent, that is, by $8/$100, the rise in manufacturing costs divided by the original price. Thus, even a massive rise in the costs of psychoactives at early stages in the distribution process will have only a minor effect on the prices paid by consumers, and therefore a negligible effect on consumption of the drugs themselves.

The essential features of this example are borne out by experience. In the late 1980s, the United States was spending about $2 billion per year on efforts to stem the flood of incoming cocaine.[24] Using resources ranging from drug-sniffing dogs to radar-equipped blimps, the government succeeded in confiscating record amounts of cocaine and in making smuggling operations more difficult and more costly. Despite this, a recent study by the Rand Corporation came to a sobering conclusion: The total impact of the nearly $6 billion spent on coast guard helicopters, Customs Service jets, and radar-equipped blimps succeeded in raising the street price of cocaine in the United States by only 4 percent relative to what it otherwise would have been.[25] The study also estimated that for each additional 2 percent hike in the street price of cocaine, an additional $1 billion per year will have to be spent on protecting our borders from smugglers.

The compact physical bulk of most psychoactives compared to their street value makes the battle against smuggling especially difficult. An ordinary automobile tire weighs roughly eighteen pounds (about eight kilograms). Imported to the United States from South America or Asia and hidden within a shipment of 40,000 other tires, that tire can be used to smuggle in $1 million worth of cocaine, or $10 million worth of heroin. A few handfuls of hollow plastic bananas can be filled with $500,000 worth of cocaine and secreted within a twenty-ton shipment of bananas from South America. A million dollars worth of heroin can be hidden inside just one of the hundreds of thousands of personal-computer terminals imported to the United States each year. The list of items within which illegal drugs can be and have been imported is almost limitless. Inspecting every one of the steel cargo containers used to bring in 90 percent of America's imports would require the full-time services of more than 300,000 customs inspectors, and would bring the country's international trade to a grinding halt.[26]

Even if officials could somehow inspect every item of imported commerce, the United States still has more than 12,000 miles of coastline, and 7,500 miles of land bordering Canada and Mexico. Across these shores and borders each year pass 574,000 airplanes, 177,000 ships and boats, and 118,000,000 automobiles. Every one of them is a potential smuggling vehicle, as are the bodies of the 422 million people who come into this country every year. It is little wonder that one expert has remarked that our search for illegal drug imports makes looking for a needle in a haystack seem like child's play.

THE ACTION-REACTION SYNDROME

Recognizing many of the difficulties we have noted, the U.S. government has turned to sophisticated technology in the war on drugs. The problem—as drug-enforcement officials are now admitting publicly—is that the drug dealers frequently have the technology first, and obtain it more cheaply as well. The enforcement agencies must deal with the cumbersome congressional budget process to obtain the funds for new technology, and then must meet all the rules of the government procurement process to convert the money into enforcement tools. The drug dealers have plenty of money and play by their own rules. When new technology comes along, they pay cash, on the spot. As one veteran customs agent put it, "They are inherently flexible; we're not. That's why we always lose."[27]

Then there is the matter of cost. The drug dealers can strike with anything anywhere, but when they do, enforcement officials must be prepared to react to the exact methods chosen by the drug dealers. As a result, according to Anthony Bocchichio, the head of the Drug Enforcement Administration's technical operations unit in Washington, D.C., devices that counteract a smuggling innovation cost ten to fifteen times as much as the innovation costs. For example, since conventional telephones (used to place and take orders for drugs) are fairly easy to tap, the drug dealers switched to cellular telephones, which cost $500 to $1,000 apiece. To tap cellular phones, the government must buy devices that cost $15,000 apiece.[28]

The technology duel between drug agents and drug dealers has gone on for years and the process of action and reaction seems to escalate on a monthly basis.[29] To track planes flying drugs out of Colombia, U.S. Customs agents managed to conceal radio transponders on a few of them. The transponders enabled the agents to keep track of the planes in the air, and thus capture the smugglers when they landed. To counteract this, the smugglers purchased radio frequency detectors ($30 each at the local Radio Shack) to inspect their planes for transponders before takeoff. Customs agents reacted by implanting transponders that did not begin sending their signals until the planes had reached a certain altitude. The smugglers simply took their detection devices along with them in the planes. Exasperated, drug agents resorted to exotic transponders that did not begin broadcasting until the planes on which they were implanted turned north, as they commonly did only when nearing the U.S. coast. Smugglers counteracted by flying in circles around their home airports, thereby triggering the transponders' signals and alerting the smugglers to their presence. The drug warriors finally gave up on the idea of implanting transponders on smugglers' planes. And the taxpayer money spent on the devices? Gone, with nothing—save for a few stories—to show for it.

BRINGING OUT THE BEST

Who is more motivated—a drug trafficker, or the enforcement agent trying to stop him? A drug smuggler, describing the duels between drug runners and Drug Enforcement Administration (DEA) agents in fast boats along the Florida coast, gave this answer:

> There are places [along the coast] where the water is two feet deep and less, and the channels that you have to use are unmarked. Now, a good doper knows those channels because he studies them. He's also making ten, twelve, fifteen thousand dollars—it depends on the load—for four hours' work, and for that kind of money he is expected to take the risk of getting it wrong. The guy chasing him is making maybe a hundred bucks for a shift, on which he's going to pay tax, and if he hits that sandbank at sixty miles an hour he isn't going to collect his pension because he's going to be dead. Now, you're in the Customs' boat heading for the sandbank: Which way do you want to push the throttle?[30]

This simple story helps illustrate why both innovation and adaptation in the drug wars so often favor the bad guys. For drug dealers, the rewards of developing new ways of bringing drugs to market (or of adapting to the latest methods of the drug warriors) are enormous, compelling enough for them to risk prison terms or death, or to murder anyone who stands in their way.

Compare this with the incentives facing law-enforcement officials, who are paid whether they catch the dealers or not. Quite simply, the drug warriors have little economic stake in the success or failure of their efforts, and equally little incentive to risk life and limb. Certainly, some may get publicity, and others may even get salary increases; but these are small compensations for risking their lives. Because their expected rewards—huge profits—are so much greater, drug dealers are willing to face a far greater risk of violent death than are drug-enforcement agents, and they are more willing and able to innovate and adapt as well. The common notion that drug warriors are a group of dedicated individuals constantly thinking up ways to outsmart the bad guys surely has an element of truth to it, but by and large, it is the bad guys who spend their time trying to figure out ways to outsmart the good guys. It is the drug dealers who are constantly seeking new products and delivery systems to give them a competitive edge, and it is the dealers who adapt the most quickly to changing conditions, because the bad guys—the dealers—have greater incentives to do so. The rate of innovation and adaptation in the drug-enforcement agencies is much slower than it is within the drug trafficking business, simply because the rewards are structured to make it so.

WHEN THE BEST IS NOT ENOUGH

Many military personnel who served in Vietnam learned firsthand about the *balloon principle*: A military thrust into one part of the country yielded a temporary inward bulge at the point of attack, but no change in the overall size of the enemy presence. The military personnel who have entered the drug war have found the same principle at work. Consider a recent eighteen-hour drama involving the armed forces of the United States and Canada, as well as numerous law-enforcement agencies on both sides of the border.[31]

On the morning of March 12, 1989, a twin-engine executive turbojet loaded with half a ton of cocaine and thirty-eight seven-gallon cans of extra fuel took off from a small airfield in northern Colombia. As part of a $300 million supplement added to the defense budget for drug interdiction, extra radar had been installed at critical points along the East Coast of the United States in anticipation of just such an occasion. But the Colombian plane flew along a path outside the new land-based radar. As luck would have it, an Air Force E-3 Air-borne Warning and Control System (AWACS) plane on a training mission happened to pick up the turbojet blip on its radar. Customs agents aboard the AWACS plane decided the turbojet might be on a drug mission.

In response to the customs alert, two Air National Guard F-16 fighter planes were launched from a North American Air Defense Command base in Maine. The lead fighter saw the Colombian jet as it was nearing the coast of Nova Scotia, flying without running lights. Staying far enough behind to avoid alerting the drug-runners, the F-16s shadowed the turbojet until their fuel ran low. Two more F-16s, launched by Vermont's Air National Guard unit, took their place. Meanwhile, a U.S. Customs Service interdiction unit with a specially equipped airplane and a Blackhawk helicopter crew happened to be at the airport in Bangor, Maine. Three customs agents piled into the plane and joined the chase. The Blackhawk crew waited at the airport for a team of Canadian Mounties, just in case arrests had to be made in Canada.

At 11:00 P.M. the Colombian jet landed at Sorel, a small town fifty miles northeast of Montreal. Unfortunately, Canada had not yet given the pursuing customs plane permission to land, so it had to circle overhead. Viewing the field through night-vision goggles, the customs pilot saw a small truck pull alongside the Colombian plane and un-load numerous duffel bags. As the customs plane began its long-delayed landing, the truck sped away into the night, headed south with at least half a ton of cocaine. Without the evidence, the pilots of the Colombian plane could be charged only with a few minor offenses, including bringing a stolen plane into Canada. They were fined $23,000, which they paid in cash. The Colombians were deported a few days later. Nobody went to jail.

An F-16 costs $2,300 an hour to operate; an AWACS plane, $3,000 an hour. How much is the American taxpayer getting for his or her money? Not much. The vast majority of the 700 or 800 airplanes the Customs Service chases each year are on legal flights. In 1987 alone, the Air Force spent $2.6 million flying AWACS planes on antidrug missions that resulted in only six drug seizures and ten arrests. In round numbers, that works out to $260,000 per arrest, or $433,000 per seizure.

Both the Customs Service and Congress seem undaunted by such numbers. After all, the reasoning seems to be, if the cause is just, what does it matter how much of the taxpayers' money is spent? Thus, the Customs Service is now pumping an additional half a billion dollars into its efforts to stop drug smuggling across the southern U.S. border.[32] The heart of the system is a chain of overlapping, blimp-mounted radar stations backed with sophisticated aircraft and command centers. The first of these blimps was raised over southern Florida. In response, some air smugglers began dropping their drugs well offshore, and ferrying them to shore on small boats virtually invisible to the radar. Others simply diverted their planes into Alabama, Mississippi, and Louisiana. Still others began flying drugs in via Mexico. Most likely, when the blimps are finally in place across the southwest border, planes will simply dart into U.S. airspace, drop their drugs, and return to Mexico before aircraft interceptors can reach them.

As it turns out, the customs project was doomed before it began, because air smuggling across the southern border was already declining. The Medellín and Cali cartels have vastly expanded their ground-based smuggling through Mexico, hiding cocaine in some of the millions of cars and trucks that cross the U.S. border each month and using human "mules" to bring it across the border by foot on routes also used by illegal aliens.[33] Even more ominously, the cocaine cartels have discovered the wonders of cargo containers, stacked ten-deep within and upon giant container ships. These sealed twelve-by-eight-by-twenty-foot steel boxes can be inspected only if they are thoroughly unpacked, and it takes customs officials eight working days to inspect one container. Since there are currently almost 9 million cargo containers entering the United States every year, it would take more than 65 million agent-days to inspect them all.[34] The probable cost of such a venture would be $27 billion a year, not including the costs of disrupting international trade. The probable outcome would be that smugglers would find a new route before the program was ever in place. Sometimes it seems that even the mightiest government in the world can do no more than dent the balloon.

SUBSTITUTION

Suppose we made a real breakthrough on the interdiction front, perhaps by simply shooting anyone attempting to smuggle psychoactives into the country.* Such a policy would obviously reduce smuggling, possibly dramatically. But the effects on drug use would be much less substantial, simply because domestic production is a remarkably good alternative to imports. Recall that domestic production of marijuana was negligible until government efforts to halt its importation began to have some modest successes in the late 1970s. Now domestic cultivation comprises 25 percent of U.S. consumption and the average potency of marijuana has risen.[35] Given the ease with which marijuana can be grown indoors, and the huge tracts of public land on which it can be grown outdoors, further reducing marijuana imports will serve chiefly to stimulate additional domestic cultivation.

By contrast, domestic cultivation of coca bushes or opium poppies is less likely to result from success against imports of cocaine or heroin. For one thing, the likelihood of subfreezing winter temperatures rules out year-round production of either crop throughout much of the United States. The fact that about 500 pounds of coca leaves are needed to make a pound of cocaine also makes domestic cultivation of this plant unlikely. Commercial coca production would require plantation-sized operations, which would be too easy for the authorities to detect. Large-scale domestic production of opium poppies is equally unlikely, because harvesting the poppy's sap (the basis for heroin) is labor-intensive, and thus inordinately expensive given the relatively high wages in this country.

In any case, the marvels of modern chemistry would come to the rescue of cocaine and heroin users in the event of a reduction in imports. There already exists a superb substitute for cocaine—methamphetamine hydrochloride, or "methedrine"—and many experts believe it will soon supplant cocaine. This powerful stimulant was developed in Japan, where its use became widespread during World War II when it was given in liquid form to soldiers and munitions workers to enhance their stamina. Widespread abuse of the drug after the war prompted Japan to make it illegal, but production simply shifted to South Korea.[36]

In recent years, a smokable form of methedrine, called "crystal meth" or simply "ice," has been developed. Ice produces an intense, euphoric high much like that of the cocaine derivative "crack," but

---

*While this may sound absurd, in 1989 there was active discussion at the highest U.S. government levels of the possibility of shooting down planes that were suspected of drug smuggling. Conceivably, we could extend a similar policy to ships, cars, and trucks suspected of being involved in smuggling.

it has three distinct advantages over both cocaine and crack. First, it is cheap: $50 worth of crystal meth is sufficient to keep someone high for a week. Second, it is potent: Its effects routinely last eight hours or more, whereas the effects of crack last only twenty or thirty minutes, and the high from cocaine only about an hour. Third, it is convenient: It can be made at home, using raw materials that can be purchased legally. The use of crystal meth is currently spreading rapidly through the United States. Any significant disruption in cocaine imports would simply serve to hasten that spread.[37]

Chemistry would come to the aid of heroin users as well, should interdiction efforts make any significant inroads on the importation of their drug of choice. III-Methylfentanyl is a synthetic, heroinlike narcotic that is 100 times more potent than heroin ounce for ounce. It can be, and is, manufactured in back-room laboratories using chemicals available from reputable pharmaceutical and chemical companies. Although production appears to be on a small scale so far, a number of emergency rooms across the country have already reported cases of overdoses involving this potent depressant. Moreover, in 1989 an industrial chemist was arrested with enough III-Methylfentanyl in his possession for 10 million doses of the stuff, enough to keep every heroin addict in America satisfied for a long time.[38]

The unfortunate circumstances facing us have been aptly summarized by an official of the U.S. Drug Enforcement Administration:

> Even if the drug lords decide to stay with cocaine and heroin, these substances can be chemically synthesized from scratch, and the day may come when the drug merchants can get along without the natural raw materials—coca and opium. But for the time being, the economics are against it.[39]

Simply put, ample, low-cost supplies of nature's own raw materials have kept the back-room chemists at bay so far, but any significant disruptions in the existing supply chains will be met with a flood of synthetic substitutes.

A GRIM FUTURE

The battle to undo drugs in America cannot be won in the mountains of South America, in the shallow waters of Biscayne Bay, Florida, nor in basement laboratories scattered across America. Even the best efforts of today's drug warriors are rendered futile by the nature of supply conditions. First, there are literally millions of square miles on the earth's surface suitable for the production of these drugs. Even major success in closing down current production sites would simply cause production to begin elsewhere. Second, the incentive structure in producer nations—prosperity for those who participate, imminent peril for those who do not—makes it wishful thinking to hope that the residents of those nations will voluntarily curb their exports of psychoactives. This same incentive structure, of course, makes it unlikely that we could ever offer sufficient inducements or penalties to force people to acquiesce to our wishes. Third, the low production costs and high street value of psychoactives, combined with the multitude of methods by which they can be brought into the country, make it inconceivable that we can stop the flood of drugs at our own borders. Finally, the possibility of domestic U.S. production, either in basement grow rooms or back-room laboratories, means that even if we quash imports of psychoactives, consumption will continue, largely unchecked. Stemming the supply of illegal psychoactives nationwide is simply not in the cards.

CHAPTER 3

....

Home Front

COLOMBIA, BOLIVIA, AND PERU ARE THE PRINCIPAL SOURCES OF CO-
caine and coca leaves. When the leaders of these South American
nations met with President Bush in 1990, they tried to make one thing
perfectly clear: Cocaine is a problem in the United States because
American consumers demand cocaine. Without this demand, most
Peruvian and Bolivian farmers would grow other crops, and Colombian processors and smugglers would find other jobs. If Bush were
to have a similar meeting with the leaders of Laos, Thailand, and
Myanmar, the Golden Triangle nations of Southeast Asia, he would
be told the same story about heroin. Without the demands of American consumers, most opium poppy cultivation in the Golden Triangle
soon would become a money-losing proposition, instead of the profitable source of 60 percent of the heroin consumed in the United
States.[1]

The American demand for drugs is at least half of the story behind
the drug crisis in this country, and so we must discover what fuels
the demand for drugs in America, and if we can effectively reduce
this demand. Drug use, abuse, and addiction in America are far more
pervasive—and difficult to stop—than the drug warriors would have
us believe. The common stereotype is that illegal drugs are largely
confined to the inner cities—a plague that strikes the disadvantaged
and the poor. There is an element of truth to this picture: Drugs *are*
more prevalent in the inner cities than elsewhere. But most of America is white, and most of America is middle class; consequently, most
drugs are used by white, middle-class Americans who live in Any-
town, U.S.A. Psychoactives are pervasive and systemic throughout

our land, as much a part of our lives as our friends, our children, ourselves.

Just as important is the *nature* of drug use in America. Most of the tens of millions of drug *users* are casual users, but most drug *use* is engaged in by abusers and addicts. Even if we eliminated all casual drug use in America, we would leave perhaps 70 percent of all drug use untouched. Although drug abusers and addicts comprise but a small proportion of the population, they populate all strata of American society, and both the strength and nature of their attraction to psychoactives make their long-term drug use largely immune to the current tactics of the drug warriors. Current tactics are thus largely ineffective in reducing *total* drug use, and hence incapable of eliminating the ready market for drugs. If we are to undo drugs in America, these facts must be accepted, and our policies changed to reflect them.

WHO ARE THE USERS AND THE ABUSERS?

Drug use in America is widely perceived to be concentrated among inner-city blacks. Casual statistics seem to confirm this view. Blacks account for almost 40 percent of all drug arrests, and most of these arrests are concentrated in large cities. Moreover, blacks account for 50 percent of the individuals who receive emergency-room treatment for heroin overdoses, 55 percent of those given emergency care for cocaine abuse, and 60 percent of those treated for adverse reactions to PCP (angel dust).[2]

When one considers that blacks comprise only 12 percent of the nation's population, numbers such as these appear staggering. Taken at face value, they suggest that drug use and abuse are three to five times more prevalent among blacks than among whites. Countering this impression, however, are numerous surveys revealing that drug use among blacks—especially inner-city blacks—is only modestly higher than that among whites. Moreover, the impression created by the arrest and emergency-room figures runs counter to what we know about the distribution of spending power in the United States. It takes money to buy drugs, yet the inner cities are ravaged by poverty. Nationwide, blacks earn at least 30 percent less than whites and their poverty rate is three times higher; inner-city residents are poorer still.[3] How can people who earn so little spend so much on drugs? Alternatively, how have inner-city drug dealers become so rich selling to customers who are so poor? The answers are simple: They can't and they haven't.

Consider one Washington, D.C., dealer, Rayful Edmond III.[4] At the time of his 1989 arrest, Mr. Edmond owned over a dozen automobiles (including assorted BMWs, Mercedes, and Jaguars), half a dozen real-estate properties, and several legitimate businesses, all purchased with profits from drug deals. The bonuses he gave to members of his sales force included Super Bowl trips and foreign vacations. Salesmen and bossman alike were draped in gold jewelry.

Every major city in America has dozens of inner-city drug dealers like Rayful Edmond III, all of them awash in cash, luxury cars, and gold chains, and each of them a model for inner-city youngsters seeking to make their mark. Yet the combined income of the residents of a typical inner city—including their welfare checks—cannot account for the wealth accumulated by even a handful of the inner-city drug lords. Indeed, the bulk of the money is coming in from the outside.

Exactly how much outside money feeds the inner-city drug trade is a matter of disagreement. Some observers argue that the figure is 65 percent, while others claim it is up to 90 percent.[5] In any case, the majority of the drugs sold in the inner cities are consumed outside them—by white Americans, many of them middle class, and most of them residents of communities far removed from the inner city.[6] Half of the nation's youth experiment with an illicit drug sometime before they leave high school; most of them are white. Roughly 30 percent of all Americans have smoked marijuana; most are white. An estimated 35 to 40 million Americans used one or more illegal drugs during the past year; the majority are white. And roughly 80 percent of all the patients at the 7,000 or so drug-treatment centers in the United States are white.

The geographic distribution of drug use in America is incredibly diverse and notably egalitarian. "Cocaine," says the Northeastern University criminologist Paul Tracy, "is not only an inner-city drug anymore."[7] Indeed, many crack dealers have left the fierce competition of the larger cities in favor of smaller, but more profitable, cities and towns.[8] Crystal methamphetamine (ice) is being manufactured chiefly in clandestine labs well hidden in rural landscapes, and although most of it is brought into urban centers for initial distribution, much of it is ultimately consumed out in the suburbs and beyond.[9] Most of the potent sinsemilla marijuana grown commercially in the United States is produced in rural areas of Kentucky,

California, Hawaii, and Oregon.[10] And given its price tag of $200 an ounce and up, most of it ends up in the hands and lungs of upper- and middle-class America.

Drug seizures, arrests, and the scope of drug corruption further illustrate the wide spread of illegal psychoactives. In Kentucky a judge and a county sheriff were recently convicted of accepting bribes from a cocaine ring. In Tennessee seven sheriffs and two former sheriffs were jailed for their involvement with illegal drugs. Some 86 percent of the drug cases prosecuted in the rural Western District of Wisconsin in 1989 involved cocaine, while in the predominantly rural Northern District of Iowa, cocaine seizures are doubling every year.[11]

Even crack, a drug most often associated with the inner city, has made steady headway into the hearts and pocketbooks of white America. According to Dr. Arnold M. Washton, the director of a New York drug-treatment center, the white middle class harbors more crack addicts than any other segment of the population. "Despite all the poor black crack addicts you see on TV and Page One," Dr. Washton says, "these new addicts are business executives, and house painters, and doctors, and receptionists. And if you met them on the street or at the Little League game, you wouldn't have a clue they're smoking their brains out on crack back at home in the basement."[12]

Perhaps it shouldn't be surprising that crack has spread to the middle and upper class. Several years ago a similar type of smokable cocaine, called "freebase," became popular among affluent drug users. Today's crack is simply mass-produced freebase cocaine, and it is proving itself attractive to people of all income levels and races. To be sure, we hear more about crack and other illegal drugs proliferating in the ghettos of Detroit, St. Louis, and New York than in the bedroom communities of middle-class America. But this is because the users and abusers in the inner cities get into trouble with the law. The upstanding middle- and upper-class citizens who use illegal drugs also have jobs, and savings accounts, and four-bedroom homes with green lawns. With so much to lose if they are caught, they are careful to keep clear of the police.[13]

For example, middle-class crack users from the suburbs of New York don't go en masse into Harlem to buy their drug of choice. Instead, a single member of a select group of acquaintances makes the buy, and then doles out his friends' shares in the back of a Wall Street elevator. When the drugs are smoked, it's not in a dilapidated crack house known to police. Yuppies light up behind locked doors, hidden away in the suburbs or in their private offices in midtown Manhattan. "They smoke it in tight little cliques," says William Hopkins of the New York State Division of Substance Abuse. "But there are oh-so-many of them. We see their cars streaming through Harlem to make buys all the time. There is an extraordinary amount of crack in the American workplace. Crack is definitely an equal-opportunity drug."[14]

Fundamentally, then, white money from Hometown, U.S.A., makes the drug dealers rich. Drugs are consumed by all socioeconomic classes, by all races, in all geographic areas, and by virtually all age groups in America. Inner-city blacks consume their share of illegal drugs, but they can't—and don't—foot the bulk of the $100 billion illegal-drug bill in America. Most of America is white, and most of the illegal drugs in America are consumed by whites. The middle class is the largest income group in the United States, and it consumes the largest share of the illegal drugs in the United States. We have found the users and abusers and they are us.

USE, ABUSE, AND ADDICTION

Much of what is written these days about illegal drugs, including what we have chronicled thus far, treats the terms "casual drug use," "drug abuse," and "addiction" as though their meanings were etched in stone and universally agreed upon. In many contexts, there is no great harm in adopting such an attitude. But as we begin to understand what can and cannot be accomplished in the drug wars, it is important to be precise about these terms. Not everyone who has read and thought about these issues will necessarily agree with our usage, but at least everyone will know what we mean, and why the distinctions we make are important.[15]

By casual use of drugs we mean the ingestion of psychoactives (including alcohol, caffeine, and nicotine) in quantities and under circumstances that produce no material physiological or psychological harm to either the user or to third parties (such as spouse, unborn child, or front-seat passenger). Consuming a cocktail occasionally before dinner qualifies as casual use of alcohol; drinking four double martinis every night does not. Snorting a line of cocaine to celebrate one's birthday constitutes casual use of cocaine; snorting a gram of cocaine a day does not. Sharing a marijuana joint with a friend on

Saturday night is casual marijuana use; smoking three joints a day is not. Casual drug use produces no material harm at the time of consumption, nor is there measurable harm due to cumulative effects of the drug over time.

Drug abuse comes in two varieties: acute and chronic. In either variety, abuse is use that causes either physiological or psychological harm to the user or to third parties. The distinction between acute and chronic simply refers to the time period over which the use takes place. Acute abuse entails consuming a large amount of a psychoactive over a relatively short period of time. Chronic abuse means repeatedly consuming amounts of a psychoactive that, even if the amounts consumed at each point in time do little if any harm, ultimately produce damage due to their cumulative impact. Getting drunk enough on New Year's Eve to pass out (or throw up) constitutes acute alcohol abuse, while regularly getting "tight" before (or after) dinner is an example of chronic alcohol abuse.

Most discussions of psychoactive abuse either implicitly or explicitly treat the abuse involved as chronic. Since the notion of chronic use is such a common component of the popular conception of abuse, we shall adhere to this usage in our discussions, treating the chronic behaviors cited above—several martinis, joints, or lines of cocaine consumed on a regular, frequent basis—as examples of drug abuse.

The notion of addiction is more difficult to define, in part because it appears to involve mental processes that are not fully understood, and in part because the outside observer cannot easily distinguish between addiction and abuse. Certainly, it is easy to measure the impaired lung function of a marijuana or cigarette abuser or the elevated liver enzymes of an alcohol abuser, and in this way distinguish them from casual users of each drug. But doctors are not infallible, smoking is not the only cause of impaired lung function, and alcohol abuse is not the only possible cause of liver damage. If someone refuses upon advice to give up his or her drug of choice, is that person an abuser, rationally judging that the pleasures of continued use outweigh the dangers, or an addict, irrationally denying the existence of a problem evident to co-workers and friends? Consider the cigarette smoker whose stated reason for not quitting is that he or she "doesn't *want* to." Most of us would judge that, more likely, the smoker simply *can't* stop. Yet how many of us would make the same judgment about an acquaintance who has two martinis for lunch each day? The amount of use can be measured, and the extent of damage at least roughly gauged. But the distinction between abuse and addiction lies in the mind of the user—territory off-limits to the observer.

To appreciate this, we must recognize the difference between addiction to a drug and physical dependence upon a drug. During World War II, tens of thousands of wounded American soldiers were injected with massive doses of morphine to ease the pain of their wounds. These doses often continued for days, or even weeks in the case of men who were severely wounded. Many soldiers developed physical dependence on morphine as a result: If the drug was withheld, they went into physical withdrawal, with symptoms including profuse sweating, severe cramps, nausea, and so forth. But if the morphine injections were gradually reduced in potency and frequency, the men were weaned from their physical dependence, and exhibited no physical signs of withdrawal upon the ultimate cessation of the drug.

The vast majority of the soldiers who went through this process emerged with no desire to continue using morphine. Despite fond memories of miraculous pain relief, these individuals had no more long-term interest in morphine than they did in, say, sulfa drugs or foot powder. Nevertheless, a very small percentage of the soldiers exposed to morphine in this manner became addicted to it. Long after its use was discontinued, and in the complete absence of any physical manifestations of withdrawal from the drug, they ultimately felt obsessed with the desire to recapture the feelings they associated with the drug. Upon their return to civilian life, months or even years afterward, they either returned to morphine, or turned to its street cousin, heroin, to recapture that "special something" they associated with the drug.

Physical dependence lies in the province of the biochemist. It is measurable by the outside observer, and the withdrawal symptoms manifested upon removal of the drug can be immediately and completely eliminated simply by readministering it. Addiction, however, involves psychological elements that are beyond the reach of the test tube. In the case of marijuana (and possibly cocaine), there appears to be no physical dependence associated with addiction. And in the case of heroin and alcohol (where physical dependence can be enormous), an addict who is deprived of the drug continues to be mentally obsessed by it—compelled to resume using it—long after physical withdrawal symptoms have passed. Casual users, and even abusers, think in terms of what their drug of choice does *to* them; addicts and alcoholics think in terms of what their drug of choice does *for* them. To the outside observer, this distinction is inherently unmeasurable—except, perhaps, in terms of the lengths to which addicts will go to feed the monkey on their back.

For the addicted person, these lengths are extraordinary indeed. Heroin addicts routinely risk hepatitis and AIDS every time they shoot up with a dirty needle, often the only kind at hand. Crack addicts send tens of thousands of dollars up in smoke in a matter of weeks in their obsession with getting and staying high. Nicotine addicts bedridden with emphysema continue to smoke cigarettes, despite having to turn off their oxygen tank every time they light up. Alcoholics lose their jobs, their homes, and their families, seemingly oblivious to everything except their next drink. People such as these have crossed the invisible but fundamental line separating abuse from addiction. The horrors they inflict upon themselves make the drug warriors' threats of fines and imprisonment pale in comparison, a point that is central in what follows.

HOW ADDICTION SUSTAINS THE MARKET FOR DRUGS

The current federal approach to fighting the war on drugs, which is essentially identical to that used during Prohibition seventy years ago, is based on two fundamental errors concerning drug use, abuse, and addiction. First, the drug warriors believe that drug consumers can be permanently and effectively dissuaded from ingesting their drugs of choice if the costs of doing so are high enough. For casual users of psychoactives, this stance is no doubt basically correct; most casual users will respond to an increase in the cost of an activity by doing less of that activity. Thus, Prohibition reduced alcohol consumption in America, and the fear of being arrested today induces many casual users to "just say no."

In principle, this theory also applies to addicts whether the costs are self-inflicted or externally imposed. After all, a dead addict is no longer a practicing addict. And there is evidence to suggest that death is not the only deterrent to drug use by addicts. For example, during Prohibition, the number of actively practicing alcoholics probably fell by as much as 20 to 30 percent, a (very) rough estimate based on the observed decline in cirrhosis deaths and other alcohol-related deaths during Prohibition.[16] World War II proved even more disruptive to practicing heroin addicts in America, whose numbers may have fallen by as much as 50 percent during the war due to the worldwide disruption of heroin supplies.[17]

Nevertheless, the approach of the drug warriors ignores a fact that is recognized by every specialist in the field of drug and alcohol treatment: Addiction and alcoholism are diseases.* Addicts and alcoholics who are forced to abstain from their drug of choice due, say, to imprisonment or threat thereof are, in the nomenclature of the field, "dry" rather than "sober." They are still addicts and alcoholics, whose practice of their addiction has merely been interrupted. Short of being executed or physically isolated from their psychoactive of choice, the overwhelming majority will sooner or later (and more likely sooner than later) return to drugs or alcohol, thereby starting the cycle anew. Involuntary incarceration, or the threat thereof, at best produces abstinence; it does not produce recovery from the underlying disease.

Addicts and alcoholics are not hopeless cases, however, fit only for abandonment or permanent incarceration. Treatment programs have been developed (and are steadily being improved) that empower these individuals to refrain completely from consuming their psychoactive of choice, and to do so in a manner that enables them to live "as though" they are not addicts or alcoholics. These programs, which generally require a lifelong commitment to self-monitored follow-up programs (such as Alcoholics Anonymous or Narcotics Anonymous), help addicts and alcoholics become recovering addicts or alcoholics—sober (or "clean") rather than merely dry. Those treated remain at risk of returning to the depths of practicing addiction if they resume drug or alcohol use, but they learn how to establish an effective set of barriers against such resumption of use, barriers that the dry addict or alcoholic does not have.[19]

The current approach to the drug wars is imperiled by its refusal to acknowledge addiction as a disease rather than a crime. When it comes to their psychoactive of choice, addicts (and alcoholics) simply don't respond to incentives the way rational people do, because they are not—in this dimension—rational. By the very definition of the term, an addict has "given himself up" to his drug. Truly draconian

---

*They have been defined as such by the American Medical Association since 1956.[18]

measures, including punishment, will induce some addicts to temporarily forgo their drug of choice, but most will refuse or simply switch to legal substitutes (such as alcohol) while awaiting the opportunity to return to their drug of choice. Unless they obtain treatment (and not just punishment), they are at best "just one hit away from their next high."

Another fallacy underlying the current approach to the drug wars is the belief that if casual users can be prevented from consuming drugs, the market for psychoactives will collapse. Let's consider the facts. The consumption of psychoactives generally follows the lognormal distribution, which means that the vast majority of the population either does not use the psychoactive or uses it only casually, and a small minority of the population accounts for the vast bulk of the total consumption of the psychoactive. Consider alcohol. About 80 percent of all adult Americans either don't drink, or drink in such moderation that, as a whole, this part of the adult population drinks only 20 percent of the alcohol consumed in the United States.[20] The other 20 percent of the adult population—the "heavy drinkers"—consume the remaining 80 percent of the alcohol. In fact, the 10 percent of adult Americans who drink the most consume more than 50 percent of the total amount of alcohol drunk in the United States.

This pattern has been true in the United States for as long as such statistics have been kept, and holds (plus or minus a few percentage points) in all countries for which statistics are available. And although the percentages that fall into each category differ across different psychoactives, the character of the lognormal distribution generally holds true: Most people consume drugs either not at all or casually, but most of the consumption is accounted for by a small percentage of people, who systematically either abuse or are addicted to the psychoactive in question. This pattern is true not just when most people are nonusers, as with heroin. *Even when casual use is widespread, as it is with marijuana and cocaine, most of the drug in question is being consumed by the abusers and addicts.** This point cannot be overemphasized. Casual users ingest less than half of the illegal drugs in question, while the bulk of all illegal drug consumption (between

---

*Nicotine and heroin—generally recognized as two of the most addictive psychoactives—exhibit perhaps the most extreme version of the lognormal distribution, since the fringe of casual users of each is so small relative to the population of nonusers: Addicts consume nearly 100 percent of both drugs.

60 percent and 80 percent) is engaged in by abusers and addicts.[21] And it is these individuals who are the least responsive to the measures advocated by today's drug warriors.

The upshot is sad but simple. If we spend enough money and deprive enough people of their liberties, we can, in principle, dissuade people from casual use, and even induce some addicts to give up. But a core of abusers and addicts will remain who, though small in number, will keep overall consumption high. This core demand is sufficient to keep the basic infrastructure of the drug market profitable and in place. *We can dissuade 70 percent of the users; we cannot eliminate 70 percent of the use.* And achieving even this would require efforts on a scale far beyond what we are trying now; after all, not even the most ardent proponents of today's policies claim that we have eliminated casual drug use. Perhaps more importantly, and distressingly, even a 30 percent reduction in total consumption by means of today's policies would require significant additional resources permanently devoted to this task. The moment we lessen our efforts or relax our constraints, casual users will return to the market, and drug dealers will immediately leap into the breach, ready, willing, and able to supply all comers.

History is clear on this point. Despite fourteen years of all-out war against alcohol during Prohibition, the suppliers survived, and when Repeal brought a resumption of legal production, the cocktail hour returned to millions of homes across the country. Despite seventy-five years of all-out war on heroin in this country, the suppliers and addicts remain. One out of 400 Americans is addicted to heroin today, just as roughly one out of 400 was addicted eighty years ago. The faces and names have changed, but the addiction has not.

The resilience of users, addicts, and suppliers is not unique to the United States, nor does it exist simply because we haven't been "tough enough." Malaysia and Singapore, for example, both impose the death penalty for drug trafficking. For run-of-the-mill drug users, the penalties range from whipping to two years in boot-camp-style "rehabilitation" facilities, where push-ups and hard labor are the order of the day.[22]

"Punishment must be strict, or otherwise the penalty has no meaning," says Roh Geok Ek, the director of Singapore's central narcotics bureau. The assistant director of the Malaysian antinarcotics force, Tey Boon Hwa, claims that "we hang anyone convicted who exhausts their appeals." Apparently, officials in both countries mean what they say. Since Malaysia introduced the death penalty for trafficking in 1983, some 235 people have been sentenced to death; as of early 1990, 81 had been hanged. Singapore, whose population is about the same as that of Dallas or Boston, has imposed the death penalty for drugs since 1975. Thirty-seven people have received the death sentence for trafficking; at last count, twenty-five of them had been executed.* According to the prime minister of Singapore, Lee Kuan Yew, "death is the best deterrent we have." It's difficult to argue with the prime minister's logic, but drugs have not disappeared from the streets of his nation. Despite the prospect of whipping and forced labor, the arrest rate for drug possession in Singapore is still only about 30 percent below that in the United States. Meanwhile, the rehabilitation camps in both Malaysia and Singapore continue to grow in size, and hangings continue unabated.[23]

On the home front, it appears that even the weight of the presidency is not enough to swing the scales. Early in 1989, President Bush vowed to make Washington, D.C., a "test case" in the war on drugs. Assisted by U.S. marshals and led by Drug Enforcement Administration agents, the Washington, D.C., police began the most intensive drug-eradication effort in our nation's history. Within six months it was clear that the effort had been an abysmal failure, as the use of drugs in Washington was as high or higher than ever. Publicly, William Bennett, Bush's first drug czar, said, "From April to October, the length of a baseball season, may be enough to establish a winner in the World Series. It is not enough to win the war on drugs in this city or in any other city." One of Bennett's aides privately admitted to journalists that "twenty-five years was probably not enough either."[24]

1984 IN THE MAKING

An illegal drug transaction involves a voluntary exchange between buyer and seller. The sale, purchase, and consumption of illegal drugs therefore constitute what are commonly labeled "victimless" crimes, in the sense that there is generally no aggrieved party who is likely

*In interpreting these numbers, it is worth remembering that Malaysia (population 16.5 million) and Singapore (population 2.7 million) are both small nations. Since the death penalty was reinstituted in America in 1976, we have executed fewer than 150 persons for all possible crimes, including murder.

to serve as a criminal witness. As a result, the legal authorities must do without the most important ingredient in a successful prosecution—the victim. Without victims to report drug deals and drug use, and to serve as material witnesses at trial, the drug warriors typically must rely on covert operations, including the use of informants and undercover activities, in their endeavors. Most Americans rightly regard such operations as being inherently antithetical to the heritage of our nation—suitable perhaps against foreign spies, but surely not appropriate for everyday police work. Unfortunately, covert operations have quickly transformed the federal government's war against drugs into a war against its citizens.

Americans are an intensely private people, as is evident in our lifestyles. Single-family dwellings are far more prevalent in the United States than anywhere else in the world, in part because houses offer more privacy than do apartments. Once ensconced in single-family dwellings, we continue our quest for yet more privacy by purchasing houses with larger lots, building fences, planting dense shrubbery around our homes, and so forth. Our craving for privacy even shows up in our modes of transportation, for Americans are notoriously averse to using public transportation, preferring the privacy of cars. Our entire lives are structured in ways that maximize our privacy— which is to say, in ways that make it difficult and costly for the government (or our neighbors) to spy on us.

Even more fundamentally, the American people are intensely individualistic. Many people who originally immigrated to the United States did so in part because it offered freedom from the intrusions of others—government officials and nosy neighbors included. Some immigrants had been repelled by the repressive governments of their homelands, and the secret police and informants that accompany such governments. Others were attracted by a country in which individual freedom was prized above all else. The U.S. Constitution reflects this spirit of individual freedom, for it protects our fundamental rights to say, believe, and worship what we choose. And although the Constitution does not specifically guarantee our right to privacy, opinion polls reveal that most Americans either think it does, or feel it should. The bottom line is that the government's use of covert operations against its own citizens is antithetical to the foundations on which America was established, and thus is likely to be met with both resentment and opposition by those citizens.

Nonetheless, the drug warriors have persisted in urging Americans to inform on each other. Television commercials have appeared urging viewers to "rat on a rat," the rodents being alleged drug dealers, or even drug users. In some cases, police departments have advertised openly for private citizens to serve as buyers in sting operations, offering the citizens a share of any assets confiscated from dealers as a result.

To date, appeals such as these have met with relatively little success, perhaps because the thought of informing or being informed upon is so repugnant to most people. As a result, the government has relied heavily on the use of undercover agents in its efforts to ferret out participants in drug deals. But even this approach is unlikely to produce much success in the long run, in part because there are tens of millions of Americans who consume illegal psychoactives each year. Undercover operations also take months (and sometimes years) to develop properly, as undercover agents must work slowly and carefully if they are to uncover the evidence without breaking the law or being uncovered themselves. Short of reimposing the military draft and putting the draftees under cover, we are not likely to uncover more than a trivial percentage of the drug trade through covert operations.

WAR IS HELL

Drug use in the United States is not confined to some narrowly defined, easily excised subculture. Tens of millions of Americans use illegal psychoactives each year, and they come from all walks of life. If we are to undo drugs in America, our policies must reflect the fact that *we* are the users, the abusers, and the addicts.

Although the bulk of all users of psychoactives are casual users, the bulk of all use is by abusers and addicts. And most of the damage done to and by users occurs as a result of addiction and abuse. This is true whether we focus on the adverse health consequences for the users (such as lung cancer for nicotine addicts), adverse health consequences for third parties (such as people killed by drunk drivers), or other adverse effects (such as crimes committed by heroin addicts). Thus, only if we materially alter the behavior of addicts and abusers will our policies yield substantial benefits.

Unfortunately, the users whose behavior is the most difficult to modify successfully are the addicts. Not only is it difficult to get them to abstain or refrain for any given time period, but modifying their short-term behavior (e.g., via incarceration) is unlikely to have beneficial long-term effects on their drug use. Today's punishment-oriented policies will not generate long-term success with addicts, even if they manage to discourage some casual users. Eventually, addicts will simply return to their addictive behavior. Unless and until public policy is shaped to yield a permanent and substantial reduction in *use* rather than *users*, few beneficial consequences are likely to result from drug policy.

Although the battlefields are different, our tour of the home front reminds us of the Civil War general William Tecumseh Sherman's proclamation that "War is hell." When the opponents are psychoactives, it would appear that Sherman understated the nature of the problem—but, of course, Sherman had considerably more success than today's drug warriors are having.

PART TWO

THE COSTS OF CONTROL

CHAPTER 4

································

The Rape of the Inner City

NOWHERE IS THE PREVALENCE OF DRUG USE MORE APPARENT THAN in the inner city. Nowhere is the impact of our war on drugs so severely felt. And nowhere but in the inner cities is that war so likely to fail, leaving the cores of our cities drug-infested and battle-ravaged, dying anew with each passing day. Nearly all of America's heroin addicts live in major cities, more than one-third of them in New York City alone.[1] Both PCP and "speedballs," a potent mixture of heroin and cocaine, are almost exclusively consumed within the inner city.[2] And although cocaine was initially popularized by yuppies in the late 1970s, it is in the inner cities that crack cocaine and crystal methamphetamine are taking their greatest toll in addiction, violence, and death.[3]

The tragedies that repeat themselves endlessly in the inner cities are the most appalling and most revealing manifestations of the scourge that America faces today. Here the inducements to sell and use drugs are the greatest, because the alternatives are so poor. Here the wounds inflicted by the drug wars are the greatest, because the targets are so easy. And it is here that the rewards will be the highest if an alternative for today's errant drug policies can be found. It is in the inner cities that we can—and must—begin undoing drugs. As we will see, we cannot hope to do so by continuing with current policies.

THE LURE OF DRUGS

The appeal of psychoactives lies in their ability to alter the states of our minds and bodies. Stimulants, ranging from coffee to crack, alleviate depression and relieve fatigue. Depressants, from Valium to heroin, induce sleep and soften the jagged edges of living into euphoric peace. Hallucinogens, including LSD and mescaline, recast the tedium of reality into shapes and colors beyond the imagination of Hollywood's special-effects masters.

Drugs offer the illusion of the promised land, a state of mind that, however spurious and ephemeral, at least seems preferable to immediate circumstances. Drugs compete with the reality that confronts individuals every day, and the lure of psychoactives becomes stronger as the disparity grows between the illusions they offer and the reality they leave behind. Nowhere is this disparity between what is and what might seem to be greater than in the inner cities.

Life in the ghetto is harsh. It is a reality as demanding, demeaning, and deadly as those experienced in many of the poorest nations on earth.[4] Average income is less than one-half the U.S. average, and the poverty rate is triple the national rate. Infant mortality in the inner cities is more than twice the national average, and the homicide rate is more than three times higher than the nation's as a whole. And, because the incidence of heart disease, cancer, and hypertension is also higher in the inner cities, the average life expectancy there is ten years lower than elsewhere in the country. The inner cities also lead the nation in the incidence of illegitimate births, broken homes, unemployment, and crime. In short, if one compiled a list of the tragedies of human existence, inner cities of America would prove to be national leaders in most categories.

The oppressive, unyielding conditions of life in the inner cities contrast starkly with the states of mind possible under the influence of drugs. Stimulants offer euphoria and a sense of power; depressants promise peace and oblivion; and hallucinogens transform the grotesque into the acceptable. From alcohol to barbiturates, and PCP to cocaine, psychoactives offer escape. If the grass is always greener, it is at its most luxuriant when viewed from the ghetto.

In the inner cities, the lure of drugs is transformed into the horrors of abuse, addiction, and overdose by many of the environmental elements that make the drugs so appealing in the first place. Consumed infrequently in modest doses, psychoactive drugs push the mind and the body toward the extremes of what is possible. Taken abusively or consumed compulsively, extremes are exceeded and the results become catastrophic. When the potential adverse consequences of consuming psychoactives do not deter usage altogether, they usually moderate it. Yet the caution with which many Americans approach the use of psychoactives (including alcohol) is often cast away by inner-city residents. The dangers associated with the use and abuse of psychoactive drugs are routine to people surviving at the ragged edge of human existence.

Over the past decade, the rate of unemployment among minority teenagers has averaged almost 40 percent nationwide, and in the inner cities teenage unemployment approaches 80 percent.[5] The danger of losing a job because one is high on drugs is little threat to someone who has never held a job. The chance of being murdered is more than six times as high for inner-city black males as for the average white male.[6] In such circumstances, the risk of a heroin overdose is simply another fact of life. The structure of the welfare system offers many unmarried mothers in the inner cities a substantial loss of income if they take a job.[7] For them, the risk of destroying a career because of drug or alcohol dependency is nearly meaningless. On both sides of the coin, then, psychoactives exert their strongest attraction for residents of inner cities. The altered states offered by drugs are worlds away from the gruesome reality of life, and the downside risks are little worse than those that must be faced every day. It is little wonder that drug use and abuse is at its greatest in the ghettos.

TARGETS OF OPPORTUNITY

Given the greater incidence of drug use in the inner cities, it is no surprise that both politicians and police principally direct their drug-enforcement efforts there. There is nothing sinister in targeting specific areas for drug enforcement. Basic economic principles and good management practices dictate that enforcement resources be devoted to those activities that will yield the greatest returns. Since the per capita incidence of using and dealing drugs is highest in the inner cities, it is there that any given amount of law-enforcement resources will yield the highest arrest and conviction rates.

Moreover, a number of factors, including minimum wage laws, racial discrimination, and decaying school systems, severely limit economic opportunities in legal markets for the residents of inner cities. This makes criminal activities relatively more attractive for them, not because they are inherently bad people, but because the economic returns from legal activities are so low. As a result of the higher overall crime rate, the police presence in the ghettos tends to be greater to begin with, making the transition from nabbing muggers to arresting drug dealers and users much easier.

There are other, less appealing, but no less accurate reasons why the inner cities are targeted for drug enforcement. First, the high crime rates and low income levels of these areas imply that residents are both accustomed to the inherent violence of the criminal justice system and unlikely to hire high-priced legal assistance in the event that the law is misdirected toward them. An errant drug bust in middle America is apt to earn the police an expensive and embarrassing lawsuit by the wronged individual. The same mistake inflicted on the resident of an inner city will likely produce little more than a futile vocal complaint. Quite simply, the inner city is an expedient locale for police to rack up impressive arrest numbers, with little fear of the consequences if mistakes are made.

For politicians, too, the inner city is a convenient place to demonstrate one's commitment to fighting the drug wars. Voter registration and voter turnout rates tend to be low among inner-city residents and, given their income levels, these individuals are unlikely to be significant campaign contributors. Moreover, based on both exit polls and precinct voting records, inner-city residents tend to be fairly distant from the political mainstream. It is difficult for a liberal candidate to lose the inner-city vote and almost impossible for a conservative to win it. As a result, it is cheap for politicians of any stripe to transform inner-city residents into the arrest statistics that make the war on drugs appear successful to mainstream voters.

FORM AND SUBSTANCE

All life is composed of a blend of form and substance—of what really is, and what merely appears to be. As individuals, we try to put our best foot forward, just as businesses attempt to maintain public relations that offer a flattering corporate image. Nowhere is the distinction between form and substance more important than in government. Many of the services provided by government are difficult for individual voters to measure based on firsthand experience. The decision by voters that the government should, say, prevent crime, does not normally result in the majority of voters being directly affected by the government's actions in any readily measurable way.

Rarely does one actually observe a police officer apprehend a would-be burglar just as the thief is about to enter one's house. Rather, voters must rely largely on whether or not the government *appears* to be preventing crime. The profits that keep a private firm in business come solely from those customers who actually experience the substance, or reality, of its products by purchasing them. In contrast, the votes that keep a government in office come primarily from citizens who are judging government programs based on their outside perception of them.

Ultimately, of course, perceptions catch up with reality; as Abraham Lincoln put it, "you can't fool all the people all the time." But Lincoln also told us that "you can fool all the people some of the time."* And so the government spends a great deal of its efforts working on form rather than substance, hoping that "some of the time" extends through the next election. Given the important role of appearances in sustaining a government in office, it will clearly spend a great deal of effort on keeping those appearances good. How does it do this? By publicizing simple, quantifiable measures of "performance" that are largely under its direct control.†

If the task at hand is to "prevent crime," the number of arrests made by the police is likely to be one measure used. For example, although police departments routinely deny the existence of traffic-ticket quotas, policemen know that if they don't write tickets, their superiors are likely to doubt that they have really been doing their job. If the crime at issue is the use of drugs, then the total number of drug arrests is routinely adopted as one measure of the effectiveness of the prevention of drug use. Consequently, of the more than one million drug arrests per year, three-fourths are for simple possession, and the drug in question has most often been marijuana. Why? Because marijuana possession arrests are the easiest: Roughly one out of ten Americans use the drug, and almost none of them carry Uzis or have lookouts posted when they light up. In the inner city, where crack and heroin are so popular, arresting users becomes as easy as

---

*The full quote goes as follows: "You can fool all of the people some of the time and some of the people all of the time, but you can't fool all of the people all of the time."
†A classic example of this was observed during the Vietnam War. How could the government demonstrate that we were "really" winning? It relied on daily "body counts" of the number of enemy soldiers purportedly killed. The counting was performed by the government, of course. If the daily count was not high enough, it became standard practice to send soldiers out to count again—with the clear understanding that if the recount did not show a higher total, another recount would likely be required.

shooting fish in a barrel, and so they become convenient targets of opportunity for police and politicians hoping to rack up impressive "crime prevention" statistics.

If the crime at issue is drug trafficking, then the amount and purported value of the drugs seized by the government are likely to be publicized. Most of the drugs seized are intercepted early in the distribution chain, when the value of the drugs is quite low relative to their ultimate street value. Nevertheless, when these seizures are announced, reports emphasize the "street value" of the drugs, a number that is grossly inflated relative to their market value at the time they are seized. Indeed, this method of reporting is equivalent to claiming that the value of a bale of cotton is equal to the retail price of the custom-tailored shirts that might someday be made from the cotton. It is a fiction, but it makes good headlines.

Do massive arrests of users and inflated dollar values of drug seizures provide unassailable proof that drug use and trafficking have been significantly reduced? No, but if arrests and seizures are up, at least it appears that the government is doing its job. In principle, arrests and seizures could be the means by which the harmful use of illegal psychoactives is prevented. But despite all of the publicity that is given to arrests and seizures, the use of, abuse of, and addiction to drugs have continued to mount throughout the nation, particularly in the inner cities.

CASUALTIES OF CHANCE

The domestic distribution chain for drugs in the United States begins in the cities. Sometimes cities are the ports of entry for drugs, and sometimes the incoming drugs cross our borders or shores at remote locations and are then transshipped in bulk to metropolitan areas. In either case, our major cities—from New York to Los Angeles, from Miami to Seattle—form the initial links of the domestic drug distribution chain.

There are a variety of reasons for this fact. First, per capita consumption of drugs tends to be higher in urban areas than in suburban or rural areas, for many of the reasons mentioned earlier. Starting the drug distribution chain in cities thus helps dealers keep transportation costs down, because so many of the drugs can stay where they start. Second, crime rates are higher in cities than elsewhere, which means that relatively more urban dwellers, particularly in the inner cities, are experienced in dealing with the wrong end of the criminal justice system. People with prior criminal experience tend to have some advantage in dealing drugs, since they are knowledgeable about avoiding police detection and experienced in coping with the justice system once caught. Cities are thus a convenient place for major dealers to recruit the lesser dealers who will move the drugs down the distribution chain. Finally, the high population densities and large volumes of commercial activity within cities serve as natural screens for the comings and goings of both suppliers and customers, and the strange faces and out-of-state license plates that would cause comment elsewhere go unnoticed in the urban sprawl.

The large volume of drug transactions in cities at the importing, wholesaling, and retailing levels means that there is a large amount of money on the line. Money attracts people, and since the activity that is generating the money is illegal, the people who are attracted to it are, on average, experienced in conducting criminal activities. As such, they are more likely than average to be schooled in the principal means of illegal competition: corruption and violence.

Consider an importer who is bringing in 500 to 1,000 kilograms (kilos) of cocaine at a time, and selling to primary wholesalers in lots of 10 to 50 kilos. Each successful sale can easily bring gross profits of $250,000, but several obstacles stand between the seller and the profits. Since the transaction is illegal, the police may prove troublesome. To ensure success, the seller may wish to pay the police to "look the other way." As we have seen, corruption is a regular part of the drug trade in countries such as Colombia and Mexico where psychoactives originate. Over the last decade, drug-related police corruption has been equally well-documented in the United States. Recently, in one year alone, twelve New York City police officers were arrested on drug-related corruption charges, and seven Miami police officers were indicted for similar crimes. And less than four months after President Bush announced a major expansion of the war on drugs in 1989, several agents of the U.S. Drug Enforcement Administration were jailed on corruption charges. Many observers now argue that drug-related police corruption is present to varying degrees in virtually every major city in the country, and in many smaller jurisdictions as well.[8] The corruption occurs not because the police involved are inherently prone to bribery, but simply because the dollar amounts involved in large drug deals are overwhelming.

The high cost of legal means of competition and contract enforcement also induces buyers and sellers of drugs to turn to the most effective illegal means of doing business—violence. Just as the bootlegger's Thompson submachine gun offered a low-cost method of doing business during the era of Prohibition, the drug dealer can rely on a MAC-10 machine gun today. Over the last several years, cities across the country from Miami to Los Angeles to Washington have reported sharp increases in the number of drug-related murders, assaults with firearms, and other acts of violence.[9] Sometimes the targets are other parties in drug deals gone bad, or competitors engaged in turf battles. At other times the victims are simply innocent bystanders caught in the wrong place at the wrong time. Most of the time, however, the cause is the same. The illegal nature of the product has eliminated legal means of settling disputes, so the parties turn to the next best alternative—violence.

The role of violence in the illegal market for drugs, and its impact on innocent citizens, is nowhere better illustrated than in the market for crack. By the time crack finally came to the attention of the national press in late 1985, it was deeply entrenched in New York City's poorer neighborhoods. Indeed, turf wars were already breaking out as dealers sought to consolidate control over the most lucrative locations. At about the same time a new set of traffickers came into the scene: illegal immigrants from Jamaica. Organized into groups called "posses," these Jamaicans now control about 35 to 40 percent of the nation's crack network. Authorities estimate that there are at least 10,000 members spread among the forty or so major posses. Their distribution network extends from Miami to New York and is rapidly spreading westward.[10]

Posses emerged as effective organizations in the violence surrounding the 1980 Jamaican elections, and violence has become their trademark in grabbing control of the crack market in this country. According to the U.S. Bureau of Alcohol, Tobacco and Firearms, the Jamaican posses have been responsible for at least one thousand murders since 1985, mainly in the inner cities of the East Coast but extending as far as Kansas City, Dallas, and Denver. Indeed, in some cities the murder rate recently has started to *fall* because the posses have already killed most of their competitors.[11]

Jamaican posses are not the only gangs that have gotten into the crack business. The Bloods and Crips are two major American gangs that got their start in Los Angeles and are now battling over crack distribution territories throughout the country. Authorities believe that the combined membership of these two predominantly black gangs exceeds 10,000, and estimate that between them they control crack distribution in fifty cities.[12] Just as the posses spread along the East Coast and turned westward, the Bloods and the Crips have largely monopolized the West Coast and rapidly moved eastward. As with the Jamaicans, their modus operandi is vicious but simple: Do away with your competitors before they do away with you. As Thomas Repetto, head of the Citizens Crime Commission, put it, "The drug gangs have set the tone that life is very cheap."[13]

The nexus of the major drug distribution gangs is the inner city, where the steadiest appetite for drugs is found, where the recruitment of new dealers is easiest, and where drug-related violence is at its worst. During the early 1980s, most drug killings were directed toward specific individuals, such as the other parties to a drug deal that had soured, or competitors who strayed from their turf. By the mid-1980s, however, "drive-by" shootings had appeared, with semi-automatic weapons fired indiscriminately from passing cars at buildings or groups of pedestrians. What had begun as premeditated murder became random mayhem. Lawrence Sherman, Professor of Criminology at the University of Maryland, called it "a real innovation in homicide."[14] In 1989 alone, thirty-two innocent bystanders in New York City were killed as a result of drug shootouts. Nationwide, the drive-by homicide toll in 1989 was estimated to be between 200 and 300 persons, most of them inner-city residents.

Perhaps most tragically, children in the inner cities are facing some of the greatest danger. Black children from ages ten to nineteen are being killed at seven times the rate of young whites, most of them the innocent victims of inner-city drug-gang violence.[15] Concerned parents in many inner cities keep their children locked in their houses because playgrounds are too dangerous. Some children are forced to sleep on floors to protect them from stray bullets crashing through windows. According to Clementine Barfield, the director of the Detroit-based group Save Our Sons and Daughters (SOSAD), black children who live in the inner cities of Detroit, Washington, Los Angeles, Chicago, and New York are living in "war zones." It is little wonder that in many drug-plagued areas of the country, children are reacting to the violence in ways similar to the post-traumatic stress syndrome suffered by Vietnam combat veterans.[16]

BARKING UP THE WRONG TREE

Fundamentally, it is the illegality of drugs that produces the drug-related violence of the inner cities. The illegal nature of the drug trade induces traffickers to turn to violence, just as the illegal nature of alcohol during Prohibition induced bootleggers to rely on violence in plying their trade. The illegal nature of drugs is what makes them so profitable and lures posses and street gangs into the trade, just as the illegal profits of Prohibition whiskey attracted Al Capone, Dutch Schultz, and others.

Ironically—and tragically—although the inner cities have been subjected to the vast bulk of this violence, it is there that our laws against drugs are likely to have the least impact in reducing the use and sale of drugs. This is because the very factors that encourage drug use and trafficking there also make dealers and users most resistant to attempts at altering their behavior. Moreover, the pitched battles currently being fought in the inner cities, among dealers and between dealers and the police, perversely offset whatever beneficial effects might be expected from the war on drugs.

Consider first the drug users. We might usefully think of the initial motivations to use drugs as falling into one of two categories. Some people are first attracted to psychoactives as a means of exploration—drawn by a desire to experiment, a sense of boredom, or peer pressure. Others first begin using drugs as a means of escape—perhaps from chronic pain due to injury, or from environmental stresses. For people who embark on drug use as a means of exploration, a rise in the risk of arrest and imprisonment is likely to cancel out the hoped-for positive aspects of drug use, thus curtailing their use, and possibly even inducing users to refrain altogether. For these individuals, the prospect of punishment is truly a deterrent. But for people driven to drug use as a means of escape, punishment does not alter the fundamental factors from which they seek escape. Indeed, imprisonment without drugs may be little worse than a drug-free existence on the streets. For such people—and many inner-city drug users surely qualify—legal penalties border on having no deterrent effect whatsoever. As one judge in Phoenix, Arizona, describes the users who appear before him: "the huge majority are young, black. They don't have jobs, they don't have skills, they don't want treatment, they don't care about a criminal record."[17]

The weak deterrent effect of punishment in the inner cities is further dampened by the havoc produced by the drug wars. In city after city, drug use in the ghettos has been met by police tactics seen nowhere else in the United States. In Los Angeles, police sweeps directed at drug gangs have produced mass arrests, netting many actual gang members but also nabbing innocent citizens along the way. In Boston, police have undertaken large-scale searches in the predominantly black communities of Roxbury and Dorchester, accosting, frisking, and sometimes strip-searching residents whom they call "known gang members." According to Massachusetts state senator William Owen, the police are simply "stopping hundreds of people just because they are young and black." The inner cities are becoming police states, compounding the stresses created by the violence dealers employ against each other (and against innocent bystanders). When layered atop the existing ravages of poverty and unemployment, such conditions surely must make the temporary escape offered by drugs seem all the more appealing.

Consider drug dealers. Many inner-city dealers, particularly at the retail level, arrive at their trade by one of two routes. Either they are dealing to support a habit, or the lack of decent employment opportunities has made dealing the only means of achieving even modest prosperity. For the first group, giving up dealing would mean giving up their own consumption of drugs—an unappealing alternative for an addict. For the second group, life without the income from dealing would be little harsher than time spent in jail. For both groups, then, imprisonment seems little worse than the alternative they must face if they give up dealing.

Just as importantly, the high incidence of drug use and trafficking in the inner cities, combined with the generally high crime rates there, mean that the risks of being caught are pitifully low. In addition, the court systems are staggering under unprecedented caseloads. As a result, more than 90 percent of all drug arrests end up as plea bargains, entailing little or no jail time. Thus, despite the seemingly impressive number of drug arrests—more than 1.2 million a year nationwide—the chances are small that any given dealer will actually go to jail for an extended period of time. As a result, dealers in the inner cities, like users there, rightly regard the laws against drugs as being simply one more obstacle in their mazelike existence. And so they press on, drawn by the lure of drugs, fleeing the carnage around them.

THE WORST OF BOTH WORLDS

Productive social policy weighs the pros and cons, the benefits and costs, of alternative courses of action. The goal of action is the attainment of a beneficial objective. In the war on drugs, this objective is presumably a reduction in the human misery and economic and social havoc caused by addiction and abuse of psychoactive agents. Yet balanced against this objective should be a consideration of the possible adverse consequences of government action. Just as the destructive repercussions of drug abuse and addiction should militate against the allure of psychoactives, so too should a clear-eyed reckoning of the costs of social policy steer us away from false promises of policies that are doomed to fail.

A superficial view of the world suggests that the war on drugs should concentrate on our nation's inner cities, where drug use is most pervasive, and where the ravages of drug abuse are most likely to be felt. This view is complemented by the ease with which success, at least when measured by the body counts of arrests, convictions, and imprisonments, can be achieved in the inner cities. On the surface, it is a marriage of ideals and outcomes without peer.

Yet this view is sadly flawed. As we have seen, the very conditions that make the inner cities fertile ground for psychoactives also make them impervious to frontal assault. In focusing the war on drugs upon the inner cities, the government has arrayed an indomitable force against an unyielding object, dissipating the available resources and accomplishing no productive end. Indeed, our efforts have had results that can only be considered perverse. We have created horrors that were absent before, and have failed to alleviate the misery that preceded them, leaving the residents of the inner cities with the worst of both worlds. Even as the inner cities reveal in extremis the adverse effects of the war on drugs, they suggest the immense gains that are possible from an alternative policy—a policy that we will outline in chapter 11.

CHAPTER 5

....

Blinding Justice

AT FIRST GLANCE, THE EASIEST WAY TO UNDO DRUGS IN AMERICA would seem to be to arrest more drug dealers and drug addicts. If the people who sell drugs and the people who consume drugs are behind bars, they won't be using law-abiding citizens for target practice or burglarizing homes to support their habits. The result, it seems, would clearly be a safer, drug-free environment.

The data show that we are indeed putting more drug kingpins, street dealers, and drug users in jail. Drug arrests are up, mandatory minimum sentences for drug offenses are growing in popularity, and drug offenders are being sentenced to longer terms. Moreover, drug seizures have increased dramatically. In 1982, federal authorities seized just over 12,000 pounds of cocaine, or roughly 6 tons. In 1990, federal cocaine seizures exceeded 100 tons. Over the same period, seizures of marijuana and heroin also rose sharply; quantities that once would have been respectable totals for an entire year are now being seized every month.

Despite the impressive statistics, however, the amounts of drug trafficking and drug use have not been significantly reduced. Even in the face of the huge increases in drug arrests, in drug convictions, in drug prisoners, and in drug seizures, the drug *problem* is worse today than it was ten years ago. Indeed, all the evidence seems to show that the amount of drug trafficking, lawlessness, and violence in the United States has *increased* along with the increased efforts to capture, prosecute, and imprison traffickers and users of illicit drugs. Indeed, the federal government's emphasis on drug seizures, arrests, convictions, and imprisonment has led to a more dangerous society, one in which drugs are causing more damage rather than less. In this chapter, we show how we come to this conclusion.

THE PRISON POPULATION BOMB

In 1989, officials in northern California opened a 1,000-bed maximum-security prison at Pelican Bay. A 1,200-bed wing was added soon thereafter, bringing the capacity of the nation's largest state prison system to almost 50,000 inmates. There was one slight problem: By the end of 1989, the California state prison system already had 87,000 people in custody, with 250 being added every week. The California prison system now routinely operates at almost 200 percent of capacity, with two prisoners packed into one-person cells, and prison gyms and dayrooms being used to house the inmates for whom there is no cell space.

The California story is no anomaly; it is being repeated across the country. The federal prison system was designed to hold 29,000 inmates, but at last count, there were almost 60,000 prisoners crammed into federal jails. The total of state prison populations exceeds 700,000 inmates, up over 100 percent since 1980, and more than 250,000 above capacity.[1] Eighty percent of the states have prison populations at historic highs, and within a few years, all of them will likely have record numbers of inmates jamming their prison systems. At the county and city levels across the country, there are estimated to be 300,000 inmates, far more than those facilities were designed to hold. Overall, there were more than one million Americans in jail at the beginning of the 1990s.

We now have a larger percentage of our population in prison than any industrialized country in the world.[2] Moreover, our prison population is growing faster than at any other time in our nation's history. From 1989 to 1990 the number of persons in state and federal prisons rose by more than 85,000, an increase of nearly 15 percent in one year alone.[3] If current growth rates in the prison population continue, we will see a doubling of that population every five years. At current growth rates, there will be nearly 2 million people in jail by 1995. In the year 2000 the prison population will number almost 4 million persons, and by the year 2010 there will be 15 million Americans in jail. Look around you: In less than twenty years, one out of every fifteen adults in America will be in prison.

THE COST OF THE PRISON SYSTEM

As the number of arrests and incarcerations in the United States increases, the cost of building and operating prisons is increasing in lockstep. We need 1,700 new prison beds a week to handle the current inflow of prisoners, and they do not come free of charge. The average cost of construction per prison bed ranges from $50,000 at a minimum-security site to $100,000 or more in a maximum-security facility.[4] When operational costs are included and construction costs are amortized over the life of a facility, the cost of sentencing one person to one year in jail averages between $25,000 and $40,000.[5] Thus, the annual nationwide cost of building, maintaining, and operating prisons is about $35 billion today. Given the projected growth in the prison population, within fifteen years we will be spending more on prisons than we are currently spending on national defense.

Even impressive dollar amounts like these don't reveal the full picture. The real cost of our exploding prison population lies in the fact that we are giving up more and more of other desired goods and services as we spend more and more on our prison system. We are giving up potential teachers and schools. We are giving up health-care systems that would improve the lives of our elderly. We aren't supporting the prenatal care and nutritional assistance that would reduce the high infant mortality rate that ravages impoverished families. We are even giving up the opportunity to protect and enhance the environment.

Incurring the cost of these tradeoffs would make sense as a course of action if the growing prison population were producing demonstrable beneficial results—fewer muggings, fewer random killings, or a smaller chance of having one's house robbed. But just the opposite is happening: Crime rates are rising throughout the land, particularly for serious crimes. The fear of being a victim—of assault, burglary, or even murder—is spreading like a cancer through the land. Moreover, as we show, the rise of serious crime is happening *because* of the best efforts of our law-enforcement officials, not *despite* their efforts. Let's see why.

THE PERVERSE EFFECT OF DRUG ARRESTS

More than one million Americans are being arrested each year on drug charges, and tens of thousands of them are going to prison for extended sentences. The proportion of prisoners who are in jail on drug charges—often simple possession charges—is growing at a record rate. Presently, more than 10 percent of the inmates in state prisons are drug-law violators, and more than a third of all federal prison inmates were jailed on drug charges.[6] As early as 1987, the number of persons in New York State prisons on drug-law violations actually surpassed those who were there on first-degree robbery charges. Between 1983 and 1988, the number of people imprisoned on drug-law violations in Florida grew more than 500 percent, and roughly 30 percent of all felonies in Florida are now drug felonies.[7] Throughout the country, from Washington, D.C., to California, drug offenders are the fastest growing segment of the prison population. The U.S. Sentencing Commission has predicted that by the year 2000, the number of federal prison inmates will have at least doubled, and possibly tripled, and that fully one-half will be there on drug-law violations.[8]

The drug warriors have been pouring drug-law violators into our nation's prison system at double or triple the rate at which that system can accommodate them. As a result, our prisons are now literally, as well as figuratively, overflowing into the streets. Because prisons are filled so far above their designed capacities, judges in states across the country are imposing "cap laws" on inmate populations. Under a cap law, as soon as the number of inmates hits the maximum allowable number, every new admission to the prison system legally must be accompanied by the release of an existing prisoner—regardless of the dangers that might result. In Connecticut, one sheriff faced with the application of a cap law ordered his deputies to forcibly commandeer a little-used National Guard armory to house inmates from his overflowing jail! Law-enforcement officials in Florida have simply complied with their cap law; partly as a result, the average inmate in Florida prisons serves only 35 percent of his or her sentenced time, down from 50 percent just a few years ago.[9]

The experience of Jacksonville, Florida, illustrates the dangers of overflowing jails. In one recent year, the convictions obtained by the Jacksonville prosecutor's office resulted in 1,167 people receiving prison sentences of at least one year. Within five months, 712 of those had been granted early release from the overcrowded state prison system; many of these convicts had actually been sent directly to work-release programs without spending a day in the state prison. By March of the next year, 359 of the 712 who had been released had been rearrested for serious new felonies. Because most of those arrested had already committed several crimes before their actual arrest, more than 1,000 new felonies were thus committed by individuals who should have been in prison.[10]

Consider the implications on a nationwide basis. According to the Federal Bureau of Investigation, the average professional criminal commits more than 150 crimes per year. The FBI also estimates that the average cost of a single crime is $2,300, and thus the typical professional criminal costs us nearly $400,000 every year he or she is on the street.[11] Every time a marijuana smoker is incarcerated in a state with a cap law, an existing prisoner must be released prematurely. Because the majority of all prison inmates have been incarcerated for crimes such as assault, larceny, fraud, burglary, car theft, rape, or murder, they are the ones who are most likely to be released. A pot bust may relieve us of the fear that our neighbor might be getting stoned on Saturday night, but the price we pay is the premature release from jail of a car thief, or perhaps a burglar or rapist. *This* is the tradeoff we face every day in the war on drugs.

Thus far, the drug warriors have decided that it is, indeed, more important to put casual drug users *in* jail than it is to *keep* professional felons there. Partly as a result of this decision, there is now a 20 percent chance that a household of four will be victimized by a serious crime in any given year. Moreover, criminals are today less likely to go to jail for their crimes than they were thirty years ago. In 1960, there was a 6 percent chance of going to jail for committing a crime; today the chance is only 4 percent.[12] All the drug arrests, the drug seizures, and the drug imprisonments add up to one thing: Criminals who avoid breaking the *drug* laws—the felons who "just say no"— are having a field day.

THE USE OF POLICE TIME

Clearly, prison populations can only rise if people are arrested, and drug arrests are rising at a record pace. Between 1984 and 1988, drug arrests increased nearly 60 percent, and the number of drug arrests each year now totals over 1.2 million.[13] And because the number of police is growing much more slowly than is the number of drug arrests, police have less and less time to do other things, such as enforcing the laws against assault, theft, and murder.

The case of Desmond Legister, age twenty-four, graphically illustrates this point. Legister was arrested in June 1989 for selling cocaine to an undercover New York City police officer. His arrest was the culmination of a five-week-long surveillance operation involving eight New York police officers. When Legister's case came to trial in the summer of 1990, the officers each spent an average of six days in the courtroom, either testifying or waiting to testify. The total police commitment involved in putting Legister behind bars exceeded 200 working days—nearly the equivalent of a full year's worth of a police officer's time.[14]

Again, we see the tradeoff that exists in the war on drugs. For every hour (or week, or month) that a police officer devotes to capturing someone like Desmond Legister, that police officer is *not* spending it doing something else—perhaps preventing one of the 215 or so murders that took place in New York City during the five weeks that Desmond Legister was under surveillance, or the 85 rapes committed in New York while his trial was under way. The reality of today is that urban law enforcement has become all too often synonymous with drug-law enforcement; and so the enforcement of our other laws often falls by the wayside.

Removing Desmond Legister from the streets of New York no doubt conferred benefits on the city's residents. Legister admitted that he had been involved with drugs since he was seventeen, and it is likely that, had he not been convicted, he would have returned to using and selling drugs. Nevertheless, one may well wonder whether the effort was worth it. Was Desmond Legister a "Mr. Big," racking up millions in profits each year? Was he a drug kingpin, distributing hundreds of kilos of cocaine throughout the country? Apparently not. Legister merely purchased cocaine on behalf of the undercover officer who arrested him, using money provided by the officer. According to Legister's testimony at trial, his sole payment for acting as the courier in the deal was a share of the cocaine, "about the size of a quarter." Yet in New York, couriers are just as culpable as kingpins. Desmond Legister is now serving twenty years in the New York State penitentiary. His arrest and trial cost the city of New York almost $150,000; his incarceration will cost the citizens of New York an additional $1,000,000 or so. In return, the authorities have guaranteed that Legister will not imperil the city's residents again until the year 2010.[15]

CRISIS IN THE COURTS

Our judicial system has a drug problem. The problem is not drug deals on the courthouse steps (although that happens). The problem is not drugs being sold in the halls of the U.S. Department of Justice (although that happens too). The real problem is the inability of the courts to handle the growing number of cases involving drugs. In the words of Chief Assistant District Attorney Robert Sieberling, "The system is just being overrun by drug cases."

Federal Courts

The crisis begins in the federal courts. In 1980, there were approximately 1,700 drug trials in federal district courts. By 1990 that number had grown to 3,500.[16] The doubling in the number of criminal drug cases means that *civil* cases no longer can get to trial. Consider one important civil case filed in 1986. The state of Florida accused Great Lakes Chemical Corporation of contaminating ground water at twenty-two sites throughout the state of Florida, exposing tens of thousands of residents to carcinogenic chemicals. Yet the lawsuit to determine how much cleanup is required and who should pay for it cannot get to trial; all of the federal courts in which the case might be tried are booked solid with drug cases.[17]

Why do civil cases—even ones involving environmental damages, civil rights violations, and job discrimination—take a backseat to criminal cases? Because of the Speedy Trial Act, which requires priority handling for criminal cases, and thus puts drug and other criminal prosecutions on the docket ahead of civil suits. As the federal government and Congress step up drug-enforcement efforts by hiring more federal prosecutors and concentrating investigative personnel on drug cases, the court-crowding problem is becoming increasingly severe. A decade ago, less than a quarter of the criminal trials in federal courts involved drug cases. Today almost 50 percent of these trials involve drugs, and the number is growing.[18]

Politics also play a role in swamping the federal court system with drug cases. In Manhattan, an arbitrary number of drug arrests are randomly assigned to federal courts. Everyone arrested on drug charges on one particular day, called the "federal day," is prosecuted on federal rather than state charges. This maneuver keeps the "body count" up for federal prosecutors, presumably demonstrating their commitment to winning the war on drugs. In some districts every case involving crack is being brought to federal court. As we shall see below, this is partly because state courts are themselves overwhelmed with drug cases. But there is also little doubt that federal authorities want the political credit for being seen in the front lines of the war against crack.

The drug problem in federal courts is not confined to border areas such as Miami or San Diego. Drug cases now overwhelm the trial dockets of federal judges in Arizona, Arkansas, New Jersey, New Mexico, North Dakota, Tennessee, and West Virginia. Moreover, the cases are becoming far more complex than they used to be, and often involve numerous defendants. Drug trials often last up to six weeks, consuming all the court's resources—the judge, clerks, and security personnel—during that time. In some federal courts, 70 percent of trial time is spent on criminal drug cases. In one eight-month period, two federal judges hearing cases in Tallahassee, Gainesville, and Panama City, Florida (an area of nineteen counties) hadn't heard a single civil trial.[19] Nationwide, the number of civil cases that have been pending in federal courts for more than three years has increased almost 70 percent since 1984. Unless you've committed a drug crime, the chances that you will find justice in a federal district court are rapidly disappearing.*

In October 1989 the Judicial Conference of the United States, headed by Supreme Court Chief Justice William Rehnquist, made a plea to Congress for more money and more judges to help handle the

---

*Every delay in a civil lawsuit inevitably raises the costs of that suit. Because many of the civil cases that are being stalled involve corporate America, the delays are adding staggering sums to the legal bills of many corporations. There is little doubt that part of those higher legal bills are passed on to consumers in the form of higher product and service prices. You are paying for America's war on drugs in more than one way.

growing crisis. Claiming that "the war on drugs will fail if the judiciary is not given the judgeships necessary to do the job," Rehnquist asked Congress to create immediately 59 new federal district court judgeships, raising the total number to 634. The Conference further requested 16 new judges for the federal appellate courts, raising their total to 184.[20] Now, the $10 million that these judgeships would cost each year doesn't sound like much, compared to the billions we are already spending on the drug wars, and adding about 10 percent to the size of federal district and appellate courts seems modest considering the exploding number of drug cases. But consider this: During the first two centuries of our nation's existence, we expanded from thirteen states to fifty states, and our population grew from 3 million people to 250 million. We accomplished this enormous national development with fewer than three new district court judges per year, and one new appellate court judge only every fifteen months. The Judicial Conference's request for fifty-nine district court judges and sixteen appellate court judges thus amounts to twenty years' worth of new federal judges, just to catch up on the work load imposed by new drug cases.

State Courts

If the federal courts are feeling the heat of the frying pan, the state courts are already in the fire, because the vast majority of all drug prosecutions—well over 95 percent—are handled in state and local courts. Indeed, drug cases are rapidly becoming the principal business of many state and municipal court systems. In New York City, the percentage of felony cases involving drugs nearly doubled during the last half of the 1980s, and by 1990, alleged drug-law violations accounted for 45 percent of all felony indictments. In Washington, D.C., drug cases account for nearly two-thirds of all felony indictments. In some jurisdictions, state judges have backlogs of up to 250 drug cases waiting on their dockets, and the prosecutors appearing before them are often working on forty or more drug prosecutions at once. The courts in New York City alone process more than 100,000 drug cases a year, half of them felony cases.[21]

Events in the state of Washington—seemingly located far from the mainstream drug trade—illustrate the nationwide character of the problem. State prosecutors are so overwhelmed with the growing backlog of drug cases that they are now deputizing volunteer lawyers from private law firms to serve as prosecutors—at no charge to the state. Although *pro bono* work for indigent defendants in criminal trials is a well-established tradition in the legal profession, *pro bono* work for the prosecution is almost unheard of in criminal law.*

Additional measures have also been taken in Washington to bring on more judges. Trial judges from counties without backlogs have been temporarily moved to King County (the location of Seattle), where more than 500 drug cases were awaiting disposition. Retired judges have agreed to return to the bench temporarily. Charles B. Johnson, the presiding judge of the King County Superior Court, has even appointed lawyers from private practice to serve as *pro tem* judges—temporary judges for particular cases.[22]

Not everybody thinks these programs improve the judicial system. Most of the volunteer prosecutors, for example, are quite young and have little experience. They receive a scant three days of training by senior prosecutors before taking drug cases to trial, and are rarely supervised during such trials. And, as one public defender pointed out, many cases that might have been removed from the court's docket through plea bargaining will end up being tried. Even the efforts to beef up the judiciary have been criticized. To some observers, shuttling judges around the state simply to get rid of backlogs smacks more of expediency than of justice. Moreover, bringing in attorneys to serve as *pro tem* judges for isolated cases threatens to introduce an unpredictable, arbitrary element into the criminal justice system. Nevertheless, Washington, like many other jurisdictions around the country, felt it had little choice. With drug cases piling up at an extraordinary rate, it seems that extraordinary measures are the only answer.

CRIMINAL INJUSTICE

Effective law enforcement begins with self-enforcement, the choice to obey the law even when "no one is looking." Short of having a police officer on every street corner, the only way citizens will choose

---

*Why would private law firms donate time to prosecuting criminal cases? There are two reasons: First, it gives their young, unseasoned attorneys valuable practical experience in court; second, if the drug-case backlog is reduced, this will free up court time in which the private firms can proceed with their stalled civil cases.

to obey laws is if legally proscribed behavior is generally recognized by the citizenry as unacceptable, improper behavior. Self-enforcement of the law depends on the belief that the law and the legal system are *just*, which is to say both impartial and evenhanded. But for many people in America, our drug laws are neither impartial nor evenhanded, and this engenders disrespect not only for the drug laws but for the entire legal system. The result is growing disregard for legal statutes other than our drug laws, and a rise in lawless behavior throughout all of society.

We saw in chapter 4 that inner-city residents have become "targets of opportunity" for those who enforce the drug laws. These citizens, predominantly black and lower-income, have come to feel that they are being unjustly singled out for harsh treatment in the application of the drug laws. And since the police, the prosecutors, and the courts that administer the drug laws also administer the laws regarding theft, assault, and murder, it is little wonder that many inner-city residents believe they are treated unjustly in the application of these other statutes. This perception of injustice brings with it a sense of contempt, both for the law and the administrators of the law. The result can only be a decline in the extent of self-enforcement and a rise in lawless behavior generally.

But the issue extends far beyond the inner city, and beyond the divisions of white and black, or rich and poor. Roughly 40 million Americans violate our drug laws every year, yet fewer than 3 percent of them are punished for doing so. The million-plus drug arrests each year are enough to overwhelm our police and jails and courts, but the 35 to 40 million *non*-arrests each year are enough to convince many Americans that the drug laws are not being applied uniformly.[23] The problem is not that the police and the courts aren't *trying*, but that the mandate from the politicians—particularly the ones in Washington, D.C.—is just too broad. Faced with orders to deter 35 to 40 million drug users, but given the resources to catch less than 3 percent of them, the police and the courts simply *can't* mete out evenhanded justice. Thus, one person smokes a marijuana joint and goes to prison for a year, while forty of his neighbors commit the same crime and go back to work on Monday morning.

Even among those drug users and dealers who are caught, the outcomes make a mockery of justice. There just aren't enough judges and prosecutors to bring to trial all persons arrested on drug charges each year.* And so, the authorities attempt to induce drug defendants to enter plea bargains, in which the defendant pleads guilty in return for a reduced sentence. In the courts of some major urban areas, individual judges process anywhere from 70 to 100 plea-bargained drug cases a day, dispensing what one commentator has called "fast-food justice." Where does this leave the person who believes he or she is innocent? To face the wrath of a trial judge who may well impose the maximum legal sentence if the jury returns a guilty verdict. The result is that the penalty for *exactly* the same alleged violation of the drug laws can result in probation for one defendant and twenty years in the penitentiary for another. Disparities such as this may be the inevitable outcome of a judicial system that is overwhelmed, but they just as inevitably create the belief that the product of our legal system is not always justice.

Sadly, it is the police who may be placed in the most difficult position by our drug laws, a position that has been tragic for both law enforcement and the officers who enforce the law. The idealized role of the police officer—"to protect and serve," as it says on the doors of Los Angeles police cars—exists no more. Nationwide, state and local law-enforcement agencies spend approximately 25 percent of their enforcement budgets on drug-law enforcement. In major urban areas, the percentage is much higher, transforming law enforcement into drug-law enforcement. Increasingly, the police are finding that their mandate is one of intruding upon, ensnaring, and sometimes entrapping people who don't steal or rape or murder, but who do occasionally smoke a joint or snort a line of cocaine. Do not misunderstand: The police are simply enforcing the drug laws they are sworn to uphold. But doing so has left them with considerably less time to protect citizens from the violators of the *other* laws—and left many people wondering just who is being served. The result has been growing animosity toward the police, and a growing sense that they have become enemies, rather than allies.

This animosity has made the job of the police more difficult and more dangerous. For the 35 to 40 million Americans who violate the

*The reason there are not is that we can't afford them. Consider New York City, where the 100,000 drug arrests each year are equally divided between misdemeanors and felonies. If all of these felony drug defendants were brought to trial, the annual cost to the city would be $6 billion—requiring additional taxes of $750 per year for each man, woman, and child in the city. And, of course, this calculation ignores the costs of bringing to trial the 50,000 additional persons accused only of misdemeanor drug violations.

drug laws every year, the appearance of a police officer represents a direct threat to their freedom. More than one law officer has been shot down while trying to issue a routine traffic ticket, simply because the driver had drugs in the car and thought the officer suspected their presence. The personal safety of police officers is also threatened by the structure of the penalties attached to the very drug laws they enforce. As drug penalties have become tougher, dealers and users have been driven to greater lengths to avoid being caught, lengths that often involve violence.

After sending Desmond Legister to twenty years in prison for selling cocaine to an undercover officer, the sentencing judge remarked, "The crime of selling drugs is just as serious, if not more so, as the crime of murder." The chilling implication of such reasoning is that Desmond Legister might have been better off killing the cop to whom he sold the drugs; at least the officer would not have been able to testify against him at trial. This very thought must have crossed the minds of all too many of those dealers and users who have killed police officers in the drug wars.

IS THERE AN ANSWER?

Justice is depicted as a blindfolded goddess, carrying a sword in one hand and a set of scales in the other. The blindfold symbolizes her obligation to judge solely according to the guilt or innocence of those who stand before her, while the scales weigh the balance of the evidence. And with the sword, she dispenses the consequences of her judgment.

Laws reflect our attempts to implement the ideal of justice, but they rarely match the lofty goals depicted by our symbols. Laws are imperfect, and it is tempting to conclude that the failings of our drug laws are no more than confirmation of this fact. But in the zealous pursuit of the battle against drugs, the drug laws have blinded justice to the balance of her scales and to the victims of her sword.

The value of imprisoning casual drug users has been weighed against the costs of freeing violent felons, and the perpetrators of assault and rape have been set free. Drug dealers have been weighed against murderers, and the dealers have gone to jail. The urge to do something has been judged against the desire to do the right thing, and expediency has vanquished equity. In the process, we have all become the victims. We have not rid the streets of drugs, dealers, or users. We have not achieved the security and freedom from fear that we seek. Instead, we have transformed our streets into battlegrounds, and our prisons into overflowing cesspools. We have forced our judges to process the faceless case numbers that fill their dockets, rather than weigh the fate and the futures of the human beings who appear before them. We have turned our police into our antagonists, and ourselves into their enemies. And we have consumed an ever-increasing share of our scarce and valuable resources, depriving ourselves of other benefits that could have been reaped instead.

Is there an answer to the crisis that grips our criminal justice system? One approach is to spend more money for prisons, judges, prosecutors, and police. Yet during the last decade, our spending on the drug wars has doubled and then doubled again, with little apparent benefit. Continuing on this path will create a society in which all of our social goals are subservient to our obsession with drugs. An alternative approach is simply to give up—to seek to return somehow to an era in which our government largely ignored drugs and the potential adverse consequences of their use and abuse. Whatever reduction in the financial burden of government such action might bring, few of us would care to contemplate a society in which PCP, crack cocaine, and heroin would be as readily available as a gallon of milk or a loaf of bread. Somewhere between these extremes there must be a middle ground in which to strike the balance symbolized by justice's scales and to deliver the equitable outcomes we expect of her sword. Finding this middle ground will be no easy task, yet we cannot even begin until we fully unmask the horrors brought on by today's misguided policies.

CHAPTER 6

······························

Organizing Crime

TAKE A WALK ON THE WILD SIDE. GO UP BROADWAY AND THE UPPER WEST Side of Manhattan into the area known as Washington Heights. When you reach streets numbered in the 150s and 160s, turn right or left on to one of them. What you will see is an American nightmare come true: tough teenagers standing in groups, displaying gold rings on their fingers, $180 Nike "Air" shoes, telephone pagers, and something else—$3 to $5 vials of crack. On virtually every block, four or five different groups stand around, each touting their own brand of the drug. In some sections of the Upper West Side, crack is available twenty-four hours a day, seven days a week. Washington Heights is the crack capital of America.

But crack is everywhere. Even in Fort Wayne, Indiana—known as the City of Churches—there are over 100 crack houses, making it the crack capital of Indiana. How has crack moved from New York City to Fort Wayne—and to Seaford, Delaware, and Ashton, Idaho, and hundreds of other towns and cities across the hinterlands? By the efforts of a small cadre of street gangs, whose young, predominantly black members make a handsome living distributing crack across the United States. In the eastern half of the country, from New York to Dallas, the crack trade is dominated by the Jamaican immigrant posses—gangs that didn't exist a decade ago. In the West, from San Diego to Seattle to Kansas City, the trade is run by the Los Angeles–based Bloods and Crips—gangs that once spent most of their time squabbling over who got to smoke cigarettes in the high school parking lot after basketball games. To understand how these street gangs have emerged out of nowhere to become organized and potent forces in American society, we must first know a bit more about the origins and economics of crack cocaine. Along the way we shall come to understand how and why the war on drugs is the catalyst for the rise of organized crime in the United States.

THE ORIGINS OF CRACK

Until about 1983, cocaine hydrochloride (known simply as "cocaine") was used almost exclusively as a powder, ingested by being snorted into the nasal passages. Only a daring handful of individuals had tried "freebasing," which required treating cocaine powder with ether, thereby reducing the drug to a smokable crystalline base. Freebasing produced a sharp, pleasurable "rush" that was far more intense than that achieved by snorting ordinary cocaine. Yet the procedure was complicated, messy, and risky—as the comedian Richard Pryor discovered when he was severely burned in a freebasing explosion. Fearful of the risks of homemade freebase, but searching for higher highs, users began asking their dealers to supply them with ready-made freebase.

Dealers were faced with a business dilemma. When cocaine is converted to freebase, it loses much of its weight. In effect, it "shrinks," which made it difficult to sell at popular prices—unless dealers could add an undetectable filler that would increase the weight and bulk of the product.

The dilemma was first solved by Dominican gangs in New York, who came up with a filler they called "comeback." They found that when a chemical similar to the prescription anesthetic lidocaine was blended with cocaine powder and cooked, the resulting blend crystallized into a relatively homogeneous, smokable "rock." This concoction was the prototype for today's crack.

Comeback was expensive, however, and dealers continued to search for a cheaper filler. They found baking soda. The formula thus devised required two parts cocaine hydrochloride, mixed with two parts comeback and one part Arm & Hammer baking soda. Water was added and the mixture brought to a boil. After cooling, the resulting crystalline mass was broken into little pieces and smoked. Two ounces of cocaine powder, plus two ounces of comeback and one ounce of Arm & Hammer, yielded enough product for 2,000 "hits." In 1983, Dominican dealers were selling these hits for $5 to $10 each.

The ready-made freebase was soon named "crack," a term derived from the crackling sound that the drug makes when smoked.[1]

For several years cocaine had been the drug of choice for upper- and middle-class yuppies. The advent of crack made cocaine available, albeit in diluted form, to the unemployed dropouts and impoverished drifters of American society. And just about anybody could get into the business of supplying crack, because all it took was an ounce of cocaine (costing about $2,000 in 1983) and some easily purchased comeback and baking soda. Since cocaine was already arriving in New York by the ton, fledgling entrepreneurs were soon distributing crack on side streets throughout the city.

The rapid proliferation of hundreds of independent crack dealers became the distinguishing feature of the early days of the crack trade, and set the distribution of the drug apart from the other major drugs with which it competed. The distribution of heroin in the United States, for example, has always been well managed and controlled by a few organizations. Similarly, the distribution system for Colombian cocaine has also always been in the hands of a few well-managed cartels. The distribution of crack initially differed from these two systems because getting into the business required so little money. Any one of the two million Americans who buy cocaine in any given month was a potential manufacturer and distributor of crack. Even a well-heeled crack organization could consist of as few as seven or eight individuals: two or three street sellers, a "steerer" to direct the customers, a weigher, a manager, and a guard—plus, of course, a "Mr. Big" who counted the profits.

A NEW BREED OF STREET GANGS

Crack came to the attention of the national press in late 1985. By then it was already deeply entrenched in New York's poorer neighborhoods, and turf wars were breaking out over the most lucrative locations. Since crack is illegal, dealers cannot use the legal system to establish exclusive rights over their commercial territories; thus, the only effective method of establishing property rights over sales locations is violence. Turf wars have nothing to do with the drug per se; they arise because the sellers cannot utilize the police and the courts to enforce property rights.

Sometime late in 1985, one of the most vicious groups of individuals ever to set foot in America burst upon the crack business. Legal and illegal immigrants from the island nation of Jamaica used an effective blend of violence and intimidation to establish themselves as the premier crack traffickers in the United States. Along the way, they transformed what had been a little-noticed, locally based trade into a nationwide distribution network.

History is sketchy on exactly when this transformation took place, but it appears to have been pioneered by Delroy Edwards, who had grown up in the shanty towns of Kingston, Jamaica. In 1980, at the age of twenty, Edwards was a street enforcer for the Jamaican labor party of Edward Seaga. Seaga was in the midst of a bitter election campaign against Michael Manley, the head of the People's National Party, and each side in the election used armed gangs to intimidate the other. By election day almost a thousand Jamaicans had been killed by these gangs. When Seaga was elected, he cracked down on the gangs, which had become difficult to control. Many gang members, including Delroy Edwards, fled to the United States.

Edwards started out peddling marijuana, but soon learned to make crack. Doing business out of two choice locations in Brooklyn, he soon was able to buy a $300,000 home on Long Island, for which he paid cash. Edwards wanted to expand his crack business, but found that New York was already crowded with competing dealers. Other areas, however, including Washington, D.C., Philadelphia, and Baltimore, were wide-open territories. In the autumn of 1986, Edwards went to D.C. and set up shop selling crack. In the spring of 1987, he established operations in Baltimore and Philadelphia. By this time Edwards's organization (known as the "Rankers") was one of the nation's biggest crack networks. There were about fifty workers, and they grossed about $100,000 a day.[2]

Edwards was nicknamed "Uzi" because the Israel-made Uzi submachine gun was his favorite weapon when business got serious. His penchant for violence was legendary in the trade. Those who crossed Edwards were pistol-whipped, beaten with baseball bats, or doused with scalding water. And if these methods did not succeed, there was always the Uzi. Edwards was eventually indicted and convicted on forty-two counts of murder, kidnapping, assault, and drug dealing. His incarceration led to the disintegration of the Rankers, but word of his early successes had already attracted considerable attention back in Jamaica. By the dozens, and then by the hundreds, veterans of the 1980 Jamaican election gangs were entering America with one goal in mind: to get rich selling crack.

THE RISE OF THE POSSES

Today there are estimated to be between 10,000 and 20,000 Jamaicans, mostly illegal immigrants, organized into a crack distribution chain that extends from New York to Miami to Dallas and encompasses dozens of cities and towns in between. Each of the territories within this chain are controlled by armed posses, some of which have as few as twenty-five members, others of which claim membership totals in the hundreds. Together, the Jamaican posses control an estimated 40 percent of the nation's crack sales.

The posse members who have followed in "Uzi" Edwards's footsteps have adopted many of the business practices that made him successful, including, above all else, the use of violence. According to the U.S. Bureau of Alcohol, Tobacco, and Firearms, the Jamaican posses have been responsible for well over 1,000 murders since 1985.[3] When they enter new territory controlled by local dealers, the posses simply murder their competitors. Indeed, some law-enforcement officials report being tipped off to the entry of posses into their jurisdictions by a sudden rise in the violent death rate of established crack dealers. Eventually, these "trademark" murders tail off, signaling that the Jamaicans have firmly established control of the local market.

The violent habits of the Jamaicans do not interfere with their good business sense. When crack is selling for $5 a vial in New York, but $12 in Kansas City, they move into Kansas City. But to make sure that new territory is properly cultivated, the Jamaicans use New York as a training ground. Once a posse member does well in Harlem or Brooklyn, he might be sent to open up an office in, say, Ames, Iowa. Upon arrival in a new area, he rents a motel room and does a market survey to determine where he should set up business. Then he rents an apartment in the appropriate location and begins selling.

The posses move crack across the United States with ease, partly because of their considerable forethought. For long-distance travel, commercial airlines are the preferred mode. The couriers who fly are overweight women who can easily conceal one- or two-pound packages of crack on their persons. For shorter trips, posse members simply rent cars and drive the interstates, obeying the speed limit all the way. Wherever they go, the Jamaicans follow the path of least resistance. A city with a well-organized criminal group already in power does not appeal to them as a new territory, simply because it is too much trouble to displace the resident gangs. Thus, the Jamaicans have stayed away from St. Louis, Newark, and Chicago, where homegrown gangs have the crack trade locked up.[4]

But wherever the Jamaicans do decide to move, they come in with guns blazing, using AR-13 assault rifles and Uzi submachine guns acquired in such states as Virginia, Texas, and Florida, where gun laws are lax. As a result of their good business sense and penchant for violence, the Jamaican posses are thriving today in Hartford, Connecticut; Newburgh, Kingston, and Sarasota Springs, New York; Martinsburg and Charleston, West Virginia; Chambersburg, Pennsylvania; Roanoke, Virginia; and a host of other towns and cities across the eastern half of the United States.[5]

THE BEST OF THE WEST

On the wall of the sheriff's office in Whittier, California, twelve miles southeast of downtown Los Angeles, there is a map of the United States. Early in 1990 there were two dozen dots arrayed upon it; today there are undoubtedly many more. The map went up several years ago to track the migration of drug-dealing, Los Angeles–based gangs into markets outside of southern California. Many of the dots are placed on medium- and large-sized cities where the appearance of gangs might seem unsurprising. But some of the locations are distinctly unsettling. The twenty-third dot, for example, was placed on Ashton, Idaho (population 1,200), a town with a one-man police force. Detective Bob Jackson of the Los Angeles Police Department's gang division explains that the appearance of Ashton on the map simply illustrates one of the fundamental links between drugs and gangs: "If there is a market, they'll go there." The map in the Whittier sheriff's office seems to confirm Jackson's opinion. If one connects the dots, the lines that result form a web across the United States.

The Rise of the Bloods and the Crips

Most of the dots on the map in Whittier, California, mark the locations of branch offices of two gangs that originated on the streets of Los Angeles—the Bloods and the Crips. Ten years ago these two organizations were penny-ante street gangs squabbling over Los Angeles turf nobody else wanted. Then crack gave them the opportunity to become big-time players. When the prototype for crack was developed in 1983, word of the production process and its profit potential spread rapidly westward from New York. In Los Angeles, gang members tried crack, liked it, and started selling it in a big way. Employing the tactics used so well by the Jamaicans—violence and intimidation—the Bloods and the Crips dominated the Los Angeles crack scene, and then began looking for new markets. Spreading ever eastward, they established branch after branch in cities across the western half of the country, killing any competitors who threatened their profits. As law-enforcement officers were soon to learn, the Bloods and the Crips had an unerring nose for profits.

The Balloon Principle, Again

When you press your finger against an inflated balloon, the air inside simply stretches the balloon outward somewhere else. The drug warriors have seen the same results in fighting the crack gangs, as the case of the Kansas City, Missouri, drug wars illustrates. Late in 1986, after months of arduous effort, the Federal Organized-Crime Task Force succeeded in virtually destroying the Kansas City crack operation that had been established by Jamaican posses. At one point the Jamaicans had employed as many as 1,000 people, with headquarters in a fortresslike house in the heart of the city. But the Feds raided the headquarters as well as its satellite ghetto crack houses, and rounded up virtually all of the local Jamaican leadership, plus many of the posse street dealers. All in all, 178 of the Kansas City traffickers were prosecuted here in the United States, and 25 more were deported to Jamaica. By the beginning of 1987 no more than 75 posse members were known to be left in town. Kansas City was the success story of the year in the war on drugs.[6]

There was one small hitch, however. The Jamaican posse organization in Kansas City had originally grown to 1,000 members for the simple reason that Kansas City was an extremely lucrative crack market. When the Feds wiped out the Jamaican suppliers, they did nothing to alter the demand for the product the posses had been providing. Kansas City was still a crack dealer's paradise, and it didn't take the Bloods and Crips very long to figure that out. Early in 1987, the Los Angeles gangs, drawn by the profits of crack, began arriving in force, like air into a vacuum. Within less than six months, it was "business as usual" in the Kansas City crack trade.[7] And the ultimate impact of the well-publicized federal war on Kansas City crack? Now the sales, the murders, and profits belong to gangs who have their roots in Los Angeles rather than Jamaica.*

The Beat Goes On

By the end of the 1980s, the Bloods and the Crips together claimed over 10,000 members spread across more than fifty cities—often cities that had no previous experience with street gangs. In Denver, for example, the police department initially claimed that the city didn't have gangs, merely "unruly juveniles." The police have now identified more than 1,500 gang members in Denver and the suburb of Aurora.[8]

Omaha, Nebraska, now realizes that it, too, has a gang problem. Omaha's rude awakening occurred when four men were shot, two students assaulted, and two houses riddled with bullets after members of the Bloods and Crips moved into that city's low-income North Side. Omaha's police have since identified several hundred hard-core members, plus several hundred more "wannabes," or would-be gang members. One of the public housing projects in Omaha is even called "Vietnam" because of the daily warfare over drug turf there.

The citizens of Minneapolis have witnessed gang membership increase from about thirty known gang members in the middle of the 1980s to several thousand today. Because the gangs were attracted by the high prices for crack in Minneapolis, prices much higher than in Chicago, the newly arrived gangs dubbed the city "Moneyapolis." In a futile attempt to fight back, Minneapolis schools have banned the wearing of gang colors, and have prohibited telephone pagers (used to facilitate drug sales) on school grounds. Nonetheless, the gangs, their crack deals, and the violence continue to flourish.

*The remnants of the Kansas City posses moved on to Omaha and Des Moines, where they thrive even today.

PROMOTING THE GANGS

Earlier in the chapter, we noted that when the crack business started it was populated by small-time operators, most of whom operated alone or with a few other kindred souls. It did not take long for the independent operators to be displaced by large organizations, and within a few years the industry was dominated by highly organized gangs operating on a nationwide basis. Why gangs? And, perhaps more importantly, why *national* gangs?

As we noted in chapter 1, organized crime—the gang—predominates in the market for most illegal goods. This was true in the alcohol market during Prohibition; it has been true in the heroin trade since soon after the passage of the Harrison Act; and it is true today in the crack trade. The marketing of illegal commodities is the perfect breeding ground of the criminal organizations we call gangs, whether they are headed by Al Capone or by "Uzi" Edwards.

Gangs are simply partnerships or agreements between individuals or business firms who ordinarily would compete against each other for the business of their customers. The gang organization enables the suppliers of illegal goods to make supranormal profits by restricting competition among themselves. *All* business firms would like to earn the high profits of restricted competition, and many try to do so by merging to form monopolies or colluding to form price-fixing conspiracies. But American firms who sell legal commodities face powerful forces that generally prevent them from successfully forming monopolies or price-fixing conspiracies. First, monopoly and price-fixing are both illegal in this country, and any business executives involved in a price-fixing conspiracy face the risk of months in jail, plus hundreds of thousands of dollars in fines. Second, the higher profits of monopoly and price-fixing soon attract new, competing suppliers whose entry into the business drives prices and profits down. Third, buyers who dislike the high prices charged by a monopolist or price-fixer can easily complain to the legal authorities or to potential new suppliers, thus facilitating the operation of the first two forces.

For suppliers of illegal commodities, such as crack, these "forces" become no more bothersome than the buzzing of an insect. They are *already* engaged in an illegal activity that carries the risk of years of imprisonment, or death in a shootout with police. Even if the legal authorities chose to prosecute gang leaders for restraint of trade, the prospect of a few months in jail or a fine that amounts to, say, an hour's worth of illegal profits would be trivial for the drug lords.

The problem of competing suppliers is also little worry for the gangs that supply illegal goods. First, they can simply murder or intimidate rivals who might try to grab their profits. Firms that sell legal goods generally don't dare try this route (even if they might like to), because legal sanctions against violence threaten their reputations and the legitimate profits that flow from the rest of their operations. But for suppliers of drugs, the extra penalties from an aggravated assault charge (or even a murder charge) add little to the potential penalties they already face due to the illegal nature of their business. In fact, for illegal firms, being known for violence actually *enhances* their reputation, and helps keep potential competitors out of the business!

The second reason that drug gangs don't have to worry about competition from other firms is the diligent work of the police, who unwittingly *enforce* the monopolies of the gangs. When a new competitor tries to set up business, if the gang doesn't feel like killing him it simply informs upon him to the police, who, naturally enough, are happy to arrest the would-be competitor. (Note that law officers do not have to be in the pay of the drug gangs to be cooperative: The police benefit from making arrests, and are quite happy to utilize anonymous tips whatever the source.) The police also make sure that drug buyers don't complain about the high prices and profits of the gangs: Complaining to the authorities that you think the price of the cocaine you just bought is exorbitant will simply land you a lengthy stay in jail yourself. If a disgruntled buyer might be foolish enough to risk arrest, there is once again the favorite gang tool to make sure he doesn't: sudden death.

All in all, then, illegal markets are the perfect environment for organized gangs. But why *national* gangs, like the Jamaican posses and the Bloods and the Crips? The answer lies in the nationwide structure of drug policies and drug-law enforcement. Even though all the states have their own drug laws, all of these laws are heavily influenced by, and often directly patterned after, nationwide federal legislation. Virtually all of the original state laws outlawing marijuana, for example, were passed at the behest of the federal Bureau of Narcotics, and incorporated the specific language recommended by that agency. State laws regarding opiates and cocaine are also patterned after the wishes of the federal government. Not only does the U.S. Congress like it this way (because it increases congressional control over the states), but state legislators find it makes life easier for them: They don't have to bother to find out what's best for their constituents, and they have the unbeatable political cover of being able to say, "Our law is just as good as federal law."

There is a similar pattern when it comes to enforcing drug laws. Even though state and local police forces are involved in the process, it is federal agencies, such as the Drug Enforcement Administration (DEA), that take the lead. DEA agents like (and indeed insist upon) running the show, because doing so increases their power. State and local police tolerate orders from the Feds, because federal involvement means federal money. Moreover, if anything goes wrong (a common occurrence), state and local police can point the finger at federal bumbling.

The nationwide uniformity in laws and enforcement methods is a dream come true for the leaders of national drug gangs. It didn't take the Jamaican posses long to learn that business practices that beat the law and the police in New York would beat them in Fort Wayne and Richmond and Charleston. Similarly, members of the Bloods and Crips who earned their colors on the streets of Los Angeles could use their skills successfully against the prosecutors and cops in Seattle and San Diego. Moreover, on the rare occasions when DEA agents figured out a new trick to use against the traffickers, word of the innovation spread to the far-flung gang subsidiaries even faster than the police could put it in place against them. The only traffickers who got nabbed were small-time local dealers who weren't part of the national organizations. Just as national safety and auto pollution standards (rather than state-by-state standards) make it easier to mass-produce cars on a national scale, the heavy federal involvement in drug enforcement makes it easier to mass-market illicit drugs on a national scale.

The federal domination of drug-law enforcement even increases the incentive of the national gangs to employ violence as a competitive tool. Murdering one's rivals is a form of investment that pays off most handsomely when other potential rivals are convinced that you will be willing to murder them if they intrude. A local drug dealer has little incentive to risk a murder investigation simply to get rid of his competitor on the next block. But the national gangs know that word of their carnage in, say, Washington, D.C., will spread elsewhere, making entry into other markets that much easier. Thus, whenever the Jamaican posses or the West Coast gangs come into town, they have their Uzis set on full automatic.*

THE KIDS' CONNECTION

Kids are becoming crooks. Over the last decade, the crime rate among juveniles has soared in this country. Today's connection between kids and crime is forged with drugs, but it is a link that is unique in our history. As recently as ten years ago, most juveniles who came in contact with drugs did so solely as users. Only a few of the many young people who experimented became addicted, and it was here that their connection with crime began in earnest, for they were forced to turn to dealing or stealing to finance their habit.

Today, kids start out as criminals, and only later move on to consume the drugs in which they deal. Inner-city youths as young as eight or nine years old are getting their start in a life of crime by working for drug dealers in a variety of capacities: as spotters, who alert street sellers that the cops are coming; as couriers, who move money and drugs between headquarters and the street; and even as dealers themselves, handing over crack for cash. If and when they get around to using the drugs themselves, they may already have a police record worthy of a career criminal. Not surprisingly, it is the organized drug gangs who have made the most of the kids' connection. What may be more surprising is what has made the connection so lucrative—and so socially devastating.

The Drug-Law Lottery

Rayful Edmond III is an alleged murderer and a convicted drug kingpin. He is also a leading role model for poor youngsters in inner-

---

*The home front is not the only place that the federal drug effort is organizing crime. Our efforts to interdict drugs send their prices skyrocketing, which in turn creates enormous profit potential for those who supply the U.S. market. Fidel Castro of Cuba, for example, is believed to have used drug profits to finance a substantial amount of his country's armed intervention into Angola. Similarly, it appears that drug profits may have played an important role in keeping Manuel Noriega in control of Panama until U.S. military forces ousted him. In South America, two communist guerrilla groups, the "Shining Path" in Peru and "M-19" in Colombia, owe virtually all of their financing to drug trade profits—profits created almost solely by U.S. drug policy.

city Washington, D.C. At age eighteen, Edmond barely graduated from high school. By age twenty-four, he was tooling around inner-city Washington in a gold-wheeled Jaguar luxury sedan, wearing a $45,000 diamond-encrusted Rolex watch. And every time he pulled out the cash to buy Thanksgiving turkeys for the poor, or hot meals for the homeless, he was sure to flash a two-inch thick wad of $100 bills.

From 1986 until 1989, Edmond was head of D.C.'s largest cocaine operation, which at its peak was taking in $20 million a month. Indeed, throughout the entire city, only seven legitimate Washington-based companies had revenues greater than Edmond's operation. When he was finally arrested, role model Rayful Edmond III was charged with three counts of murder, assault, and running a criminal enterprise. Alleged partners in the operation included his mother, three sisters, two half-brothers, three brothers-in-law, a cousin, and an aunt. It was truly a family enterprise.[9]

Edmond is in jail today, but he remains a popular hero in the inner city of Washington, D.C. And though the names are different, his story is repeated in ghettos throughout the United States. It is not legitimate businessmen, or politicians, or educators who are the daily heroes of black youngsters in poor neighborhoods. It is the drug dealers, especially the leaders of the drug gangs.

We detailed some of the reasons for this in chapter 4. The drug wars have driven legitimate businesses out of the inner cities, leaving youngsters there with few legal employment opportunities. Gone, too, are many working-class families, who have taken their children to the suburbs rather than subject them to stray bullets. With them has gone the economic base needed to support decent inner-city schools. Thus, educational standards in the ghetto have plunged, leaving the kids left behind with little hope for learning what they need to know in the legitimate business world.

But the drug wars have had another insidious effect on the career choice of inner-city kids: Our drug laws and their enforcement have *created* the Rayful Edmonds of the world, and made the drug business the perceived means of escape from inner-city poverty. Millions of Americans every month use drugs, and hundreds of thousands of Americans support themselves in the drug trade. By casting its drug net so broadly and indiscriminately, the government has made sure that many of the people in the trade won't get caught, and thus *will* get rich.

The "tax" of criminal prosecution that is levied on drug dealers ends up being applied unevenly. Those who are detected and prosecuted are big losers—but they simply disappear from sight. On average, profit margins must compensate dealers for this risk. Hence those who happen to be lucky enough or skillful enough to avoid prosecution end up earning enormous profits—and thus enter the hearts and minds of inner-city youngsters. What attracts millions of everyday, law-abiding citizens to buy tickets for state lotteries in Pennsylvania or Illinois or Florida is not the large chance of making a small amount of money. It is the chance—no matter how tiny—of winning millions of dollars. It is the "main chance" that they seek, and the youngsters in the ghetto are no different. They do not care that the chances of great success in the drug trade are slim; what they care about is the chance, no matter how tiny, that they will hit it rich, just like Rayful Edmond. The drug wars have helped destroy legitimate opportunities in the inner city, replacing them instead with the drug-law lottery. And so, just as people drive hundreds of miles to buy lottery tickets, many inner-city youngsters will, in their own ways, go to almost any lengths to buy into the drug trade.

Beating the Rap

While dreams of hitting the "main chance" draw kids into the drug trade, our legal system does no more than slap them on the wrist if they get caught. Juveniles (generally defined as persons under the age of sixteen) do not face nearly the same penalties as adults. In New York City, for example, anyone under the age of sixteen who commits a crime is remanded to the family court system, which rarely ever actually incarcerates a juvenile. Even juveniles who end up being tried as adults rarely go to prison unless they have committed heinous crimes.

A recent Justice Department report estimated that nationwide, nearly half of juveniles picked up for violent offenses are simply put on probation or released outright. And if a youthful criminal is sent to prison, in many states the jail term cannot extend beyond age seventeen, even if murder is involved. In effect, then, the cost to young teenagers of engaging in criminal activities is often negligible. They thus become willing pawns of the drug gangs, who recycle them in and out of family and juvenile courts across the land. Ultimately of course, the kids get old enough to be prosecuted as adults. But by this time, they have learned the drug trade—and the violent tactics they need to survive in that trade. Thus, with visions of Jaguars and diamond-encrusted Rolexes dancing in their heads, they are lost to society forever.

A NATION OF CRIMINALS

The next time you see your neighbors, take a closer look at them. If you are a typical American, the odds are good that several of them are criminals. After all, the production, sale, purchase, or possession of many psychoactives, such as marijuana and cocaine, are crimes in and of themselves. More than 35 million Americans committed one of these crimes last year. Roughly one of every three Americans has committed one of these crimes sometime in their lives. The land of the free may well be the home of the brave, but it is also the home of one of the largest collections of criminals ever assembled on the face of the earth. And for more than a million Americans this year, that fact will be brought home in an unmistakable manner: They will be arrested for possessing, purchasing, growing, or consuming an illegal psychoactive.

The reason we put drug users in jail is presumably because we want them to stop using drugs. There is little doubt that, by making the potential adverse effects of drug use more severe, jail time for drug users does tend to reduce the number of people who use drugs.*
Nevertheless, jail time for drug users also has serious adverse effects on society, which extend far beyond the overflowing prisons, clogged court systems, and overtaxed police forces discussed in chapter 5. As we investigate these social effects, several important facts need to be borne in mind.

First, although we often associate drugs with the horrors of drug abuse and drug addiction, the fact is that the vast majority of all users of psychoactives are not abusers or addicts. As we saw in chapter 3, with the exception of heroin and tobacco users, most of the people who use drugs are *casual* users, who light up a joint once a week, or snort a few lines of cocaine each month. Second, fully three-fourths

---

*This is true even for addicts: If the unpleasant effects (including incarceration) of using some psychoactive are sufficiently great, some addicts will seek treatment for their disease, while other individuals will refrain from using the drug in the first place.

of all drug arrests in America are for simple possession, and the drug involved has most often been marijuana.

Third, most of the people arrested on drug charges are otherwise law-abiding citizens; indeed, an exhaustive study recently completed by researchers at Florida State University reveals that more than three-fourths of all people arrested on drug charges had no prior criminal record. The typical American who goes to jail on drug charges is a casual user who has never been in trouble with the law before. Tragically, as we shall see, the typical American who *emerges* from jail is likely to look considerably different. Obviously, only a small percentage of the people who use drugs go to jail for doing so. However, the criminality of the drug trade has a peculiar tendency to *promote* other types of criminal behavior among drug users. We've seen in earlier chapters that the illegal nature of the drug trade tends to attract criminals as suppliers of drugs, and most of the millions of Americans who buy drugs on a regular basis would probably never come into contact with such criminals, except for the fact that they buy drugs from them. There is little doubt that each of us is influenced—sometimes in small ways, sometimes in large ways—by the people with whom we associate. The millions of people who buy drugs from the "real" criminals who sell them are influenced by those criminals—by their contempt for the legal system, or their disregard for the value of human life, or by their myriad knowledge of how to successfully break the law. In subtle but important ways the users of drugs are likely to incorporate elements of such attitudes and practices into their own lives. In this way, the antisocial, anti-legal mindset of the purveyors of drugs comes to pervade society.

Crime U.

The best vocational crime schools in the world are supported by your tax dollars: our prisons. Every time we send drug users to prison, we expose them to the best-trained "Professors of Crime" in the country—their fellow prisoners. After all, most of the people in prison are, in fact, criminals. Perhaps 15 percent have broken the drug laws, but the other 85 percent or so are skilled shoplifters, burglars, car thieves, safe crackers, contract killers, extortionists, and arsonists. These knowledgeable individuals are able to transfer many of their skills to minor criminals who end up in the prison system. Want to learn how to burglarize a home? Ask somebody who burgled forty of them before the police finally caught him. Want to know how to make money "torching" buildings to collect on the fire insurance? Ask the arsonist in the jail cell next to yours. Interested in picking up an automatic pistol that can't be traced by the police? The murderer you met at lunch probably can tell you where to buy one. The best source of knowledge about a trade is the people who make a living practicing that trade, and the trade practiced by most of the people in prisons is crime. Sending a marijuana smoker to prison won't automatically make him into a car thief, but he'll certainly have a better idea of how to steal cars when he leaves.

Drug Bazaar

Drugs are readily available and widely consumed in virtually every U.S. prison. Indeed, prison can be the first place that an individual is introduced to illegal drugs. One survey of state prison inmates found that about half of the inmates who had used illicit drugs did not do so until after their first arrest and incarceration.

The mix of drugs found in prisons *is* a bit different from the typical mix on the street. Since prison guards routinely search both prison visitors and prison cells for contraband, the drugs that are smuggled into prisons are those that can be easily hidden and offer a fast-acting, intense high. These drugs include high-purity heroin and cocaine, high-THC hashish, and high-potency black-market tranquilizers and stimulants. No one bothers with beer or low-grade marijuana. Moreover, the nature of consumption is different in prisons. The greatest risk of being caught occurs while ingestion is actually taking place. To minimize this risk, inmates do their best to swallow, inhale, or inject as much of the drug as they can within a short time period. *Abusing* drugs becomes the normal way of *using* drugs in prison— producing patterns of behavior that inmates are likely to carry with them upon their release. Pot smokers don't all leave prison as heroin addicts, but the experience is nonetheless likely to have a lasting, postincarceration impact on both the drugs they consume and the way they consume them.

Ex-Con

Whenever we arrest and convict drug users, we burden those persons with permanent criminal records, whether or not they actually do time in jail. Moreover, users sent to jail are taken out of the legitimate job market for the duration of their sentences, during which time their job skills will atrophy. On both counts, criminal sanctions against users of drugs reduce the attractiveness of legitimate, legal work relative to illegal activities. Arrest and conviction are likely to cost users their original jobs, the resulting criminal record will exclude them from numerous future jobs, and the decay of legitimate job skills that takes place while in prison will reduce the wages they can earn if they eventually do find a job. All in all, a life of crime may well be the best career opportunity for which the ex-con can hope.

So What?

We don't send people to prison because *they* want to go there. We send them to prison because *we* want them there. Do we really care if drug users lose their jobs or careers because they smoke marijuana? Does it matter to us if they fry their brains smoking crack while they're in jail? Indeed, to the extent that such outcomes discourage *other* persons from using drugs to begin with, these consequences might be exactly what we *want* to happen. Prison is, after all, supposed to be a deterrent, not an expenses-paid vacation.

But there are many different ways to deter behavior. Suppose, for the sake of argument, that the deterrent effect of these three penalties is the same: 1. three months of hard time in the state prison; 2. one year of weekends in the county jail, with release time during the week to perform community service; and 3. a $10,000 fine, paid in twenty monthly installments of $500 each. By assumption, each of the three punishments deters just as many people from smoking pot or snorting coke. Yet the consequences of imposing them may be quite different in other respects. In the first case we may end up with a freshly trained car thief who has developed a taste for heroin; in the second case we may get a year's worth of antidrug lectures in the state high schools; and in the third case we may get much needed funds to refurbish the county library. Clearly, we should consider *all* of the consequences of a legal deterrent before imposing it. If those consequences are sufficiently adverse, we might even want to reconsider the advisability of imposing the deterrent at all. And we should certainly compare it to alternative deterrent systems.

Because of such considerations, ten state governments in America, as well as the Netherlands in Europe, have made the decision to "decriminalize" the possession of small amounts of marijuana. Users who are caught don't end up with a criminal record, and generally pay a fine or perform community service instead of going to jail. Interestingly, the deterrent effect seems to have been maintained: There is no evidence of a surge in marijuana use in any of these locations, and use in the Netherlands actually declined significantly after decriminalization.

Policies like decriminalization may not be the preferred outcome everywhere in the United States. But because of current federal policies (which still strictly prohibit marijuana) and federal politics (which strongly discourage states from liberalizing their policies), the people in many states may never have the opportunity to seriously consider options such as decriminalization. Under the current rules of engagement in the drug wars, we routinely run the risk (and sometimes incur the cost) of cutting off our nose to spite our face.

CRIMINAL JUSTICE AND VIOLENCE

One of the most terrifying aspects of the spread of drugs has been the spread of violence. Record homicide rates, sleeping children killed by stray bullets, drive-by shootings, and drug-bust shootouts have all become routine stories in the daily newspapers. The Uzi, the AR-13, and the AK-47—automatic weapons all—have become part and parcel of our vocabulary. We have become a nation under siege, and under fire.

Our politicians tell us that drug dealers are the cause of the mayhem. The solution to the violence, it would seem, is to increase the penalties for dealing in drugs, particularly when the dealers are the big fish in the pond—the "drug kingpins." And so our governments have pushed the penalties for drug dealing to record levels, imposing long sentences, mandatory sentences, even life sentences. Yet the violence has continued, even increased, as we have sought to bring the dealers to justice.

Will anything stop the violence? The answer is yes—but the answer lies not in tougher, longer sentences for drug *dealing*. The solution is harsher penalties targeted at drug *violence*. Policies that impose mandatory ten- or twenty-year jail terms for dealers, and sentences up to fifty years for drug kingpins, not only encourage violence in the drug trade, but actually *compel* the dealers and kingpins to practice their trade in the most murderous manner possible. Let's see why.

Consider a jurisdiction in which both drug dealing and murder are illegal. Suppose that the penalty for dealing is five years in prison, while the penalty for murder is fifty years in prison. Despite the presence of these penalties, some individuals will still deal in drugs and some will still commit murders. But a drug dealer will think long and hard about risking a shootout with the police, or exterminating a stool pigeon, because a murder conviction means not only the end of his career but also the end of his freedom for life.

Now, imagine that the jurisdiction raises the penalty for drug dealing to fifty years. The objective is to deter drug dealing, and indeed, some would-be dealers will decide that other pastures are greener. But look at the incentives facing those who stay in the business. Since being convicted for drug dealing means the end of their careers and freedom for life, being convicted of another crime at the same time has effectively zero deterrent value. Even if a fifty-year murder charge is tacked on to a fifty-year drug dealing charge, the dealer likely won't even live to see the beginning of the second sentence. Once the penalty for drug dealing is high enough, other crimes committed in the course of dealing—extortion, assault, even murder—cost the drug dealer nothing.

This conclusion is chilling: *Raising* the penalties for drug dealing is equivalent to *lowering* the penalties on other crimes committed in the course of the illegal drug business. *The result is more intimidation, violence, and lawlessness by drug dealers.* When the police show up with an arrest warrant, it costs the dealer almost nothing to kill a few of them. If there is a risk that a disgruntled customer or envious competitor will "shop" him to the police, the best course for the drug dealer is homicide—a murder rap means little to someone who already faces the prospect of life in jail. In fact, violence and intimidation become the only sensible ways for the dealer to conduct business. If he is caught for dealing, he loses *everything*; therefore, he is willing to do *anything* to avoid being caught. The result today is exactly the result we observed sixty years ago during Prohibition: Murder and assault rates are on the rise in virtually every city in the land. In 1930 it was the bootleggers and rum-runners; in the 1990s it is the drug dealers and their kingpins. In both cases, the high penalties for violating the psychoactive laws actually *promote* the violence.

What is true for dealers and kingpins is true for users as well, albeit on a more modest scale. Raising the penalties for drug *use* effectively *lowers* the penalties for other lawless activities associated with use. If the penalties for smoking marijuana or snorting cocaine are sufficiently high, it matters not a whit to users of those drugs what they do while they are using them. Imposing lengthy, mandatory sentences for drug use will discourage some would-be drug users, but those who remain users will behave every bit as viciously and murderously as today's drug kingpins.

If what really concerns us is the thought of some hopeless addict getting a buzz on heroin, if what really frightens us is a college student dealing a few joints to his fraternity brothers, then the appropriate action is clear: Throw them both in jail for fifty years. But if it is the prospect of our children being shot on their way to school that terrifies us, and if it is the sound of gunfire that keeps us awake at night, then we must target legal penalties toward assault and intimidation and murder. Only then will our laws accomplish the objectives we truly desire.

THE LINK BETWEEN DRUGS AND CRIME

We all know there is a link between drugs and crime. This link is often emphasized when politicians in Washington tell us of the need for more—more drug laws, more penalties for drug users and dealers, and more taxes to pay for the courts and police and jails needed to enforce those laws and implement those penalties. But what we (and our politicians) don't always appreciate is the *nature* of the link between drugs and crime.

First things first. There *is* evidence that some psychoactives induce some individuals to engage in "antisocial" acts, including violent criminal behavior. Nowhere is this clearer than in the case of alcohol, which produces the most violent effects of any psychoactives.* According to the U.S. Justice Department, more than half of all prison inmates report having used alcohol immediately prior to committing

---

*One physician we talked to in the course of our research put it this way: "When I see lung cancer, I'm 95 percent certain that cigarettes are involved; when I see a stab wound, I'm just as sure that alcohol is involved." Another physician, the director of emergency care at a major metropolitan hospital, was even more emphatic, stating "I have *never* seen a stab wound in which alcohol was not involved."

their crime.[10] A recent survey of inmates in state prisons found that among prisoners who had been under the influence of a psychoactive at the time of their crime, far and away the most prevalent drug involved was alcohol. And, of course, alcohol is involved in more than 40 percent of all highway traffic fatalities.

Alcohol is not the only culprit, however. Phencyclidine (PCP), also called "angel dust," produces a bizarre mixture of hallucinogenic and stimulating effects that sometimes drives its users to violent acts, often committed without any apparent reason. Crack cocaine and methamphetamine (ice) are also stimulants that can produce violent, lawless behavior on the part of their users. Nevertheless, most other drugs, including marijuana, heroin, and LSD, generally do not produce violent behavior, and their consumption does not seem to be particularly associated with criminal behavior—except for the criminal act of buying and consuming them.

What are the other links between crime and drugs? First and foremost in the minds of many Americans are the murders, drive-by shootings, and violent turf wars associated with the drug trade. Second (a close second in some major cities), there are the crimes committed by drug consumers to support their habits. Indeed, drug shootouts, burglaries, and larcenies seem difficult to escape, even for those who have never used an illegal psychoactive.

The one underlying feature of these crimes that must be understood if we are to make sensible drug policies is the same fact that the makers of current drug policies are most loath to discuss: The violent crimes associated with drug dealing, and the property crimes committed to finance the habits of users, are *not* committed because drugs are drugs. They are committed because drugs are illegal. The evidence on this point is both unequivocal and overwhelming. Drug dealers threaten our lives because our drug laws have made it profitable for them to do so. Drug addicts steal our possessions because our drug laws have made it necessary for them to do so. The single most important reason that drugs cause crime is because we have caused drugs to be criminal.

Consider alcohol. Sixty years ago, alcohol was illegal in this country, and because of that, the profits from successfully delivering alcohol to thirsty customers were astronomical. As a result, bootleggers and rum-runners went to any lengths in their drive to succeed. And since their business was illegal, most of those lengths were also illegal and violent. We no longer have drive-by shootings, turf wars, and "cement shoes" in the alcohol business because alcohol today is legal—not because alcohol no longer intoxicates people, not because alcohol is no longer addicting, and not because alcohol dealers have suddenly developed a social conscience.

Consider marijuana. In 1920, many Americans began using this psychoactive because their old standby, alcohol, had suddenly been declared illegal. When they purchased marijuana, did they wonder if their supplier was going to pull a gun on them? Did they run for cover because of turf wars between rival pot dealers? No, because marijuana was legal in this country, and no one selling it seventy years ago would have risked the possibility of running off his customers (or going to jail) by engaging in such behavior.

Consider heroin. Today it is illegal to consume heroin in America. As a result, heroin prices are 100 times higher than they were eighty years ago, even after adjusting for inflation. As a result, most heroin addicts today can support their addictions only by committing criminal acts—burglarizing apartments, snatching purses, stealing cars, selling sexual favors, and shoplifting. Eighty years ago, heroin addicts did not commit these acts appreciably more often than the rest of the populace—not because heroin was nonaddicting eighty years ago, or because the criminal opportunities weren't there, but because the legal nature of heroin also meant that it was inexpensive, and thus could be afforded without the need for antisocial, criminal behavior.

Thousands of addicts across the country are now in publicly sponsored treatment programs in which they take the synthetic opiate methadone instead of heroin. These people are still *addicted*, but they are satisfying that addiction with legal, inexpensive methadone, instead of illegal, expensive heroin. In general, these people no longer commit crimes to finance their addictions, not because they are no longer addicts, nor because they have suddenly "gotten religion." These people are no longer stealing and mugging because they are spending $30 per week on methadone instead of $1,000 a week on heroin.*

Consider cigarettes, which are readily available and cheap. Even a pack-a-day addict can support his addiction for no more than $15 or $20 per week. How often have you ever read of a nicotine addict

---

*In the years before methadone was first used in 1965, Britain permitted heroin addicts to legally obtain heroin by prescription from physicians. The result? British addicts were law-abiding souls, because with access to low-cost supplies of their drug, they had no reason to turn to crime.

robbing a convenience store to finance his next "buy"? When did you last see a cigarette dealer threaten a competitor with death if he didn't stay clear of his turf? It's unlikely you've read about or observed either of these events, but if you'd like to, we can suggest a sure way to do it: Make cigarettes illegal.

For drug after drug, now and in the past, the story is the same. If you want to establish an unmistakable, unbreakable link between drugs and crime, the surest way to do it is to make drugs illegal. The high profits and prices that result will drive the dealers and addicts into lives of crime as surely as they always have.

DRUGS VERSUS POLICIES

Drugs are not harmless, and psychoactives are no exception. Their use can lead to abuse and even addiction. The consequences of both can be devastating, both to the individuals consuming the psychoactives and to other members of society. Indeed, the harm produced by psychoactives drives our desire to reduce or even eliminate their use. Yet in striving to achieve these goals we must also recognize that, just as drugs may have harmful effects, so too may drug policies.

Crime is surely among the most harmful potential consequences of psychoactive use, whether that crime is vehicular homicide committed by a drunk driver, or a burglary committed by a heroin addict. Recognizing the harmful effects of the crime that psychoactives may produce, policy makers have sought to eliminate their use by making their sale and consumption illegal. Yet in doing so, policy makers have created a wide array of adverse consequences that flow not from the sale or the use of drugs, but from their illegal status. If we are to have sensible drug policies, we must understand the fact that many of our government's actions have produced the very damages that we hoped to prevent. At some point, we must recognize the need for a balance between the benefits that are conferred with one hand and the costs that are imposed with the other. For if we fail to recognize this balance, any small victories earned in the war on drugs will surely be pyrrhic, leaving only ashes to stain our lives and the lives of our children in the years and decades ahead.

CHAPTER 7

....

Bathtub Gin and AIDS

LEN BIAS WAS GOING TO BE A CELTIC. FOLLOWING A BRILLIANT COLLEGE basketball career at the University of Maryland, Bias had just been selected by the Boston Celtics as the number-one pick in the 1986 National Basketball Association draft. Looking forward to a professional career that might pay him $2 million per year or more, Bias decided a celebration was in order. Some friends and acquaintances suggested that cocaine could add just the right touch to the evening's festivities. Although Bias apparently had never consumed the drug before, he agreed. Less than twelve hours later, line after line of cocaine had reduced his superbly conditioned heart to a quivering mass of dysfunctional muscle tissue. Len Bias was dead of an overdose.

Len Bias's story made the headlines, but he was just one of some 2,000 to 3,000 individuals who suffer sudden death each year as a direct result of their drug use.[1] Another 3,500 Americans will die this year from AIDS contracted as a result of drug use, most of them because they used contaminated hypodermic syringes to inject heroin or cocaine into their bloodstream.[2] To complete this macabre picture, tens of thousands of babies will be born this year to women who used illegal drugs during pregnancy; an unknown but substantial percentage of these children—many of them "crack babies"—will suffer disabling physical or mental damage due to their mothers' drug use.

PROHIBITION REVISITED

During the years from 1920 to 1933—the years of bathtub gin and bootleggers—tens of thousands of Americans died from acute alcohol poisoning. Thousands more were blinded by the illicit booze they drank. Many others suffered adverse effects ranging from lead poisoning to debilitating gastritis, caused by the methods used to produce alcohol or the additives introduced to it. These casualties were in addition to the "routine" adverse health effects of alcohol consumption, such as cirrhosis, brain damage, and cancer.* The emergence of a host of debilitating and lethal consequences of alcohol consumption was not simply due to the Roaring Twenties being a time when morals were low, people were crazier, and life wasn't worth as much as it is today. Ounce for ounce, booze became deadlier during this period because Prohibition changed the incentives of both the suppliers and the consumers of alcohol. The war on drugs has produced the same change in incentives for the suppliers and consumers of illegal psychoactives today—with equally deadly results.

More Bang for the Bulk

The consumers of drugs are ultimately interested in the pleasurable effects produced by the drugs. Suppliers of drugs make money by providing consumers with what they want. When the drugs in question are illegal, both suppliers and consumers know that if they are caught possessing them, they will go to jail. Moreover, they know that possession of large physical quantities of the drugs increases both the chance they *will* be caught, and the legal penalty imposed if they *are* caught. As a result, suppliers and consumers of illegal drugs have a joint incentive to minimize the physical volume of the drugs required to produce any given psychoactive effect.

Prior to the Harrison Act of 1914, which made opiates and cocaine effectively illegal in this country, people consumed those drugs in fundamentally different potencies and dosages than they do today, and they used different delivery systems to do it. Opium was more popular than its more potent derivative, morphine. When the even more powerful heroin was introduced in 1898, it was less popular

---

*Although the incidence of routine alcohol-related deaths (such as cirrhosis) dropped during Prohibition—which is, of course, one of the factors that motivated Prohibition.

than either opium or morphine. Most users of both opiates and co-caine utilized them in small doses spread through the day.[3] The most prevalent method of consumption was the ingestion of pills or liquids containing dilute concentrations of the drugs. Despite the fact that hypodermic syringes were cheap, legal, and readily available at the corner drugstore or through the Sears, Roebuck catalog, relatively few users of the opiates or cocaine employed them. Opium that was smoked (rather than eaten) was specially selected and refined to *re-duce* its morphine content, given the greater efficiency of smoking as a delivery system. In short, despite the fact that many people in nineteenth-century America were addicted to opiates (and some were addicted to cocaine), most of them used these drugs much like caffeine and nicotine addicts use their drugs of choice today: in small, meas-ured doses that enabled the users to integrate their addictions with the everyday business of living.

All of this changed when the opiates and cocaine became illegal. Ounce for ounce, heroin is the most potent opiate; its small physical volume makes it easy to hide from the authorities, thereby reducing the legal risk of selling or using it. After 1914, suppliers and consumers quickly switched to heroin in place of weaker, bulkier opium and morphine. The illegal status of heroin and cocaine also made intra-nasal ingestion more popular, as this was a more efficient means of delivering a given amount of the drugs to the brain. By the early 1920s, intensifying enforcement of the Harrison Act had made hy-podermic needles the preferred delivery system, and after an addi-tional toughening of the narcotics laws in 1924, users switched from subcutaneous injection to intramuscular injection, and then finally to intravenous injection—successively more efficient means of deliv-ering smaller physical amounts of the increasingly expensive drugs.[4] By making opiates and cocaine more expensive and more difficult to obtain, the enforcement of the Harrison Act reduced the number of consumers of these drugs; but it also transformed the remaining con-sumers from productive members of society into social outcasts whose only thought was how to beg, borrow, or steal the money needed for their next fix.

A similar transformation has been taking place over the past fifteen years, as the war on drugs has heated up again. In the mid-1970s, the overwhelming drug of choice for users of illegal drugs was low-potency imported marijuana. A series of successes in the federal ef-forts to interdict imported marijuana raised the risks and the costs faced by both suppliers and consumers. Smugglers looked for a product that could more easily escape detection. They hit upon cocaine, because its smaller bulk made it more difficult to detect. The same traffickers, often using the same routes, airplanes, and boats, simply began bringing cocaine instead of marijuana into the United States.

Quite apart from the pleasing novelty of cocaine compared to marijuana, many potential users of the drug were attracted to it for the same reason that suppliers found it appealing. Cocaine delivered a large psychoactive punch relative to its bulk, and it could be consumed in a manner (snorting) that was less susceptible to detection than smoking marijuana. On both counts, the risks of prosecution were reduced by switching to cocaine.*

Some suppliers and consumers preferred to stay with marijuana, but sought ways to avoid the risks of importing it. Growing the plant domestically offered a possible solution, but presented its own risk: The plants were exposed to possible detection by the authorities throughout their growing cycle. To minimize this risk, growers began perfecting techniques that yielded far more potent strains of the plant, thereby minimizing the bulk associated with a given set of psychoactive effects. Domestically produced marijuana is now more than ten times as potent as imported pot, and has captured 25 percent of the marijuana market. As a result, the average marijuana joint consumed in America today contains roughly four times more active ingredient (THC) than it did in 1975.[5]

Higher and Higher

Not only did the mid-1970s successes of drug enforcement against imported marijuana help foster the spread of cocaine and the rising

---

*The resurgence of cocaine in this country actually began in the 1960s, prompted by the success of the "speed wars." Amphetamines ("speed") are, like cocaine, central nervous system stimulants; they are legally produced by pharmaceutical firms for the prescription drug market. "Leakage" from this market is an important source of their illegal supply, although they can also be manufactured in basement laboratories.

Amphetamines had been developed during the 1930s, and their introduction had largely destroyed the market for cocaine. Cocaine had to be imported, a difficult task during the depressed world trade conditions of the 1930s and the disrupted world trade conditions of World War II. Domestically produced amphetamines provided a cheap, convenient substitute.

During the 1960s, the government began a crackdown on illegal makers of amphetamines and on doctors and pharmaceutical suppliers who dispensed amphetamines indiscriminately. In response, many consumers looking for stimulants switched to cocaine, reestablishing supply lines that had been defunct for thirty years.

potency of marijuana, but they helped alter the fundamental nature of illegal drug usage. Use of a drug obviously necessitates possession of the drug; for the users of illegal drugs, this creates the risk of detection and apprehension by the authorities. Thus, illegal drug users have an incentive to minimize possession time by consuming any given amount of the drug at a faster rate. Just as teenagers are prone to "chug" illegally obtained beer to dispose of the evidence quickly, users of illegal drugs have an incentive to snort, smoke, or otherwise ingest their psychoactives intensively. Instead of carrying an inventory of the drug in their pocket or purse and accessing small amounts of it occasionally, users simply dump the inventory into their bloodstreams. Highs of shorter duration but greater intensity are the result.

Since users are looking for a way to dispense the psychoactive effects of illegal drugs as quickly as possible, there is an incentive for consumers and suppliers alike to discover and utilize new forms of the drugs that will facilitate intensive consumption. Thus, not until the federal government began a crackdown on amphetamine pills in the 1960s did *injectable* amphetamines—which produce a much more intense high than pills—became widely marketed and utilized in this country.[6] Similarly, the development and explosive popularity of crack in the mid-1980s was prompted by the search for an inexpensive, intensive means of obtaining the stimulating effects of cocaine. Most recently, the development of "crystal meth," a smokable form of methamphetamine, was stimulated by government enforcement efforts focused on stemming the crack trade. Indeed, crystal meth is (thus far) the ultimate weapon in the illegal drug user's arsenal of higher highs: It produces a stimulating high like that of injectable amphetamines or crack, but it dispenses with the need for a hypodermic syringe, and its effects last for eight to ten hours rather than the twenty to thirty minutes offered by crack. Thus, in two dimensions, smokers of crystal meth reduce their risk of apprehension by the legal authorities. The incriminating evidence of the hypodermic syringe is gone, and the drug must be accessed only once every eight hours, instead of two to three times per hour.*

The transition to more intensive use pattern and drug forms in the

---

*It is possible that drug forms like crack and crystal meth could have been *invented* even if cocaine and methamphetamine were not illegal, just as heroin was introduced at a time (1898) when the opiates were legal. Heroin did not achieve widespread consumer acceptance until after the opiates were prohibited, however.

market for illegal psychoactives contrasts sharply with concurrent developments in markets for legal psychoactives. Over the last ten to fifteen years, millions of Americans have quit smoking, and those who continue to smoke are consuming cigarettes that are lower in tar and nicotine than ever before. Americans are drinking less alcohol, and are switching from higher-potency hard liquor to lower-potency beer and wine. We are even switching from regular coffee to decaffeinated coffee. In short, the consumption and strength of legal psychoactives have been decreasing, even as the consumption and strength of illegal psychoactives have been increasing. We can find only one plausible explanation for this observation: The growing vigor of the drug wars has induced the consumers of illegal psychoactives to consume these drugs in different and more damaging ways than they otherwise would have chosen.

The intensive consumption rates associated with illegal drug use have at least two potential adverse health effects for consumers, effects that are magnified by the development of intensive drug forms such as crack and crystal meth. Intensive consumption increases the chances of an inadvertent (and possibly lethal) overdose of the drug. Humans generally moderate their intake of psychoactives (including caffeine and alcohol) by monitoring how they feel as consumption proceeds. Thus, most of us know people (perhaps including ourselves) who have turned down another drink at a cocktail party because the psychoactive effects of previous drinks are becoming evident. Monitoring becomes much less effective as a defense against overdose when consumption is rapid, because large amounts of the drug are "stockpiled" in the body before any of the drug's effects are apparent. If the body's second line of defense (vomiting) is bypassed because the drug has been snorted, smoked, or injected, the stimulating or depressing effects on the central nervous system have an even greater chance of being lethal.

In the view of some experts, intensive consumption of psychoactives (and thus of intensive drug forms) may also enhance the risk of addiction. The ingestion of psychoactives initially produces chemical changes in the brain that users presumably find pleasurable, as well as causing a series of biochemical reactions associated with the body's attempt to return to a normal state. When consumption is moderate, the return to normalcy is often smooth and untroubling. When consumption is intensive, however, the path to normalcy may be far from pleasurable—witness the hangover following intensive consumption of alcohol. In the case of stimulants, such as cocaine and amphetamines, the aftermath of the high is depression, and as users routinely report, "the higher the high, the lower the low." In effect, the body overshoots, which produces an incentive for the user to use the drug again, simply to neutralize the aftermath of the last usage. When this cycle is repeated often enough over time, the user eventually cannot feel either physiologically or psychologically normal *except* when he or she is using the drug. Addiction has set in.

Flying Blind

As we noted in chapter 1, when psychoactives are illegal, information about product quality becomes more expensive and more difficult for consumers to obtain. Suppliers are reluctant to advertise their goods or to establish easily recognizable identities and regular places and hours of business, because to do so increases the chances of being caught by the police. Sellers also cannot use the legal system to protect brand names and trademarks, and consumers cannot readily use the legal system to punish suppliers who fail to deliver what they promise. Buyers and sellers even have difficulty establishing regular trading relationships, because the police are periodically hauling one or both off to jail. The combination of these forces produces a rise in the uncertainty about the potency of illegal drugs, and even their identity. The consequences for consumers of illegal drugs can be lethal.

As cocaine and heroin move down the distribution chain, they are "cut" (or diluted) at each stage, using any of a variety of cutting agents. For cocaine, the agents might be lidocaine, ephedrine, baking soda, or baby sugar (powdered lactose). For heroin, agents often include dextrose, lactose, and quinine. On average, the purity of street level heroin currently runs about 10 percent; the average street purity of cocaine is roughly 60 percent.[7] For both drugs, however, there is considerable variation around that average, depending on geographic location, the identities of buyer and seller, and current market conditions.

Drug overdose is the most obvious potential hazard resulting from the uncertain potency of illegal drugs. This appears to be an important problem for cocaine users, particularly among the inexperienced ones. In 1990, for example, there were tens of thousands of hospital emergency admissions due to cocaine use, and perhaps 1,500 to 1,800 deaths. Most of these admissions and deaths are believed to be accidental overdoses, and some—such as the death of Len Bias—occurred the very first time the drug was used.

Overdose per se occurs much less frequently among heroin users, despite common perceptions to the contrary. Experts now believe that many of the 1,000 or more supposed heroin "overdose" deaths each year are in fact caused by one of two other factors, although both are largely the product of current drug policy. Quinine (the same drug used to treat malaria) is often used to cut heroin; it looks like heroin, and some users even find that the quinine enhances the initial rush produced by injection. Suppliers also use quinine as a cutting agent because users sometimes taste a small amount of the heroin mixture before buying to estimate its purity; quinine's bitter taste makes it difficult to determine exactly how much cut has been used. Unfortunately, quinine produces a severe and often lethal allergic reaction in some individuals: The lungs fill rapidly with fluid, and the user literally drowns within minutes.[8]

The other factor responsible for sudden deaths among heroin addicts is caused indirectly by disruptions in the supply of their drug. Even normal dosages of heroin can be lethal when injected while the user is under the influence of alcohol or barbiturates. Under regular supply conditions, most addicts eschew these other psychoactives while using heroin, but if heroin supplies are disrupted by a bust, addicts often use alcohol and barbiturates to stave off the worst of their withdrawal symptoms while their drug of choice is unavailable. When fresh supplies of heroin hit the street, the addicts immediately shoot up; if they are still under the influence of alcohol or barbiturates, the synergistic impact of the heroin can kill them.

Even the buyers of marijuana face considerable uncertainty about the potency and identity of the drug they are purchasing, although the effects are rarely lethal. Unscrupulous dealers sometimes cut marijuana with oregano, an inexpensive herb that looks and smells like pot, but fails to produce the hoped-for psychoactive effects. The oregano produces no harmful effects itself, but a mixture of imported marijuana and oregano may have an effective THC content of 0.25 percent or lower. At the other end of the spectrum, unadulterated domestic pot may have a THC content as high as 15 percent. Thus, any given sample of marijuana may vary in potency by a factor of sixty—a fact that cannot be determined until after consumption has taken place and the psychoactive effects have taken hold. Still more danger to marijuana users arises because some dealers lace pot with angel dust (PCP). In very small amounts, PCP can help low-grade marijuana yield high-grade effects, but in only slightly larger amounts it can produce extreme psychoses and long-lasting psychological effects among unsuspecting users. Although the physical harm is modest, the mental damage can be both substantial and permanent.

AIDS AND HEROIN

More than 3,500 Americans a year are dying from AIDS contracted directly or indirectly as a result of intravenous drug use. In the New York metropolitan area, fully *half* of all intravenous drug users are believed to be infected with HIV, the virus that causes AIDS.[9] Nationwide, it is estimated that roughly 25 percent of all Americans with AIDS—including the vast majority of all heterosexuals, infants, and children with the disease—have contracted AIDS because either they, their sexual partners, or one or more parents have engaged in intravenous drug use.[10]

The initial propagators of "drug-related" AIDS generally are heroin addicts, because intravenous injection is the preferred method of administration for heroin among addicts. Neither heroin nor intravenous injection per se cause AIDS; the shared use of hypodermic syringes contaminated with the AIDS virus is at the root of the problem. Once the drug user is thus HIV-infected, he or she can pass the disease on to sexual partners. If the infected person is (or becomes) pregnant, the disease is then passed on to the newborn infant.

The drug wars play a pivotal role in promoting the spread of AIDS. Since heroin is illegal, its price averages between 100 and 200 times the pharmaceutical cost of production. To conserve on their precious drug, most users (and virtually all addicts) inject heroin with hypodermic syringes. The authorities are aware of this, and thus try to restrict access to needles. Hypodermic syringes may not be obtained legally without a prescription, and doctors cannot legally prescribe them for addicts. So addicts share the few precious needles they are able to obtain and do so under circumstances that often make sterilization impractical. If a user of a shared needle is HIV-infected, the odds are good that one or more subsequent users will become infected.

Even though heroin is illegal, it is possible to break the link between injection of the drug and the transmission of AIDS. The key is sterile needles, or, at the very least, needles that don't have to be shared. In Hong Kong, where needles are legal, there are no reported cases of drug-related AIDS.[11] In 1988, the French started distributing free hypodermic needles, and believe they have stemmed the spread of drug-related AIDS. In the United States, some private, community-based organizations have begun dispensing packets of ordinary household bleach to addicts; when needles are rinsed with bleach, the AIDS virus is killed on contact. The federal government has refused to legalize needles, and has vigorously opposed local initiatives to sterilize or distribute them, because it believes that to do so would encourage the use of heroin and other injectable drugs. And so the spread of drug-related AIDS continues.

CRACK AND STDS

AIDS is typically classified as a sexually transmitted disease, or STD. As we have seen, illegal drug use has fostered the spread of AIDS through other means, but drug use is also implicated in the sexual transmission of AIDS, as well as the spread of other STDs, including syphilis.

With the widespread introduction of the antibiotic penicillin some forty years ago, syphilis, a debilitating and ultimately lethal STD, was brought under control in this country. Syphilis didn't disappear, for penicillin is not a vaccine. Nevertheless, once the disease has been contracted, penicillin is a rapid and efficacious cure—if the infected person receives treatment. According to the U.S. Centers for Disease Control in Atlanta, there were fewer than 30,000 cases of primary and secondary syphilis reported in the United States in 1986. By 1990 that number had soared to over 50,000. Among black males, the incidence of the disease rose 132 percent over this period.[12]

To discover why there has been such an increase in a disease whose incidence had been falling for years, just visit your local "crack house"—an establishment that sells crack to its customers, typically for consumption on the premises. At crack houses throughout the country, men find that crack produces sexual arousal. Women who are crack addicts willingly sell themselves on a frequent basis in order to earn "hits" of the drug. Although crack increases sexual interest, it prevents sexual release. Frequent and long-lasting physical couplings result, leading to open lesions on the genitals of the men and women involved. These lesions are the perfect medium for the transmission of STDs, particularly syphilis.

The number of sexual partners that crack-addicted women have can be staggering—as many as 100 per *week* in some instances. In one study reported by Knight-Ridder News Service in 1989, twenty-seven teenage Miami girls who admitted trading sex for crack said they had engaged in a total of over 19,000 acts of prostitution in the previous year.[13]

The crack house transmission of STDs is not confined to inner-city areas. Consider the experiences of Nolan Phillips, an epidemiologist who works for Georgia's southeastern health district, an area covering sixteen counties that is about the size of Massachusetts. According to Phillips, known syphilis cases in his district reached 385 cases in 1988—an 800 percent increase in four years. On one recent visit to an Atkinson County crack house, Phillips tried to convince the five teenage prostitutes living there to submit to blood tests for syphilis. Only one agreed; at age fourteen, she tested positive for the second time. The girls freely admitted that they sold sex for as little as $2, pooling their funds to pay for crack. None of the girls, however, was inclined to give Phillips a list of the clients they had serviced, despite Phillips's assurances of confidentiality. The girls would face beatings (or worse) at the hands of their pimps if it was discovered that they had aided Phillips's search for syphilis carriers. Like other epidemiologists, Phillips knows that his inability to track additional potential carriers means that the true incidence of syphilis is growing even faster than the reported numbers reveal.[14]

The spread of syphilis among crack-addicted prostitutes and their clients will worsen the AIDS epidemic. Syphilis produces open sores on the genitals, sores that allow the AIDS virus easy entry into the bloodstream. Epidemiologists at the Centers for Disease Control have noted that a sharp rise in the incidence of syphilis occurred among gay men just before AIDS struck this group in the early 1980s. The crack-syphilis connection may be in the process of producing a new high-risk AIDS group—heterosexual crack smokers. Indeed, preliminary data suggests that this trend has already begun.*

---

*Heterosexuals are also at increasing risk for tuberculosis (TB), a disease that had virtually disappeared in this country. Individuals infected with the AIDS virus are

Although the link between the drug wars and drug-related AIDS is clear, the connection between our drug policies and the spread of STDs may be less obvious. After all, the root of the problem appears to be simply a combination of drug use and promiscuous sexual practices, outside the realm of government policies. This view ignores both the drug involved and the environment in which its use commonly occurs—both of which are importantly the result of the war on drugs.

CRACK HOUSES

Even the watered-down images of crack houses shown in popular movies and television programs are disgusting. The actual establishments—refuse-strewn, rat-infested, abandoned houses or apartments, reeking of urine, vomit, and human excrement—are even worse. One wonders why anyone would voluntarily frequent such disgusting environments. The answer lies in a combination of the drug involved and the government policies toward those who use and sell it.

As we noted above, the development and popularity of crack are importantly due to the illegal status of cocaine: Crack provides an efficient means of quickly delivering a large psychoactive punch. The intense twenty- to thirty-minute high produced by crack is accompanied, however, by an intense subsequent low, which creates the incentive for futher use of the drug. The preferred method of consumption of the drug is thus in the form of long "runs," often lasting for many hours, as hit after hit is taken at twenty- to thirty-minute intervals. Ultimately, either the user's money runs out, or he or she becomes exhausted and falls into a prolonged slumber.

To sustain a run such as this, a user must have ready access to 20, 50, or even 100 rocks of crack. This is enough of the drug to elicit a

---

highly susceptible to TB, which unlike AIDS can be spread through as little as a sneeze or a cough. In other areas of the world where AIDS has taken a heavy toll, a TB epidemic is in the offing, and there is growing evidence that the United States may not be far behind. In New York, for example, there has been a sharp rise in tuberculosis cases among AIDS patients, health-care workers, and those who live or work in homeless shelters. Thus we have yet another unintended adverse consequence of today's policies: The illegal status of heroin and syringes promotes the spread of AIDS, whose victims are more susceptible to TB, which is easily transmitted to other people.

legal charge of dealing if the user is caught—and dealing carries a far greater penalty then using. In return for a modest premium in the drug's price, the crack houses absorb this risk and provide other valuable services to users. They keep an ample inventory of crack on hand, giving smokers convenient access to the quantities of the drug needed to sustain a run. Since the houses sell the rocks of crack to patrons as they consume them, consumers are protected from the more serious charge of dealing. And, of course, crack houses provide a convenient venue for sexually aroused male users and addicted prostitutes to satisfy their respective desires.

There is a second element in the crack house phenomenon, however, one that also helps explain why they are commonly filthy, vile establishments located in abandoned houses or apartment buildings. Federal law permits the seizure of any assets that are in any way "tainted" by illegal drugs, either because they have been used in the illegal drug trade or because they have been purchased with the proceeds of illegal drug sales. Indeed, even the *presence* of illegal drugs in a car, boat, or building makes that asset subject to seizure by the authorities, and in 1990 alone, agents of the U.S. Drug Enforcement Administration seized more than $1 billion worth of such assets.[15] The use of abandoned, derelict buildings as locations for crack houses minimizes the financial risks to operators in the event of a drug raid. Except for the drugs on hand, nothing owned by the operators is subject to seizure. Following the same logic, crack-house operators also have no incentive to spend any money on furnishings, repairs, or even the barest sanitation. So users sleeping off their runs repose on filthy floors or lice-infested mattresses; broken windows are not repaired; and if somone happens to vomit or urinate on the floor, well, it will dry by itself soon enough.

CRACK BABIES

When a pregnant woman consumes a psychoactive, her fetus is exposed to the drug and, in principle, threatened by it. When the psychoactive is alcohol, for example, the result can be fetal alcohol syndrome (FAS). The symptoms of FAS include birth defects involving varying degrees of physical and mental damage to the fetus. Exactly how many FAS babies are born each year is not known, in part because FAS is often difficult to distinguish from other forms of fetal abuse, such as poor maternal nutrition and a lack of prenatal medical care. Rough estimates suggest, however, that FAS may affect 30,000 newborns each year, with perhaps 10 to 20 percent of them suffering profound damage.[16]

Since all psychoactives are believed to have the capacity to damage the fetus, doctors routinely recommend that pregnant women avoid them. Not all women heed their doctors' advice, and the result is sometimes physical or mental damage to the fetus—an outcome that might be termed fetal drug syndrome (FDS) when the psychoactive is a drug other than alcohol. When the drug is cocaine, the babies suffering from FDS are commonly called "crack babies," because crack appears to be the drug form of choice among pregnant cocaine users whose newborns show the most visible consequences of FDS. The potential consequences of regular crack use during pregnancy are shocking:

- The incidence of sudden infant death syndrome (SIDS) in crack babies is up to ten times greater than among other babies.
- Crack babies who survive infancy neither speak nor understand language as well as other babies during the first five years of their lives.
- The cost of the initial hospital intensive care for a crack baby is estimated to be as much as $90,000.
- For those crack babies who survive and go on to school, it can cost society an additional $40,000 to overcome that child's learning problems enough to get the child ready for kindergarten.

Numbers such as these strongly suggest that crack babies present a major public health and social policy problem for America. The exact magnitude of this problem depends, of course, on how many crack babies are born each year. The most widely reported estimate of the incidence of crack babies was produced by a congressional committee headed by Senator Lloyd Bentsen of Texas. According to his committee, some 350,000 to 400,000 crack babies are born in the United States each year. If such numbers are correct, the hospital intensive-care bill for crack babies could be in the range of $30 billion to $35 billion per year, with the additonal costs of preparing these children for kindergarten amounting to another $14 to 16 billion per year.[17]

Although Bentsen's estimate of the number of crack babies has received extensive media coverage, his number is highly suspect. In fact, it probably overstates the true incidence of the problem by a factor of at least ten to one. Senator Bentsen's estimate implies that fully 10 percent of all babies born in the United States each year are crack babies. Yet no more than 10 percent of the U.S. population is estimated to have tried cocaine at any time in their lives, much less used it intensively while they were pregnant. At most, there are believed to be three million regular users of cocaine in the country, perhaps one million of them abusers and addicts.[18] Approximately 60 percent of these abusers and addicts are men. We are left with roughly 400,000 women who are likely to be cocaine abusers or addicts. Even assuming that all of the babies born to these women are damaged due to their mothers' cocaine abuse during pregnancy, the number of crack babies would roughly equal the number of babies suffering from fetal alcohol syndrome—about 30,000 per year.*

A variety of factors could result in this estimate being either too high or too low. For example, cocaine use appears to be highest among persons aged fifteen to twenty-nine, and women in this age bracket have a fertility rate about 50 percent higher than the average for all women. Acting in the opposite direction is the fact that cocaine abuse puts enormous stress on the human body, and stress is well known to sharply reduce fertility rates. There is also anecdotal evidence that some abusers sharply curtail or eliminate their consumption of the drug during pregnancy. Finally, there is evidence that not all children born to alcohol abusers and alcoholics suffer from FAS, and that not all children of heroin addicts suffer long-term damage as a result of fetal exposure to heroin. Thus, it may also be the case that not all children of cocaine abusers and addicts suffer fetal drug syndrome.

Although the 30,000 figure is far below Senator Bentsen's estimate, it is strikingly high in one dimension: Since alcohol consumers (including abusers and alcoholics) outnumber their cocaine counterparts by an enormous factor, our estimate implies that a far larger proportion of cocaine consumers harm their fetuses than is the case for alcohol consumers. In part, this may be due to the different speed of progression of alcohol abuse and addiction compared to cocaine abuse and addiction. For reasons not fully understood, chronic al-

---

*About 75 percent of illegal drug users are white. The fertility rate for white women is a bit over 60 births per 1,000 women per year; for black women, the rate is just over 80 births per 1,000 each year. The resulting arithmetic yields about 28,000 babies born each year to women who abuse or are addicted to cocaine.

cohol abuse proceeds far more slowly in individuals than does chronic cocaine abuse. Peak rates of abuse and addiction among alcohol users are observed when those individuals are in their forties. Peak rates of cocaine abuse and addiction usually occur when individuals are in their twenties. Since the peak child-bearing years are the twenties, and most women have finished having children by their forties, the higher per-user incidence of crack babies compared to FAS babies is not surprising.

There are, however, some key features of the war on drugs that help produce the higher proportionate incidence of crack babies. First, current drug policies encourage more potent drug forms and more intensive consumption patterns, and crack smokers rather than cocaine snorters are the chief source of cocaine-damaged babies.*

There also appears to be a fundamental incompatibility between a drug policy based on "just say no," and a policy that adds, "but if you *do* use drugs, don't get pregnant." Simply put, there has been remarkably little targeting of drug education toward young women who are or might become pregnant, nor has there been any public policy effort to aid these women in preventing pregnancy. Perhaps such educational or other efforts would have no impact on the women's behavior. They might simply say to themselves, "It won't happen to my baby," or they might decide that the potential consequences to their child don't warrant giving up their drugs. But if pregnant cocaine consumers do come to such conclusions, then punishing them is likely to have equally little effect on their drug use. There is little reason to suppose that a woman who foolishly ignores the adverse effects of drug use on her unborn child would be so wise as to respond to the threat of legal punishment for herself. Similarly, an addict who is unable to give up her drug of choice to save her child from extreme mental and physical damage is not likely to give it up because there is a slight chance that she will be arrested.

Sadly, our policy of "just say no" also seems to be virtually incompatible with a policy that adds, "but if you do use drugs, we'll help you get treatment for your problem." Nationwide, public drug treatment facilities routinely have waiting lists of months (when it is too late to help the fetus) and generally don't even admit pregnant women. Moreover, many law-enforcement authorities are prone to

---

*Thus, were the data available, we would presumably observe a higher proportionate incidence of FAS during Prohibition than immediately before or after that period.

prosecuting pregnant cocaine users, thus encouraging them to avoid public drug-treatment facilities until *after* the baby is born and the damage is done. Whether these policies are appropriate or not, we do not know; we do know that they help promote the high incidence of fetal drug syndrome among the users of illegal psychoactives.

THE BAD-DRUG THEOREM

Across the board, the crack phenomenon illustrates vividly the terrible tradeoff we face in drug policy. Current policy with respect to cocaine discourages some people from using a potentially harmful psychoactive, an outcome that is surely beneficial. Yet because of current policy, those persons who do use the drug are induced to consume a more dangerous version of it, and to use it in more harmful ways and under circumstances that produce even more damage. This pattern—fewer users, but more damage to those who do use—is identical to what we observed during Prohibition, and to what occurred in the aftermath of the Harrison Act. Yet the government has shown an appalling unwillingness to admit this inevitable tradeoff even exists.

The law-induced changes in drug forms and the ways in which they are consumed have become so widely recognized by experts in this field that the phenomenon might well be expressed as a simple theorem, or law:

> *When drugs are illegal, more damaging drugs*
> *drive out less damaging drugs.*

More damaging drugs are high-potency versions consumed in abusive manners and dosages; less damaging drugs are low-potency forms consumed in nonabusive ways and amounts. Crack cocaine smoked in forty-eight-hour runs is a more damaging drug. Heroin injected intravenously is a more damaging drug. High-proof moonshine liquor is a more damaging drug. A coca-infused liquid solution (such as Coca-Cola before 1903) consumed orally is a less damaging drug. A can of light beer is a less damaging drug.

Do not misunderstand: There is no moral connotation here in the use of the terms "more damaging" and "less damaging," nor are we claiming that cocaine or alcohol are rendered harmless in dilute solutions. All psychoactives are potentially dangerous. The distinction between less damaging and more damaging is based solely on the *magnitude* and *likelihood* of the harm produced by the drugs. When drugs are illegal, *more* harmful drugs are consumed in *more* harmful ways: This is the sense in which they are "worse" than legal drugs.

Does this theorem mean that high-potency drugs and intensive, abusive methods of consumption would not exist in the absence of prohibition? Obviously not: High-proof distilled alcohol was discovered more than a thousand years ago, and both drunkenness and alcoholism existed long before that. Similarly, some nineteenth-century addicts used hypodermic syringes to inject cocaine or morphine, and heroin was invented at a time when the opiates were still legal.

The theorem asserts instead that the development of intensive drug forms and methods of administration are encouraged by current national drug policy, and that abusive patterns of use are promoted by laws against psychoactives. Human beings are inventive animals, but their innovative behavior takes a decided turn for the worse when drugs are made illegal. Our experience with Prohibition, which converted America from a nation of beer drinkers to a land of hard liquor consumers, is a classic example of the bad-drug theorem at work. The metamorphosis wrought by the Harrison Act, which converted opium eaters into heroin injectors, reveals the validity of the bad-drug theorem. And events of the last twenty years, in which we have seen every "success" in the drug wars transformed into increasingly potent and abusive drug forms and methods of administration, bear compelling witness to the bad-drug theorem: When drugs are illegal, more harmful drugs drive out less harmful drugs. As the story of Len Bias so amply illustrates, the consequences are all too often tragic.

DRUGS AND POLICY

Make no mistake about two points. The use of *any* psychoactive is potentially dangerous. Chronic and acute abuse of substances ranging from tobacco and alcohol to cocaine and heroin are implicated in higher rates of both morbidity (illness) and mortality (death). Moreover, the proximate cause of these adverse health effects, ranging from Len Bias's death to the birth of crack-addicted babies, is due to the choices made by individuals to consume drugs. Without drug use, these consequences would not have occurred.

As obvious as these points may be, they are important in understanding our third point: Current federal drug policy with respect to marijuana, cocaine, and heroin not only makes the use of these drugs far more dangerous than it otherwise would be, but actually creates new health hazards for users. If the goal of public policy is solely to reduce the *use* of selected psychoactives, regardless of the consequences, then this conclusion is surely good news: Drugs that are more dangerous to their users are less likely to be used. However, if the goal of policy is to minimize the adverse *effects* of psychoactives, this conclusion is disturbing. Unless the enhanced morbidity and mortality due to current policy discourages *all* potential users, then current drug policy toward these drugs may actually cause more harm than good.

Many of the most visible adverse effects attributed to drug use (the high incidence of crime among heroin addicts, or crack babies, or the spread of AIDS among intravenous drug users) are due not to drug use per se, but to our current public policy toward drugs. Understanding this point is essential, because the choice among alternative policies is inevitably influenced by appearances—by the obvious rather than the subtle. *Good* public policy is possible only if we look beneath appearances to find reality. If we are to have sensible, beneficial policies toward drugs, we must understand not only the effects of drugs but also the effects of our policies. We owe ourselves and our children no less.

CHAPTER 8

....

Farewell to the Founding Fathers

To MANY AMERICANS CONCERNED ABOUT THE DESTRUCTIVE IMPACT OF drugs on our country, effective action means "getting tough." And getting tough often means doing whatever is necessary to fight the war on drugs—even if it means bending the rules a bit. The drug dealers blatantly disregard our laws; the kingpins operate according to their own laws; and the addicts seem to care about little but their next fix. *They* will not follow the rules of our society, so, we reason, why should *we?*

More than 200 years ago, our founding fathers knew that times like these would come to our land. They did not, of course, anticipate crack cocaine and crystal meth, or Jamaican posses and drive-by shootings. But they did know that our nation would come upon hard times, even desperate times, when nothing save desperate action would enable us to survive. They knew this because they and their forebears had witnessed times of crisis themselves—external threats brought on by war, or internal threats occasioned by civil disobedience, or fiscal crises caused by the inability of their government to live within its means.

The founding fathers also had witnessed the responses of government to desperate times, responses that had *seemed* necessary and proper when they were enacted, but which had ultimately threatened man's freedom rather than freeing man from threat. Our founders understood that the press of events and the emotions of people are formidable threats against both the reason of law and the freedom of the individual. And so the founding fathers created a system of rules to guard against the destruction of freedom that resulted when a government of laws became a government of men. They called this system of rules the Bill of Rights, and it comprises the first ten amendments to the Constitution.

Of these first ten amendments, fully half of them are intended to ensure that the government cannot use the legal system—including the police and the courts—to deprive individuals of their other constitutionally guaranteed freedoms. The specific protections granted us by the Bill of Rights against government abuse of the legal system include the following:

AMENDMENT IV

• No unreasonable or unwarranted searches and seizures
• No arrests except on probable cause

AMENDMENT V

• No coerced confessions or illegal interrogation
• The right to remain silent
• No entrapment
• No compulsory self-incrimination
• A guarantee against double jeopardy
• A guarantee of due process of law
• No taking of property for public use without just compensation

AMENDMENT VI

• The right to legal counsel
• The right to be informed of charges

AMENDMENT VII

• The right to trial by jury

AMENDMENT VIII

• The right to reasonable bail
• No cruel or unusual punishment

Aside from the specific procedural safeguards embodied in these protections (for example, the right to a trial by jury), these elements of the Bill of Rights give us the right to conduct the affairs of our everyday lives without fear of government intrusion. The Fourth Amendment's stricture against unreasonable searches and seizures is an important foundation for our notion that "a man's home is his castle." Absent probable cause to believe that an illegal act is taking place in our homes, the police simply cannot cross the threshold without our prior permission.

Although the U.S. Constitution does not specifically mention privacy, many courts have argued that the protections of the Bill of Rights *implicitly* guarantee our right to privacy. Former Supreme Court Justice William O. Douglas, for example, was one of the strongest advocates of this reading of the Bill of Rights. He argued that the First, Third, Fourth, Fifth, and Ninth Amendments created "penumbras, formed by emanations from those guarantees that help give them life and substance," and went on to talk about "zones" for privacy that are guaranteed by these rights. The Ninth Amendment, for example, states emphatically that "The enumeration in the Constitution of certain rights, shall not be construed to deny or disparage others retained by the people." In other words, just because the Constitution fails to explicitly guarantee the right to privacy does not mean this right is denied to the people. In fact, many legal scholars believe that the Constitution's emphasis on protecting individual freedoms from government intrusion can only be understood if one recognizes privacy as one of those fundamental freedoms.

PRIVACY AND DOMESTIC ESPIONAGE

In the fall of 1989, the world was shocked to learn that the Romanian dictator Nicolae Ceauşescu had used 20 percent of that country's population to spy on the other 80 percent during his twenty-two-year regime. One favorite technique used to uncover "enemies of the state" was anonymous tips, written on slips of paper and deposited in special drop boxes located throughout the land. The downfall of Ceauşescu's regime was heralded throughout the world as a great advance in freedom. Yet in spite of its vocal condemnation of the deposed Romanian leader, the U.S. government is using—against its own citizens—a technologically improved version of Ceauşescu's espionage system in waging the war on drugs.

As we noted in chaper 1, drug deals have a peculiar property: They are "victimless" crimes, in the sense that buyer and seller are both willing participants in the transaction. In most crimes, such as assault, theft, or rape, there is an aggrieved victim who has an incentive to report the crime and serve as a witness at trial, but as long as both parties to a drug deal deliver what they promise, neither has an incentive to complain to the police that a crime has been committed. Clearly, the lack of victims in drug deals makes these crimes much more difficult to solve, and has led the drug warriors to use other methods to uncover and prosecute the perpetrators of these crimes.

One of these methods differs from Ceaușescu's favorite technique only in that it employs telephones rather than drop boxes. At hundreds of locations throughout the United States, in government buildings and U.S. Customs ports of entry (including major airports), there is an 800 telephone number posted prominently on the wall. An accompanying sign explains that the number can be used anonymously and free of charge to inform the government about anyone whom the caller believes might be involved in the use, manufacture, or distribution of illegal drugs. Persons calling this 800 number to report their suspicions need not have evidence to back up their allegations, and are not required, nor even expected, to give their names. Despite this, any of a variety of government agencies (including the Customs Service and the Drug Enforcement Administration) will be happy to investigate the allegations. In the meantime, the suspect's name is likely to be added to the DEA's computer file containing the names of more than 1.5 million other Americans who might (or might not) be involved in the drug trade.

Apparently, the U.S. government believes there is a fundamental difference between drop boxes and telephones. U.S. officials called the Romanian citizens who placed anonymous tips in drop boxes "domestic spies" and "informants." Americans who use the 800 telephone number, however, are termed "concerned citizens" who are doing their country a favor. Perhaps the difference in technology does make a difference. Nevertheless, many Americans seem to have a different opinion about the right to privacy than does either their government or the Romanian populace: Although 20 percent of the Romanian population took advantage of the drop boxes, only a few hundred Americans a week feel compelled to call the 800 telephone number.

WHAT FOURTH AMENDMENT?

The Fourth Amendment to the U.S. Constitution, ratified on December 15, 1791, guarantees "The right of the people to be secure in their persons, houses, papers, and effects, against unreasonable searches and seizures." These days, the Fourth Amendment is going the way of the horse and buggy. Neighborhood sweeps, no-knock searches, and property seizures are all routinely permitted in the name of the war on drugs. The U.S. Supreme Court has allowed police to poke through garbage, hover above people's homes in helicopters to look for drugs, and detain and question citizens based solely on their physical appearance.

Consider the use of "drug-courier profiles," which are physical descriptions or behavioral patterns the police believe are characteristic of individuals involved in the drug trade. If you fit the profile, the police are allowed to detain and question you without having any prior information that you might have committed a crime. And if you permit them to search your possessions, anything they find can be used against you in a court of law. Miami defense lawyer Milton Hersh points out that along interstate highway I-95, "If you look Hispanic and you are in a rented car, they'll stop you and ask if you wouldn't mind if they search the car." But don't think you are safe if you are not Hispanic. According to Sgt. Phil K. Moan of the Florida Highway Patrol, if your car is "riding low in the back," or you have out-of-state license plates but "no luggage or clothing visible," you are likely to get pulled over for a friendly chat. In New Mexico, you qualify for the drug-courier profile if you have Florida license tags![1]

Even more ominous are the many cases of a family's door being broken down by the police, who only later discover that they have the wrong address or that the tip upon which they were acting was incorrect. Indeed, police invasion of the homes of innocent persons has become so prevalent that it even became the subject of an episode of a popular TV series. One week after this episode was aired, TV truth became stranger than fiction. The victims were George and Katrina Stokes of southeast Washington, D.C. They were home one evening watching television when a heavily armed police S.W.A.T. team crashed through their front door. George was ordered to the floor at gunpoint and sustained a gash on his head. His wife fell down the cellar stairs as she tried to run away from the black-uniformed intruders. A camera crew from a local TV station was on hand to record the whole event. Unfortunately, the D.C. drug warriors had the wrong house. The S.W.A.T. team was still being filmed as it trooped back outside and drove off to find the right address.[2]

All too often, drug raids at the wrong addresses lead to tragedy. Jeffery Miles, age twenty-four, died on March 26, 1987, after a Jeffersontown, Kentucky, police officer shot and killed him. The officer had been sent to the wrong house looking for a suspected drug dealer. On March 12, 1988, Tommy C. Dubose, age fifty-six, was shot and killed by a San Diego police officer who had burst into Dubose's living room looking for drugs. The police had obtained a search warrant based on a tip. As it turned out, Dubose was a civilian instructor at a nearby naval station and was, according to his friends, strongly opposed to drugs. No drugs were found at his apartment after his death.[3]

Sometimes, merely a bit of inconvenience results for the victims of false drug raids. In Plaquemines Parish, Louisiana, Glen Williamson found himself handcuffed at 2:00 A.M. in his own house. When Williamson pointed out that the police arrest warrant was for a Glen Williams, a deputy simply added "on" to the name on the warrant and arrested Williamson anyway. Ultimately, the charges were dropped, but only after Williamson had spent a night in jail and was forced to post a $25,000 bond for his release.

Of course, the police do sometimes find drugs. Consider the case of Bruce Lavoie, his wife, and three children, who lived in quiet Hudson, New Hampshire. At 5:00 A.M. on August 3, 1989, the police smashed down the door of the Lavoie's modest apartment with a battering ram. They did not identify themselves, and they had no evidence that Lavoie might be armed. Nevertheless, when Lavoie rose from his bed, intending to resist the unknown intruders, he was fatally shot as his son watched in horror. What did the police find? A single marijuana cigarette.

Incidents such as these demonstrate to many concerned citizens a progressive erosion of the civil liberties—the constitutional rights—of Americans. As University of Michigan School of Law Professor Yale Kamisar says, "Throughout American history, the government has said we are in an unprecedented crisis and that we must live without civil liberties until the crisis is over. It's a hoax."[4] On the same subject, Justice Thurgood Marshall of the U.S. Supreme Court wrote that "precisely because the need for action against the drug scourge is manifest, the need for vigilance against unconstitutional excess is great. History teaches that grave threats to liberty often come in times of urgency, when constitutional rights seem too extravagant to endure."[5] For Jeffery Miles, Tommy Dubose, and Bruce Lavoie, even the right to live seems to have been too extravagant.

HELLO, BIG BROTHER

In 1949 George Orwell published *1984*, which depicted his view of what a world controlled by totalitarian regimes might look like. It was a world in which "Big Brother"—the government—heard all, saw all, and controlled all. Orwell's prescience in predicting living conditions in many Communist countries was remarkable; what he did not foresee was that the government practices he envisioned would be employed not merely in totalitarian regimes, but in democratic societies as well.

On October 25, 1989, Joseph Huberman, a hobbyist who liked to grow orchids, was tending his flowers when four cars stopped in front of his Raleigh, North Carolina, home. Six men and a woman got out, and their leader flashed a State Bureau of Investigation badge. He asked whether they could come in and look around, implying that if Huberman did not agree, they would come back with a search warrant "and wouldn't be in a great mood." Huberman was intimidated and admitted them. They searched, but found only orchids.

The frightened Huberman soon found out why his house had been chosen: He was one of the many targets of a nationwide effort, coordinated by the Drug Enforcement Administration. In forty-six states, raids had been conducted on retail stores specializing in indoor garden supplies. In those raids the government confiscated customer lists, merchandise, and records of more than three dozen establishments, and padlocked several others. Eleven store owners were arrested. All of the stores that were raided shared one characteristic: They had placed advertisements in either *High Times* or *Sinsemilla Tips*, both pro-marijuana magazines. Because Huberman had purchased his indoor orchid-growing equipment through a company that had been raided, his name was on their customer list. Huberman was thus considered to be a "hot lead"—a potential grower of marijuana, worthy of investigation.[6]

As it turns out, a variety of firms that have nothing to do with the indoor gardening business (much less marijuana growing) also advertise in *High Times* magazine. Have you purchased any products from these firms? Are you on their customer lists? Would you like to find out the answers to these questions by having law-enforcement officials show up at your front door demanding to search your house? Perhaps it was questions of this sort which stimulated George Orwell to write *1984*.

Despite the Bill of Rights, a variety of public officials ranging from politicians to high school principals believe that intrusive practices such as these are justified—as long as they are conducted on behalf of the war on drugs. Former New York Mayor Ed Koch, for example, proposed strip-searching every individual entering the United States from Southeast Asia or South America. The City Council of Washington, D.C., at least once has asked that the National Guard occupy the city and impose the equivalent of martial law. In numerous high schools across the country, school administrators have brought in specially trained dogs to give the students "sniff tests" for drugs. Students who sniff positive have been subjected to strip searches. Perhaps even more strikingly, the U.S. Supreme Court has upheld U.S. Customs agents' right to force suspects to defecate to make sure they are not carrying drugs in their bodies.[7] Not even George Orwell's fertile imagination anticipated that development.

THE LOST PLEASURES OF BOATING

The U.S. Coast Guard can legally board and search any vessel, whether it is docked or at sea, in order to check for compliance with Coast Guard safety rules. The U.S. Customs Service can do the same whenever a vessel comes from a foreign port, in order to confirm that no contraband is aboard. Not surprisingly, the two agencies have utilized their powers extensively—and often expensively—in the war on drugs.

Robert and Kay Weeks of Charleston, South Carolina, learned the hard way. Their forty-six-foot boat was boarded by the U.S. Coast Guard seventeen miles off the Florida coast and taken into custody. Using chainsaws and drills to rip into the floorings and furnishings, agents left sixteen-inch square holes in the deck of the Weeks' boat. They found nothing, but the damage totaled more than $400,000. The U.S. Coast Guard refused to pay for the repairs, forcing the Weeks to file a lawsuit in the hopes of recovering their damages.[8]

Journalism Professor Craig Klein has a similar, albeit less expensive, story to tell. He purchased a secondhand sailboat and hired a crew to transport it to Jacksonville, Florida, from St. Petersburg. When customs agents could not read two characters in its state registration numbers, they boarded the boat and found that the ownership documents were not aboard as required. The boat was taken to a dry dock where the inspectors found recent repairs to the hull. Believing there was contraband on board, they removed wood and fiberglass panels and drilled holes throughout the boat. They found no drugs, but they did manage to cause $4,000 in damage to Professor Klein's boat. Who paid for it? Not the Customs Service, which maintained that the search was reasonable under the circumstances.[9]

Law-enforcement agencies say that they have no choice but to continue the searches. After all, last year the Coast Guard seized almost 40,000 pounds of marijuana and about 8,000 pounds of cocaine from pleasure boats, and U.S. Customs agents seized another 60,000 pounds of marijuana and 21,000 pounds of cocaine.[10] The combined cocaine seizures from pleasure craft amounted to about 2 percent of U.S. consumption of cocaine last year; the marijuana seizures totaled one-half of 1 percent of U.S. consumption of that drug. Some might argue that these seizures did not warrant the methods used. We would simply suggest that if you own a boat located anywhere along the Atlantic, Gulf, or Pacific coasts of the United States, be sure your hull insurance covers Coast Guard chainsaws and Customs Service drills.

IF YOU FLY, YOU DIE

Boaters and orchid growers aren't the only ones who have to be worried these days. Private pilots are not sure whether they are safe taking their planes up into the air. The head of the President's Office of National Drug Control Policy shocked at least some of the nation by suggesting that drug traffickers flying their goods into the United States should be shot down if they ignored warnings to land.[11] Supporters of the proposal, including forty-eight U.S. senators, likened the idea to a policeman's firing at a fleeing vehicle. They argued that having such a rule would help the morale of customs agents and the Coast Guard, who normally must watch helplessly as smugglers go "merrily on their way, dropping their poison in the United States."[12]

However good the intentions of the officials proposing the rule, they cannot have fully considered its implications. Some drug smugglers do transport their product on private planes, just as some thieves run from the scenes of their crimes. Is giving the Coast Guard and Customs Service license to shoot down suspicious planes tantamount to giving police officers permission to fire at suspicious joggers? Some opponents of the proposal think so, and quickly dubbed it the "If you fly, you die" rule. Opponents noted that a radio malfunction on a private plane could prevent the pilot from responding to a customs or Coast Guard warning. Moreover, meteorological conditions and other factors sometimes produce garbled radio transmissions that might lead to fatal misunderstandings. Since thousands of innocent citizens fly private planes through airspace that is also used by drug smugglers, the results of such mechanical failures or misunderstandings could be devastating. Although the rule has not been implemented, the administration has not ruled it out as a future policy option. Keep your radios tuned.

MONEY LAUNDERING, PART I

Drug dealers like cash. It's readily transportable, and unlike checks and money orders, it leaves no "paper trail." One million dollars in $100 bills, for example, weighs only about twenty-two pounds and will fit conveniently into a stylish, inconspicuous briefcase.

Current law requires that most transactions involving more than $10,000 in cash must be reported to the federal government. Although the currency reporting law was originally developed to prevent people from hiding sources of cash income from the Internal Revenue Service, the law is now being used in an effort to trace cash from supposed drug transactions. The reasoning is that drug dealers won't want to leave their cash in briefcases forever, but will eventually want to get it into banks, where it is safe and can earn interest. Requiring that banks report large cash withdrawals and deposits thus gives the federal government a means of identifying potential drug smugglers. Not many of us have ever deposited or withdrawn $10,000 in one lump sum, but if you have, the federal government knows about it. Moreover, there is a good chance that as a result your name may be included on the DEA's computerized list of persons suspected of some involvement in the drug trade.

Keeping track of large cash transactions is no mean feat. In fact, the government has nearly 100 employees located in Detroit, Michigan, whose job is to do nothing but physically sort the 70,000 currency reports that come in each day.[13] A small fraction of reports are then sent on to still more government employees in Washington, D.C., Sacramento, California, and Tallahassee, Florida, who try to determine where and by whom cash is being moved. The vast majority of the currency reports simply pile up in federal warehouses, untouched by examiners' hands.

About $350 billion in transactions are now reported each year under the currency reporting law. This sounds like an enormous sum until you realize that the total amount of money that changes hands in the United States each year runs in the neighborhood of $200 *trillion*—nearly forty times the size of the U.S. gross national product, and almost 700 times the size of the transactions covered by the currency reporting requirements.[14] Most of this money actually "changes hands" by means of wire transfers, which are electronic messages flashed from the memory of one computer to another. In effect, money has become a series of blips in the memory banks of computers, and thus "drug money" looks exactly like any other money. Using computers, it takes only about three seconds, at a cost of forty cents, to move a million dollars halfway around the globe. A drug trafficker can "launder" his money through many bank accounts so easily that it becomes almost impossible for an outside observer (or government auditor) to figure out where the money started or even who really owns it now.

The legal authorities are aware of—and frustrated by—facts such as these. And so, over the past few years they have proposed a variety of plans that purportedly will help them prevent the traffickers from hiding their ill-gotten gains. Among these proposals are the following:

- *Every* wire transfer—all $200 trillion worth of them—would have to be reported to the U.S. Treasury.
- An offical master list would be created of all "known or suspected" drug dealers, ranging from street pushers to international traffickers.
- U.S. banks and savings and loan associations would be required to refuse to accept new deposits from these individuals, and would also have to report any existing deposits owned by these persons.
- Through a combination of international agreements and "moral suasion," foreign central banks would persuade or force commercial

banks in their nations to cooperate with U.S. government investigations of alleged drug dealers. Foreign commercial banks would also effectively be prohibited from accepting any new deposits from any suspected drug dealer.

- To make sure that none of the "little fish" escape the net, the limit for currency transactions that must be reported by banks would be lowered from $10,000 to just $1,000.
- The Treasury would also covertly print up new versions (perhaps of a different size or color) of the $50 and $100 bills favored by drug traffickers. Then, with only ten days' notice, the legal tender status of the old bills would be nullified. Presumably, anyone trying to exchange more than, say, a briefcaseful of old bills for new would be immediately identified as a drug trafficker

Presumably, if these or similar proposals were actually implemented by the government, you would still be able to buy the morning paper, and possibly even the week's groceries, without it coming to the attention of a government bureaucrat. Otherwise, however, your records would be the government's records. Nationwide, the effect would be to paralyze $200 trillion in commercial transactions in an effort to isolate the one-twentieth of 1 percent of those transactions that are directly related to drug deals. One imagines that if George Orwell were alive today, even he would be impressed at our government's ingenuity.

MONEY LAUNDERING, PART II

Joseph Haji owns the Sunshine Market in Detroit. So far as we know, he is not in the drug business. Nevertheless, some drug-sniffing dogs have stimulated his interest in money laundering—albeit of a different sort than might interest a Colombian drug lord.

The Detroit police recently brought drug-sniffing dogs on to the premises of Haji's market and set them to work. The dogs found what the police were looking for: Three one-dollar bills in Haji's cash register had the smell of cocaine on them. The police confiscated those $3, plus the additional $4,381 in the cash register. At last report, Mr. Haji was still waiting for the return of his money. To no avail, Haji objected to the seizure, noting that his store is in a drug-plagued neighborhood: "Seventy-five percent of my business is with dope dealers and users. I'm supposed to inspect the money?"[15] Apparently so, according to the police, and according to federal drug laws that allow police to confiscate people's assets *before* they have been found guilty of any crime.

In fact, before you develop too much sympathy for Mr. Haji's plight, you might want to inspect the paper money in *your* pocket—or perhaps even take it to the laundry, if you think the police might have an interest in inspecting it. Paper money in the United States is made out of a woven, fibrous paper that looks and behaves a lot like cloth. (If you look at a bill closely, you'll notice some of the blue and red fibers woven through it.) If currency is exposed to dust or powder, it tends to retain some of that material among the paper fibers. If some of that powder is cocaine, the dogs can detect it and the police can seize it.

It has been estimated that one out of every three bills now circulating in the United States has been involved in cocaine transactions. Some of the money is placed in suitcases recently emptied of cocaine. Some bills are counted by dealers or users who still have cocaine on their hands after having handled the drug. Other money is contaminated by users who snort the drug through rolled-up bills. Whatever the source, if a cocaine-contaminated bill goes into your pocket with other, clean bills, some of those bills will end up being contaminated themselves. Thus, a recent study conducted by researchers at UCLA found that over 90 percent of American paper currency was contaminated with small but readily detectable traces of cocaine. If cocaine-sniffing dogs were taken into any bank in the United States, they would have a field day, and the money in the vault would be as subject to seizure as the money in Mr. Haji's cash register.

The legal risks associated with even remote traces of drugs extend far beyond our nation's money supply. Consider this: U.S. Coast Guard personnel recently boarded a shrimp boat in the Florida Keys on a "routine" inspection. They found three grams (about one-tenth of an ounce) of marijuana stems and seeds in a crew member's wastebasket. The owner of the boat protested that the marijuana did not belong to him and that he knew nothing about it. The government seized the boat. The shrimp boat was returned forty-one days after the seizure, but only after the owner agreed to pay a $100-a-day storage charge for that period.[16]

Now, you may well feel that the owner of this boat simply got what he deserved for not strip-searching his crew before allowing them on his vessel. After all, shrimpers operating in the Florida Keys surely are well aware of the Coast Guard's intense interest in making sure their vessels are not used to smuggle drugs. Before you pass judgment, however, you may want to read further, because you may face similar risks regarding your house, your car, and, indeed, all of your other possessions.

WHO USED TO OWN THIS?

The incidents mentioned above give but an inkling of how prepared the government is to use drug laws in order to seize and permanently deprive citizens of their property without bringing criminal charges against them. Under the so-called civil forfeiture provisions of the U.S. drug laws, houses, boats, cars, and other assets are subject to seizure if they are suspected of being used in illegal drug transactions or of having been purchased with the proceeds of such transactions. These seizures are conducted under the *civil* provisions of our laws, rather than the *criminal* provisions, a fact that gives an enormous advantage to the government and places a huge burden on the private citizens who are subjected to asset forfeitures.

In a criminal prosecution, a person is presumed innocent until proven guilty. The government has the burden of proof at trial, and that proof must establish guilt beyond a reasonable doubt. In most civil cases, a much more lenient "preponderance of the evidence" standard is applied. This simply means that the government has to show proof that something is more likely than not to have happened. In a civil *forfeiture* action, the government's burden of proof is even lighter. As long as the government demonstrates there is "probable cause" to believe that the seized property was used or intended to be used to facilitate some drug-law violation, or that the asset might have been purchased with the proceeds of a drug crime, then the seizure is legal. To get his or her property back, the *owner* has the burden of proving that the seized property is not forfeitable.

In effect, the courts have decided that because the U.S. Congress calls forfeiture proceedings civil cases rather than criminal cases, many of our fundamental constitutional protections simply don't apply anymore. Thus, if the government wants to fine you $10,000 for allegedly selling drugs, it must prove *beyond a reasonable doubt* that you were actually guilty of a crime. But if the government "only" wants to seize $10,000 worth of your assets because the assets alleg-edly are tainted by drug dealing, it must only demonstrate probable cause (more than a suspicion, but less than a fifty-fifty chance) that you did something wrong. The fact that you are out $10,000 in either case doesn't seem to matter to the courts.

Proving you are innocent of any criminal act is not a sufficient defense against forfeiture. Consider poor Ruth Allen. She loaned her car to her boyfriend, Vernon Whitlock, Jr., in Mississippi. He hap-pened to use the car in the course of selling some cocaine. The judge approved the seizure of Ruth Allen's car even though he acknowl-edged that Ms. Allen "was unaware of and uninvolved in" the illegal use of her car.

You may even be subject to an asset forfeiture if, prior to your ownership of the asset, it was used in drug trafficking, or if the asset was at any previous time owned by someone who used drug money to purchase it. In other words, the forfeiture statutes make the gov-ernment's ability to seize property *retroactive*. The car or house you own today is subject to seizure and forfeiture if you purchased it from someone who committed a drug offense using that asset, no matter when that offense was committed in the past. Lack of knowledge is not a defense.

As part of the Supreme Court's continuing "drug-exception" to the Bill of Rights, it has approved virtually all types of forfeiture pro-ceedings. In one precedent-setting case, a marijuana cigarette was found on a $20,000 sailboat owned by Pearson Yacht Leasing Com-pany, and leased to two individuals.[17] The boat was seized under a Puerto Rican statute that, like federal law, allows confiscation of property used in any way to facilitate the sale, possession, or trans-portation of controlled substances. There was no judicial hearing in advance of the seizure, and the owner of the yacht, Pearson, was given no prior notice that the seizure was about to take place. The govern-ment admitted that Pearson was neither involved in nor aware of illegal activity aboard the yacht. Despite these facts, the Supreme Court turned a deaf ear to Pearson's claim that the forfeiture violated the Fourth Amendment right to due process of the law. The Court also turned a deaf ear to Pearson's claim that the seizure constituted the taking of property without compensation in violation of the Fifth Amendment.

Instead, the Supreme Court decided that forfeiture is one of the "extraordinary situations" that justify postponing notice and an opportunity for a hearing. To be immune from forfeiture, the innocent owner must not only be unaware of and uninvolved in the illegal activity but must also do whatever he can to prevent the "proscribed use of his property."[18] Why has the Court seen fit to impose such onerous burdens on people uninvolved in the commission of crimes? Because the Court believes that the forfeiture provisions may have the "desirable effect of inducing [innocent parties] to exercise greater care in transferring possession of their property."[19] The logic of the Court's reasoning is impeccable, but consider the full implications of their stance: If you buy a used car from someone who once transported drugs in it, the government may be able to seize the car. If you rent out the basement apartment in your house to someone who (unbeknownst to you) purchases drugs there, the government may be able to seize your home. As a practical matter, if the government can show probable cause that any of your assets are in any way tainted by drugs, it can seize them.

In one recent U.S. Second Circuit Court of Appeals ruling in Manhattan, a building was seized from West 141 St. Realty Corporation.[20] The defendant company argued that it took adequate measures to stop drug activity in its six-story Manhattan building, including a refusal to accept rent from tenants who were arrested in a drug raid. The court did not agree that this was enough, stating that property owners must also *prove* they didn't consent to drug activities on their property. To prove the lack of consent, the owner must show that *vigorous* steps were taken to deter drug violations. In the words of the court:

> Congress intended forfeiture to be a powerful weapon in the war on drugs. The illicit sale and use of drugs is taking an ever-increasing toll on our nation. Given the present circumstances, defining "consent" . . . as a failure to take all reasonable steps to prevent illicit use of premises once one acquires knowledge of that use is entirely appropriate.[21]

Seizure and forfeiture laws also have been used in recent years to deprive criminal drug defendants of having the wherewithal to defend themselves. Criminal defendants can now have all of their assets seized *prior* to trial, since the government merely must show that there is "probable cause" that the assets are tainted by illegal drugs. How then can defendants hire competent legal help? The court has ruled that criminal drug defendants still have public defenders to help them, and that such help is good enough. That may be the case, but in effect, the forfeiture and seizure laws still mean that we no longer have the constitutional protections that our founding fathers took such great pains to include in our Bill of Rights.

EQUALITY AND BROTHERHOOD

The erosion of civil liberties taking place under the drug laws is not just an elimination of constitutional guarantees for drug lords. It is not simply another "cost of doing business" for property-leasing companies, such as Pearson or West 141 St. Realty. And it is not something that just happens to "people who were probably guilty anyway." The government is persecuting the many to prosecute the few, and attempting to force ordinary citizens to become their brothers' keepers, so that we the people are required to do for the government what it cannot do for itself.

International drug lords and the dealers who wage open warfare on our streets are blights on our nation and our lives. Yet in the quest to rid America of these perpetrators of misery, our government is taking extraordinary actions that threaten to do us more harm than can possibly be cured. Few of us feel much sympathy for a murderous drug trafficker "deprived of his rights" to hire a $500-an-hour defense lawyer who will get him off on a technicality. Few of us are concerned that a cocaine dealer's "right to privacy" doesn't include the right to spend millions in drug profits without triggering a government investigation. It is difficult to grieve for Jamaican posse members killed in 3:00 A.M. gun battles with police S.W.A.T. teams who must shoot first to avoid being shot themselves. And few of us care that drug couriers are inconvenienced by state police determined to stop their trips north with drugs.

Yet sometimes, many times, *we* are the victims of the tactics that we applaud when used against the "bad guys." Jeffery Miles and Tommy Dubose weren't drug traffickers or gang members, yet the police who broke into their homes killed them just as efficiently. Most orchid growers and pleasure boaters have no connection whatever with the drug trade, yet Joseph Huberman and Craig Klein suffered as though they were. As soon as we permit our government to ignore the Bill of Rights as it applies to *one* of us, *all* of us are equally subject to the totalitarian horrors that can result. Just ask the widow and three children of the late Bruce Lavoie. In its rush to prosecute the traffickers and dealers, the government is trampling on the lives and rights of thousands of innocent citizens—rights and lives that all too often are gone forever.

Tragically, even though the drug warriors are increasingly able to ignore our constitutional rights, they have cast their drug net so wide that most of the fish are escaping anyway. One out of three Americans have used psychoactive substances declared illegal by our government, and one out of six fellow citizens does so every year. Just as during Prohibition, we have become a nation of criminals in the eyes of our government, and so our government has told us that we must help it do the job it cannot do itself. As "concerned citizens" we must "rat on a rat" and report our suspicions about people who keep odd hours or live life-styles that seem too sumptuous. And to make sure that we "take all reasonable steps" to ensure that no one slips through the net, our courts have decreed that we risk the loss of our homes and our property if we do not inquire far enough into the habits and past of our fellow citizens. Thus emplaced as keepers of our brothers, we shall surely become a Big Brother beyond even the imagination of George Orwell.

PART THREE

TAKING CONTROL

CHAPTER 9

············

Thinking Psychoactively

PSYCHOACTIVES ARE A FACT OF LIFE. THEY HAVE BEEN PRODUCED BY plants and consumed by animals for millions of years. They were known to and consumed by Neolithic man, and in the intervening years, humans have applied their considerable brain power and creativity to refining, distilling, repackaging, and consuming psychoactives to better suit their desires. The issue facing society today is not how to eliminate psychoactives, nor how to eliminate the *use* of psychoactives. The issue instead is how to adapt to the continued existence of psychoactives so that, on balance, we benefit ourselves and our descendants to the greatest extent.

This problem has been successfully dealt with at the *individual* level by the vast majority of people in all times and places of history. To be sure, not all individuals have successfully coped with the problem, a fact that helps explain why governments have concerned themselves with psychoactives. Unlike most individuals, however, most national governments repeatedly have either failed to recognize the relevant issue or have done a poor job of dealing with it. Indeed, our story thus far has demonstrated that our federal government has been guilty of such failures in both the past and the present. In this chapter, we begin to ask how Americans can refocus the efforts of government so that it assists, rather than impedes, our efforts as individuals to coexist successfully with psychoactives.

THE TIE THAT BINDS

For as long as man has been man, psychoactive substances have been part and parcel of his existence. Humans surely gained much of their early knowledge of psychoactives by watching the animals about them: goats suddenly energized after eating the berries of the coffee bush, or llamas performing astonishing feats of endurance after chewing coca leaves; elephants staggering drunkenly after gorging on the fermented fruit of the *Borassas* palm, or reindeer shouldering aside other members of the herd in their excited quest to nibble on the hallucinogenic *Amanita muscaria* mushroom; or even normally carnivorous jaguars gnawing on the vile-tasting stems and leaves of the *yaje* vine, whose effects include enhanced night vision when taken in small doses, and psychedelic visions at slightly larger doses.[1]

From observations such as these, as well as their own chance encounters and experimental forays, humans accumulated knowledge of the psychoactive properties of hundreds of plants over the course of thousands of years. Some of these plants, such as the coca bush, yielded nutritional value as well as psychoactive effects (stimulation and hunger suppression) valued in their own right. Other plants had medicinal value (such as the opium poppy as a source of pain reliever), but also produced pleasurable effects even when medication per se was not the objective. Some plants were originally valued for their nonpsychoactive properties (such as marijuana, whose fibrous parts were woven into rope), but ultimately came to be cultivated and consumed for what they did for, or to, the mind.

Whatever the sources of the psychoactives, and however their effects were discovered, humans learned that psychoactives could play roles in their lives that were difficult if not impossible to fill otherwise. In some cases, psychoactives enabled men to adapt themselves to a reality they could not alter, as the coca leaf did in aiding South American Indians to live high in the Andes without suffering the effects of altitude sickness. Other psychoactives enabled men to alter reality, as the opiates did in bringing sleep when it seemed otherwise impossible. And, as in the case of hallucinogens and alcohol, yet other psychoactives helped humans alter their perception of a reality which they could neither accept nor change.

Precisely why man has felt compelled to rely so often on psychoactives to fill these roles is not known, and may well not be understood in our lifetimes or those of our children. Some researchers have suggested that the urge to use psychoactives—the desire for intoxication, in its broadest sense—is simply an inherent component of our genetic makeup, much like the instinctual drives of thirst, hunger, and sex. Other experts argue that the use of psychoactives is chiefly a form of self-medication, driven either by naturally occurring imbalances in our body chemistry, or motivated by the desire to ameliorate externally imposed threats to our mental or physical health. Whatever the truth of these or other explanations, one fact seems inescapable: White or black, Oriental or Occidental, male or female, and young or old, human beings have almost everywhere and almost always chosen to make psychoactives a part of their lives.

ON BALANCE

As humans became familiar with psychoactives and experimented with them, they learned that the use of psychoactives created both negative and positive effects. In this dimension, of course, the psychoactives were, and remain, little different from virtually any aspect of the environment within which humans must make choices.

All actions have reactions. Some of these reactions, or effects, are pleasurable or beneficial. Indeed, it is the beneficial effects of action that induce us to act. But some effects are harmful or dangerous— they are the costs of our actions. These costs dissuade us from undertaking some acts, and moderate our behavior when, on balance, some action seems appropriate. Learning how to balance beneficial and adverse effects has played a central role in the human adaptation to psychoactives, just as such balance is central in adapting to every other feature of our existence.

Food has beneficial effects: It pleases the palate, satisfies our hunger, and ultimately helps keep us alive. But eating can also have harmful effects, ranging from excess cholesterol levels to obesity, which is why most of us are careful (to varying degrees) about the type and amount of food we consume. The pleasurable effects of food stimulate us to eat, but the adverse effects of eating too much food or the wrong food induce us to consume with care. Nevertheless, such effects rarely induce us to stop eating altogether, forever!

A seven-course meal is a far cry from the intravenous injection of heroin. Yet food is not so far removed from alcoholic beverages. Not only are grains and fruits the raw material from which alcohol is derived, but for many people the consumption of food and of alcohol are intimately linked—witness the prevalence in America of cocktails before dinner, or wine with it. More than two-thirds of adult Americans consume alcohol at least occasionally, most of them on a regular basis. Presumably, they do so because they judge it to have pleasurable effects. It pleases the palate, complements food, provides some nutritional value, and may even assist in "attitude adjustment" after a day of hard work. Yet alcohol consumption also has adverse effects, ranging from impaired judgment to death by alcohol poisoning. And so most people moderate their consumption, weighing the pleasurable effects against the potential adverse consequences.

What is true of alcohol is true—in kind, if not degree—of all psychoactive substances. Roughly 50 million Americans, for example, consume tobacco products, chiefly in the form of cigarettes. Presumably, they do so because smoking (or perhaps chewing) tobacco produces some pleasurable effects for them. Yet the consumption of tobacco also has well-established and widely recognized adverse consequences, ranging from throat irritation to lung cancer. In weighing the positive and negative effects of consuming tobacco, most Americans choose to refrain altogether. Yet some engage in occasional usage, and many use tobacco on a regular basis.

As with users of tobacco and alcohol, many people who use other psychoactive agents report pleasurable effects of doing so. Yet the consumption of tranquilizers, stimulants, opiates, and hallucinogens also has potentially adverse effects. Knowing this, many people deliberately refrain completely from consuming such psychoactives, even though many others choose to consume some of them at least occasionally. Valium, a prescription tranquilizer, was the most widely prescribed drug in the world during most of the 1970s. Well over twenty million Americans have tried cocaine, and government surveys reveal that twenty million people in this country report using marijuana on a regular basis. At the extreme end of the spectrum, it is estimated that more than 500,000 Americans are addicted to heroin, while many hundreds of thousands more are addicted to prescription psychoactives.

These consumption patterns result from *choices* made by human beings. To be sure, the choices are influenced by the legal framework, by genetic factors, and by a host of social, economic, and psychological forces. Nevertheless, the patterns of psychoactive use we observe are not predestined from birth, nor are they simply the outcome of random chance. They are the reflection of the preferences and pre-dispositions of individuals, expressed within the environment in which those individuals exist.

At first glance, this notion might seem absurd. Surely no one grows up wanting to be a heroin junkie or an alcoholic, not any more than anyone begins smoking cigarettes because they want to get lung cancer. Nevertheless, addiction is one of the possible adverse consequences of psychoactive use, as are a host of other diseases. With varying degrees of knowledge and forethought, people choose whether or not to use a given psychoactive initially, and if they try it, whether and to what extent they wish to continue using it. Sometimes these choices yield benefits for the individual which far outweigh the costs. In other instances, the choices turn out to have disastrous consequences. But as we try to shape public policy toward psychoactives, we must recognize that although policy can *alter* the choices people make, and may even *improve* those choices, policy can never ultimately *be* the choices. It is men and women who choose what their behavior shall be. And just as individuals make those choices in recognition—imperfect though it may be—of the benefits and costs of their decisions, so too must we weigh the effects of our choice of public policies. Only then will government policy achieve the balance that we as individuals seek in our own decisions.

BALANCING ACT

Though we live in an individualistic society, most Americans recognize that government has a valid and at times indispensable role to play. Given this recognition, we must ask what specific role the government should play regarding psychoactives. The answers each of us might give to this question would vary considerably. Yet, we may still gain some insights by considering those areas in which we the people seem willing to accept government action as an alternative or supplement to individual decision making about psychoactives.

Government rules regarding the consumption of ethyl alcohol provide perhaps the most obvious example. Americans routinely expect (and, more often than not, accept) government involvement when there are potential "third-party effects" of alcohol consumption—instances in which the consumption decisions of one individual may have significant adverse consequences on other individuals. The mere ingestion of alcohol does not by itself create third-party effects, and even the act of getting intoxicated may often not produce third-party effects. Yet there is little doubt that operating a motor vehicle while "under the influence" creates the potential for adverse third-party effects, since the impaired judgment and slowed reaction time produced by intoxication increase the chances of an automobile accident. Indeed, alcohol consumption is identified as a causal factor in more than 40 percent of all highway traffic fatalities in this country, a number that surely would be higher if we did not seek to curb the act of drinking and driving.[2] Thus, we accept laws which prohibit us from operating an automobile if our blood alcohol content (BAC) is "too high." Implicitly, we accept a restriction on our *own* consumption of alcohol because the same restriction on the behavior of *other* drivers makes the roads safer for us.

Our desire to be protected from the alcohol consumption decisions of others leads us to accept government restrictions on our own behavior; nevertheless, we expect the government to balance the beneficial consequences of those restrictions against their adverse (costly) consequences. For example, although the consumption of just one or two mixed drinks impairs our reaction times and motor skills, our laws routinely permit us to drink and drive beyond this point. Indeed, in most states one may legally drink and drive until one's BAC reaches 0.10 percent (roughly four mixed drinks consumed within an hour).[3] In effect, we are willing to accept the risk that some other driver has a blood alcohol content of, say, 0.07 percent, in return for the convenience it affords us in not having to call a taxi after having two or three drinks at a cocktail party.

Our interest in having the government balance beneficial effects against adverse consequences shows up elsewhere in government regulations which restrict alcohol consumption. For example, the potential damage that can be done by a commercial airline pilot if he or she is intoxicated far exceeds the damage that ordinarily can be done by the driver of an automobile. Thus, we accept government rules that limit airline pilots to a more stringent BAC of 0.04 percent, and prohibit them from ingesting any alcohol during the eight hours preceding takeoff. At the other end of the spectrum, there are no government rules regulating our blood alcohol content while operating a lawn mower in the privacy of our own yards, and many jurisdictions do not even prohibit drunkenness in public, unless our behavior poses a hazard to other persons.

Our interest in protecting ourselves from the adverse consumption decisions made by others extends also to the consumption of nicotine—at least when combustion is involved. It has long been illegal to smoke in the vicinity of gasoline pumps at service stations, for example. More recently, there is growing evidence that "passive smoking" (exposure to air contaminated with the smoke produced by others' cigarettes, cigars, or pipes) creates health hazards for nonsmokers. Thus, nearly all states and roughly 450 local governments now restrict smoking in public places ranging from elevators to restaurants.[4] Presumably, these restrictions are not only tolerated but demanded by the citizenry, on the grounds that the clean-air benefits that accrue to nonsmokers more than offset the loss of freedom (and possible nicotine withdrawal) imposed on smokers. Even here, however, government regulations appear to reflect our preferences for a balancing of costs and benefits, for the restrictions typically apply only to those public places (or portions thereof) where the damage done by passive smoke would be greatest. Thus, elevators are commonly required to be "smoke-free" areas, while, in most jurisdictions, only certain sections of restaurants must be set aside for nonsmokers. Of course, smoking in one's own automobile or private residence is still legal, whatever the damage that may be done to other occupants: Despite the benefits that might accrue from laws requiring non-smoking sections in our cars or homes, the resulting intrusion on our privacy is deemed to be too great.

Concern over third-party effects has not been the only area in which Americans have shown an interest in having their government take actions that restrict or influence the consumption of psychoactives. Knowledge about the adverse effects of a psychoactive is essential to individual decisions about whether and how much of the psycho-active to consume. Although the acquisition of such information is largely left up to the affected individuals, many Americans feel that the government should produce and disseminate such knowledge, and that suppliers should be *required* to advertise information about the adverse effects of their products. Thus, cigarette manufacturers are required to put health warnings on their product, and to display those warnings prominently in their advertising. Again, an element of balance is involved, for the required cigarette warnings are far less cumbersome, detailed, and expensive to produce than the voluminous package inserts summarizing the potential adverse effects of prescription drugs.

Tobacco and alcohol manufacturers are also restricted in the venues they may use to promote the consumption of the psychoactives they produce. Television and radio advertisements for both cigarettes and distilled spirits are prohibited by the federal government. Despite this, beer and smokeless tobacco (such as chewing tobacco) may both be advertised on television and radio, and all types of alcohol and tobacco advertising are permitted in the print media. Though such advertising promotes the consumption of demonstrably hazardous psychoactives, the infringement on freedom implied by complete advertising bans is apparently deemed too costly to warrant the benefits of reduced consumption.

Another area in which Americans accept and even demand government intervention in the consumption of psychoactives concerns the competency of the consumers: Quite simply, most Americans don't want their children to have unrestricted access to psychoactives, even alcohol and tobacco. This attitude probably stems partly from the widespread belief that many psychoactives have particularly adverse effects on the developing minds and bodies of children, and partly from the belief that children do not have the knowledge and maturity to make competent decisions about the consumption of psychoactives.

Despite the near universality with which Americans hold these beliefs, U.S. government policies still reflect a sense of balance between adverse and beneficial consequences. For example, even though the consumption of caffeine (a potent stimulant) has potential adverse effects, government regulations generally do not restrict the access of children to coffee or to caffeinated soft drinks, presumably because citizens do not judge those effects sufficiently dangerous. Many jurisdictions permit children as young as sixteen to decide for themselves whether to consume highly addictive, carcinogenic psychoactives (cigarettes and chewing tobacco). And despite prohibiting persons under twenty-one from purchasing alcohol, government enforcement agencies typically devote only modest resources to actually ensuring that the law is obeyed.* Finally, many Americans seem to accept the fact that parents have the right to decide about the consumption of tobacco and alcohol by their *own* children, at least within the privacy of their homes; in effect, the costs associated with government intrusion into parental decision making are deemed

---

*Indeed, until 1984 federal legislation mandating a minimum drinking age of twenty-one, many states permitted persons as young as eighteen to purchase alcohol.

to exceed the potential benefits gained by preventing juvenile consumption of tobacco or alcohol at home.

Our point is not that government regulation of tobacco and alcohol has reached some ideal state that cannot be improved upon. Tobacco and alcohol are known to cause a staggering array of debilitating and lethal diseases; between them, they kill roughly half a million Americans every year.[5] Moreover, nearly one-fourth of all adults in this country are addicted to tobacco, while roughly 10 percent are addicted to alcohol. Taken together, these two psychoactives have almost surely produced more human suffering and economic and social damage than any other psychoactives known to man. Recognizing this, many people would prefer that government regulation of these substances become more stringent.

Remarkably, our interest in more government regulation of these substances focuses on a narrow range of issues. Most obvious is the public call for more stringent laws regarding drunk driving and more diligent enforcement of the drinking and driving laws already on the books. On the tobacco front, Americans are increasingly demanding that they not be subjected to the smoke produced by the tobacco of others. In both cases, the issue involved is not the *consumption* of the psychoactive by an individual, but rather the damage that consumption does to *other* individuals.

There is also growing interest in America in toughening government-mandated labeling requirements for tobacco and alcohol products, and in restricting the extent or nature of advertising that the makers of these psychoactives may undertake. In significant respects, such measures reflect an interest in ensuring that individuals make fully informed decisions regarding the consumption of these psychoactives, an interest that is paralleled in many communities by added enforcement of laws prohibiting underage individuals from purchasing tobacco and alcohol.

Our growing awareness and concern about the hazards of tobacco and alcohol consumption is also becoming reflected in the level of taxes imposed on these two goods. At both the federal and state level, excise taxes on both products have increased substantially over the past decade. Just as significantly, the motivation for taxing these products has begun to shift. In some jurisdictions, the additional tax revenues are being earmarked for antismoking campaigns and for expansion of public rehabilitation facilities for treating alcoholism.

Across the spectrum, both the current structure of tobacco and alcohol laws and the emerging interest in extending these rules implicitly recognize the inherent human affinity for consuming psychoactive substances. In doing so, the government regulation of alcohol and tobacco reflects the fact that the decision to consume or not to consume is ultimately made at the level of the individual human being. These individual decisions regarding alcohol and tobacco are rarely perfect; just as surely, our government regulations regarding these psychoactives are not perfect. Importantly, however, our government decisions regarding our consumption of alcohol and tobacco at least attempt to balance beneficial consequences against adverse effects, and in many cases seem to accomplish something resembling that goal. Tragically, it is an accomplishment we cannot claim for government policies regarding most illegal psychoactives.

OFF BALANCE

One of the first principles impressed upon medical students is this simple rule: *nihil nocere*. Roughly translated from the Latin, it means "Guard against doing more harm than good." In practical terms, the rule cautions the physician not to prescribe a treatment which damages the patient more than if the ailment were simply left to run its course.

There are three elements involved in the successful application of the principle of *nihil nocere*. First, the nature of the disease, including its dangers if left unchecked, must be correctly diagnosed. Is the patient's cough caused by a common cold, or by life-threatening pneumonia? Second, the ramifications of the proposed treatment must be understood, including both its efficacy in curing the disease, and its potentially adverse side effects. Although antibiotics like penicillin are useful in treating bacterial pneumonia, they have no impact on viral pneumonia; and whenever they are used, possibly debilitating diarrhea can result. The third essential element is the backdrop against which the first two must be approached: the physician's knowledge of the patient. If the patient is allergic to penicillin, use of the drug could result in sudden death from anaphylactic shock.

Although the principle of *nihil nocere* has successfully guided physicians for uncounted centuries, it is a maxim that our national government has ignored (or perhaps not understood) in its approach to many psychoactives. Time and again, the federal government has failed to diagnose the nature of the "drug problem" facing society, or has adopted a drug policy responsible for more damage than caused by the original problem. And throughout it all, our government has not understood its "patient," in the sense that it has failed to distinguish between use, abuse, and addiction—distinctions that are crucial at the level of the individuals who ultimately make choices about psychoactives. In making these errors, the federal government has routinely and repeatedly failed to maintain the sense of balance that is essential if we the people are to successfully coexist with psychoactives.

The Opiates

Consider the opiates, including opium, morphine, and heroin. At the beginning of this century, the "drug problem" in America was significantly an "opiate problem."[6] Throughout the nineteenth century, opiates were legal in America and were readily and cheaply available from doctors, drugstores, grocery stores, and mail order. Opiates were contained in literally hundreds of over-the-counter and patent medicines, and were widely advertised and used as remedies for everything from diarrhea to tuberculosis. They were also the psychoactive of choice for tens of thousands of Americans who were addicted to them, and who found that, once addicted, it seemed almost impossible to "kick the habit."

The federal government's diagnosis was simple: People had been free to use opiates and when they used them they became hopelessly addicted to them. The solution seemed equally obvious: Prohibit the use of opiates, thereby forcing the addicts to stop their use, and preventing anyone else from becoming addicted. So Congress passed the Harrison Narcotics Act of 1914, which made all of the opiates (plus cocaine) effectively illegal, except under narrowly prescribed medical circumstances.

As we saw in chapter 1, the outcome of the government's solution was not exactly what was intended. To be sure, the Harrison Act did reduce the *legal* supply of opiates and as a result, ultimately drove their prices up by a factor of 100. But the act did not stop addicts from using the drugs, nor did it completely eliminate new users or new addicts. It did, however, convert a modest medical problem into a major criminal problem. Indeed, the effects were identical to the disastrous consequences of Prohibition, the government's subsequent "cure" for the alcohol problem.

The tragic fact about our government's response to the "opiate problem" is that the outcome was *not* inevitable. The British government confronted much the same symptoms but diagnosed and treated them differently, resulting in a markedly different outcome.[7] Opiates were both legal and widely used in nineteenth-century Britain, and many British citizens became addicted to them. The British responded to these circumstances with the Dangerous Drugs Act of 1920. Unlike the American government, however, the British approach was to view addiction as a medical problem, and their legal policy was designed to reflect this fact. *Existing* addicts were turned over to the care of physicians, who were free to treat them as they saw fit—a mandate that included prescribing morphine and heroin. To reduce the emergence of *new* addicts, the British government undertook vigorous law-enforcement actions against illegal distributors of morphine and heroin. Naturally, some illegal opiates slipped through, and so some new individuals did become addicts. Once addicted, however, they were free to go to physicians and receive low-cost, legal supplies of morphine or heroin sufficient to maintain their habits.

In effect, the British approach drove an almost impenetrable wedge between addicts and illegal suppliers, and thus largely eliminated supplies to nonaddicts who might be interested in experimenting with the opiates. Existing addicts had a cheap means of satisfying their addiction, so they had no incentive to pay exorbitant black-market prices, and thus no need to engage in crime to pay for their drugs. Addicts also had convenient access to sterile hypodermic syringes and to high-quality morphine and heroin of known purity, so they had no reason to risk the use of adulterated drugs or dirty needles. Potential black-market suppliers found Britain an unprofitable market, since addicts would pay them no more than the legal price, and nonaddicted, casual users typically would not pay enough to compensate dealers for the risks of imprisonment. And without the steady, well-paying addict trade to keep illegal dealers on every street corner, potential new users found it almost impossible to find supplies of the opiates.

The results of the British approach were remarkable. The incidence of opiate addiction in Britain began to decline immediately, and continued declining over the next forty years, as older addicts gradually died off and few new ones joined their ranks. The spread of infectious diseases due to contaminated needles was virtually unknown, as were addict deaths due to overdoses and adulterated drugs. British police did not have to spend their time dealing with property crimes committed by heroin addicts, simply because the addicts didn't have to commit crimes to finance their addiction. Moreover, the prevention of black-market dealing in opiates became a minor and routine part of law enforcement instead of the budget-draining war prevalent in American cities.

The comparison of the British and American experiences with opiates provides an instructive look at the importance of the principle of *nihil nocere*, as well as the dangers of failing to maintain balance between beneficial consequences and adverse effects in dealing with psychoactives. The British separated the problem they faced into two parts: addiction, a medical condition left in the hands of physicians, and use by nonaddicts, a matter dealt with by conventional means of law enforcement. American policy makers confused use and addiction, and thus not only failed to appreciably reduce addiction but also radically raised the social, economic, and medical costs of use.

Given the diagnoses arrived at by the two governments, the "treatments" chosen by the two different countries reflect a radically different appreciation of the notion of balance. At the time the two governments confronted opiates, there were only two medical approaches to treating opiate addiction: maintenance on the drug or gradual "weaning" of the addict. British physicians were aware of the extremely high relapse rate among opiate addicts, and so chose the course of maintenance. The British government permitted this choice, presumably reasoning that, on balance, it was better than recycling addicts back into the black market, where they would greatly magnify the law-enforcement problem.

This sense of balance was not maintained in the American course of "treatment." Prior to the Harrison Act, adulteration, overdoses, infectious diseases, and crime had not been associated with the use of opiates. These debilitating consequences came only with the attempt of the federal government to prohibit the use of opiates—just as adulteration, alcohol poisoning, and crime came to be the hallmarks of alcohol only after the federal government prohibited its use. Ultimately, the federal government was forced to recognize the failings of its policy toward alcohol, yet it persisted in its prohibition of opiates, despite the creation of adverse consequences that overwhelmed any demonstrable reduction in the rate of opiate addiction.

Our comparison of the British and American responses to opiate use and addiction is not intended as a plea for the legalization of heroin, nor even a claim that the British approach of heroin maintenance for addicts was the ideal solution. Our point is simply that the American government's policy toward opiates has clearly caused substantially adverse economic, social, and public health consequences, while yielding little in the way of demonstrable beneficial effects. By contrast, the policy followed by the British government for more than forty years yielded substantial reductions in the rate of opiate addiction, without producing significantly adverse consequences. Ultimately, the fundamental difference between the policies toward opiates chosen by the two governments reflected a difference in their ability and willingness to balance the beneficial effects and adverse consequences of their policies toward psychoactives.

Events of the last quarter-century provide additional evidence of the importance of changes in this balancing act. During the late sixties, the British decided to reevaluate their opiate policy in response to a modest rise in the rate of heroin addiction. Acting at least partly on the advice of American officials, the British government decided to change its policy toward one more closely resembling the American model. Private physicians can no longer dispense heroin to addicts, and the National Health Service clinics that do dispense heroin are under orders to wean addicts as quickly as possible.

Largely deprived of legal sources of supply, addicts have turned to the black market, which is now flourishing in Britain. As in America, the high prices in the British black market have induced addicts to turn to crime to support their addiction. As in America, the illegal nature of the British heroin market produces deaths due to overdoses and adulterated drugs, as well as the spread of infectious diseases via contaminated needles. And, as in America, British law-enforcement agencies now find themselves battling a budget-draining war.[8]

Marijuana

Undaunted by the results of the Harrison Act (and by the disaster of Prohibition), the federal government turned its attention to marijuana.[9] The initial disruption in alcohol supplies during Prohibition had induced some individuals to look elsewhere for recreational psychoactives. The result was an upturn in the 1920s and early 1930s in the consumption of then-legal marijuana. When Prohibition was repealed in 1933, Treasury Department officials who had been employed enforcing federal liquor law developed a sudden interest in marijuana. They began a nationwide scare campaign focusing on marijuana's alleged propensity to produce "reefer madness," a supposed mental state in which drug-crazed marijuana smokers were transformed by the drug into rapists and murderers. Despite the fact that anyone familiar with marijuana's effects knew that the drug actually produces a peaceful, introspective state of euphoria, Congress was convinced. In 1937 federal legislation was passed classifying marijuana as a "narcotic," purportedly as dangerous as heroin and so utterly without redeeming value that it could not even be prescribed by a physician.

Rising supplies of post-Prohibition alcohol turned consumers' attention away from marijuana, initially minimizing the impact of federal policy toward the drug. In the 1960s, however, the baby-boom generation came of age and began experimenting with psychoactives, marijuana included. Vigorous enforcement of federal policy toward "pot" quickly became open warfare against those who smoked the drug, and by the 1980s, hundreds of thousands of people a year were being arrested simply for possessing marijuana. Casual use of a drug that has remarkably few adverse effects when used casually was transformed into the largest single source of criminal records among the American citizenry.

As with the opiates, the fundamental problem with the approach of our government toward marijuana lies in its inability to balance beneficial consequences against adverse effects. Importantly, this is because the government fails to distinguish the use of marijuana from the adverse consequences of its use, just as the government has failed to make this distinction for the opiates. This fact can be illustrated by a simple comparison of our policies toward alcohol and marijuana.

As we noted earlier, roughly 10 percent of all adults in America are addicted to alcohol. The consumption of alcohol is implicated in nearly half of all traffic fatalities in the United States each year, and more than half of all violent crimes. Several hundred people in America die each year as a result of acute alcohol poisoning (overdose), and the chronic abuse of alcohol is known to cause or suspected of causing cirrhosis of the liver; birth defects; cancer of the throat, esophagus, stomach, pancreas, and liver; brain damage; and a variety of other minor and major ailments. Overall, the consumption of alcohol will cause the deaths of at least 100,000 people in the United States this year.[10]

What is the nature of our policy response to the dangers of alcohol? Aside from efforts to prevent underage persons from using alcohol, virtually all of the government's efforts are directed toward preventing abusers of the drug from inflicting damage on third parties. The perpetrators of violent crimes are arrested and persons who operate motor vehicles while under the influence of alcohol are ticketed or jailed. Persons who simply wish to inflict damage upon *themselves* with alcohol are generally left alone to do so.

Although marijuana use is less prevalent than alcohol use, there are still roughly 20 million people who use the drug in any given month. The incidence of addiction to marijuana among its users is not known with any precision, but it is generally believed to be smaller than that among alcohol users. Although there are no known instances of lethal marijuana overdoses, its smoke is known to be laden with carcinogenic chemicals, it is regarded as a health hazard to children and pregnant women, and many experts believe that the drug ultimately will be implicated in some cancer cases. In addition, long-term chronic abuse of marijuana is associated with loss of motivation and impairment of mental concentration and learning skills, though it is not known whether these effects are permanent or reversible. Unlike alcohol, marijuana use does not cause aggressive, violent behavior; in fact, its effect on users is just the reverse. Overall, the number of deaths attributable for any reason to the use of marijuana is apparently so small that U.S. drug-enforcement and health agencies do not even report such a statistic.[11]

What is the nature of our policy response to the dangers of marijuana? Aside from exhorting us to "just say no," virtually all of the government efforts are directed toward arresting, prosecuting, and incarcerating anyone who uses marijuana, regardless of the third-party effects of that use, or of the damage the drug might cause to the users themselves. As with the opiates, the government perceives the problem with marijuana to be its *use*.

What rational explanation can one give for the striking contrast between government policies toward alcohol and toward marijuana? A charitable explanation (and one that is routinely offered) is that alcohol use is tolerated because it is so ingrained in American society that it would be impossible to halt. There is merit in this argument, as witnessed by our disastrous fourteen-year experience with Prohibition. Yet every month, 20 million Americans subject themselves to the risk of arrest because they use marijuana, and for tens of thousands of them each month, that risk becomes an arrest record. Each year, hundreds of millions of dollars and tens of thousands of hours of law enforcement are spent on the federal government's futile attempts to prevent people from using marijuana. This effort, and its lack of success, has been going on for more than fifty years, and if marijuana does not now qualify as being "ingrained" in American society, it is hard to imagine what would qualify. No government agency has ever presented any evidence to demonstrate that the efforts to prevent the use of marijuana are warranted on any grounds other than the fact that a 1937 law is still on the books.*

Our contrast between alcohol policy and marijuana policy is not intended as a plea for a return to Prohibition, nor even a call for the legalization of marijuana, but rather as a way to focus on what we see as a critical failing in government policy toward psychoactives. The vast majority of all individuals respond to the existence of any given psychoactive by either choosing not to use it or by using it in moderation. A small minority of individuals use psychoactives in ways that cause significant harm to themselves or to other persons. Certainly any use of a psychoactive that creates significant harm to third parties creates a prima facie case for government policy to reduce those effects. This route is the one that has been taken toward alcohol in the years since Prohibition, and it is one that we would argue should be pursued even more vigorously. Marijuana provides a useful contrast with alcohol because the demonstrated third-party effects of marijuana are vanishingly small compared to those of alcohol. Even the damage done to marijuana users themselves is modest compared with that of alcohol users. We are led to conclude that either there is no rational basis for the government's disparate treatment of these psychoactives or that there is something inherent in

*One rationale given for the prohibition of the use of marijuana is that it is purportedly a "gateway" drug, whose use somehow leads to the use of other, more dangerous drugs. This argument was originally used sixty years ago when it was claimed that marijuana use somehow led to heroin use. In fact, surveys of heroin users reveal that it was their prior enjoyable experiences with alcohol and barbiturates—not marijuana—that led them to try heroin.[12]

the process of policy formulation that prevents the federal government from achieving the balance that we as individuals strive for in coexisting with psychoactives.

Cocaine

Until the 1970s, cocaine played a relatively minor role in U.S. drug consumption and in the American war on drugs. Since the 1930s, the stimulants of choice for Americans had been caffeine and amphetamines. Sadly, it was chiefly the government's success in the war against black-market amphetamines (and later, against marijuana) that revived American consumers' long-dormant interest in cocaine.[13]

As we have noted before, the principal means of consuming cocaine in nineteenth-century America was orally, in the form of dilute liquid solutions, often called tonics or elixirs. The principal use of the drug was as a stimulant consumed in the ordinary course of everyday living, much as people today consume caffeine. At one point, the Parke-Davis pharmaceutical company made fifteen different products that contained cocaine, including a cigar infused with the drug. A mixture of cocaine and wine called Vin Mariani was endorsed by such personages as Pope Leo XIII and U.S. President William McKinley.

There was abuse of cocaine, and even addiction, particularly after the drug's popularity spread in the 1880s. Most abusers and addicts simply consumed copious quantities of the cocaine solutions that were available over the counter and by mail order. Some of them snorted powdered cocaine, and a small number even injected the drug under the skin with hypodermic syringes. At the peak of cocaine's use, probably no more than about 20,000 Americans were addicted to it—a rate of addiction less than one-tenth of that observed with opiates.

The relatively low incidence of cocaine addiction meant that the drug's inclusion in the Harrison Act of 1914 drove the market for cocaine underground with few visible effects. Although Prohibition brought a modest revival of interest in the drug, the commercial introduction of Benzedrine (the first amphetamine) in 1932, followed by the repeal of Prohibition, largely eliminated the American market for cocaine. For the next forty years, Americans seeking mild psychoactive stimulation stayed with caffeine. Those pursuing more potent effects either asked their doctors to prescribe amphetamines, or purchased black-market amphetamines that had been illegally diverted from the prescription market.

In 1962 the federal government began an intensive effort to halt the black-market trade in amphetamines.[14] The attack was three-pronged: Doctors who prescribed amphetamines in quantities large enough to suggest diversion into the black market were prosecuted vigorously; pharmaceutical companies were forced to restrict the distribution of injectable amphetamines, and were required to institute new controls to prevent unauthorized persons from obtaining amphetamine pills in bulk quantities; and persons who illegally manufactured amphetamine in "basement laboratories" were hunted down and jailed. In the short run, the efforts had the desired effect, as amphetamine prices rose sharply and many users found them impossible to obtain at virtually any price. The long-term effects were less sanguine: Consumers seeking potent stimulants began looking elsewhere, and soon found the forgotten drug of their grandparents—cocaine. By the end of the 1960s, imports of cocaine were beginning to rise sharply, as supply routes unused for half a century were re-opened.[15]

Initially, the rising imports of cocaine were simply the offset to the diminished availability of amphetamines, as one potent stimulant replaced another. But beginning in 1969, with Operation Intercept, and continuing through the 1970s, the federal government began a concerted effort to halt imports of marijuana. This enforcement effort set off a chain of events whose course we traced in chapter 7. Taking advantage of supply routes reestablished during the "amphetamine wars" of the 1960s, suppliers and consumers began switching from marijuana to cocaine, which soon became the drug of choice for millions of Americans. When the federal government began moving more resources into stemming the spread of cocaine, crack was developed. And as the resulting war on crack intensified, suppliers and consumers began moving to crystal meth, a smokable type of amphetamine. Within less than thirty years, we had come full circle—except that the drugs were more potent, the prices were lower, and many more people were consuming them.

Cocaine is not an invention of the drug wars. Nevertheless, the cocaine story illustrates this simple fact: Time and again, the federal government's diagnosis has been that drug x is the problem and that the proper treatment is its attempted elimination. The response by consumers and suppliers has been simply to switch to drug y. Are we worse off because the government cracked down on amphetamines and marijuana, and then on cocaine, and then on crack? We do not know. What is disturbing about the cocaine story is that there is no demonstrable evidence that we are *better* off. And when the patient begins wondering if the doctor has forgotten the principle of *nihil nocere,* it is time to start looking for a new doctor.

RESTORING BALANCE

We cannot avoid the psychoactives and we cannot ignore them. We can, however, make choices about them. Sensible choices—those that enhance rather than impair our chances of survival—require that government policy balance the beneficial consequences of psychoactive use against the potentially adverse effects, just as the vast majority of individuals have maintained such balance in all times and places of history. In one important respect, there is a curious parallel between the imbalances that sometimes arise at the individual level regarding psychoactives, and the imbalances that arise at the government level. Some people choose not to use tobacco at all, and yet routinely abuse alcohol. Others eschew both alcohol and tobacco, preferring instead to consume a regular diet of prescription tranquilizers. In short, even when we maintain a sense of balance regarding some psychoactives, we sometimes fail to do so with others. This is indeed the pattern we observe with our government. When it comes to caffeine, tobacco, and alcohol, government at least attempts to achieve a balance between the adverse and beneficial consequences of its policies. Yet when it comes to many other psychoactives, the balancing act goes by the wayside, leaving us with policies that fail to achieve their stated objectives, and impose enormous costs on the citizenry. Where do we go from here?

CHAPTER 10

....

Perils and Prospects

THE WAR ON DRUGS OFFERS THE WORST OF BOTH WORLDS. IT HAS GUT-
ted the inner cities, filled our jails and clogged our courts, promoted
violent crime and the spread of disease, invaded our privacy, and
threatened the security of our personal possessions. Yet the war on
drugs has failed to reduce drug use or addiction substantially, nor
has it made our neighborhoods safer, nor even protected our children from the scourge of drugs. It is little wonder that however else
Americans might feel about drugs, they agree on one thing: The war
on drugs isn't working. Accompanying this dissatisfaction have been
a variety of suggestions for radically revamping the government's
battle plan. Most of these suggestions fall into two diametrically opposed categories that imply radically different directions for the
government:

1. Blanket legalization of all, or most, drugs—the laissez-faire approach.[1]
2. A get-tough version of the current war on drugs, involving more
   resources, harsher penalties, and, in the extreme, the policy that
   "if you try, you die."[2]

At first glance, each of these courses has enormous appeal. The
laissez-faire approach would free us of many of the adverse consequences of the government's current approach to drugs. The get-tough
strategy would do the job that is not being accomplished currently—
it would rid our streets of drugs and dealers. The proponents of each
of these approaches argue that their strategy offers the promise of

something that is better than the current mess. Yet, as we shall see in this chapter, neither laissez-faire nor get-tough provides a sufficient political, social, or economic balance to be a viable means of undoing drugs in America. The answer lies elsewhere.

THE BENEFITS OF LEGALIZATION

The potential benefits of having the federal government legalize psychoactives seem almost too good to be true; indeed, improvements comparable to those accompanying the end of Prohibition seem likely. An entire branch of law enforcement—including the Drug Enforcement Administration, large chunks of the U.S. Customs Service and Coast Guard, and significant portions of police forces at the state and local levels—would no longer have any raison d'etre. Resources costing $20 to $30 billion a year would no longer have to be used to fight the war on drugs, and instead could be used for environmental protection or better schools, or any of a host of other valuable activities.

Some of the most telling benefits of drug legalization derive from taking the profits out of drug prices, and thus out of the drug trade. As we pointed out in chapter 6, current drug policies act to increase drug prices and grossly inflate the profits of those drug traffickers who are lucky enough or smart enough not to get caught. If drugs were legalized, their prices would fall to competitive levels, which would cover only the pharmaceutical cost of production, plus a normal rate of return for those who manufactured and sold them. Drug users, abusers, and addicts (particularly the latter) would no longer require large sums of money to finance their habits, and they would no longer be forced to mug, burgle, and shoplift. Moreover, the violence produced by turf wars and by drug deals gone awry would fall to the level that exists in legal industries—zero.

Life in the inner city would certainly change. Legal psychoactives would end the drug-law lottery, so that youths would no longer strive for the fast-lane life of drug deals, gold chains, and black Mercedes: The profits from dealing in drugs would be no different than the profits from dealing in, say, cartons of milk. Certainly the violence associated with drug trafficking in the ghetto would disappear soon enough. The gangs that have thrived on the profits of the crack trade, such as the Bloods, the Crips, and the Jamaican posses, would go back to their former selves—small-time players protecting their pieces of backwater turf. Crack would not disappear with the legalization of drugs, but the evidence strongly suggests that it would cease being the drug of choice for many. Just as so many individuals are now choosing reduced-alcohol beverages and low-tar cigarettes, most consumers of legal drugs would choose low-potency versions, as they did before 1914.* Moreover, even if crack continued to be consumed by some individuals, suppliers would make no more money selling it than selling cosmetics or used cars.

The decriminalization of society would offer another set of benefits if drugs were legalized. Some 35 to 40 million Americans buy illegal drugs each year, and are thus labeled criminals by our current drug policies. Removing that label and stigma would likely enhance their respect for the law and might even improve the moral fabric of society, as their attitudes toward the legal system improved. Certainly the prison population would diminish rapidly, and the cries against overcrowded prisons would disappear. Spending on prisons would also decline, freeing up resources which could be used for any of a host of other priority items. The reduction in criminal activity would mean that civil litigation in the courts would once again be possible, as court dockets were freed from the burdens of criminal drug cases. Fast-food justice would largely disappear, and judges would once again be able to treat defendants as human beings instead of case numbers. Along the way, the erosion of Americans' civil liberties would likely be reversed, and the police would once again be the ally, instead of the enemy of the average citizen.

Even a major factor in the continued existence of traditional organized crime would be eliminated if psychoactives were legalized. The Mafia would not disapppear, because organized crime would be able to survive on other criminal activities, such as loan-sharking, gambling, prostitution, and child pornography. But drug legalization would remove the backbone of organized crime's profits, causing it to diminish in importance.

This list of the benefits of legalization sounds impressive. Indeed, it is impressive. But it is also one-sided, for it ignores the costs of legalization. And the costs of nationwide legalization are even more impressive.

---

*We are not claiming that large numbers of persons now addicted to crack would suddenly switch to oral ingestion of dilute liquid cocaine solutions, although it is likely that some would choose less-intensive methods of administration. More importantly, it is likely that far fewer individuals would ever begin using crack in the first place.

THE COSTS OF LEGALIZATION

Laws prohibiting drugs increase the cost of consuming those drugs. As a result, fewer people consume drugs, and fewer drugs are consumed. Legalizing drugs would reverse this process: The cost of using drugs would fall, more drugs would be consumed, and more people would consume them. First and foremost, this cost of drug legalization—increased usage of drugs—must be recognized.

Whether legalization of drugs would also produce an increase in drug abuse and drug addiction is arguable. We noted in chapter 7 that today's drug laws encourage abuse and addiction among those persons now using drugs. Legalization would probably reduce abuse and addiction among this group, because they would be induced to consume less potent drug forms in less intensive ways. On the other hand, since legalization would encourage consumption among people who currently don't use drugs at all, abuse and addiction among this group would rise from zero to some positive amount. Overall, the net effects are not certain, although the evidence from Prohibition suggests that the overall effect of drug legalization would be to increase the total amount of drug abuse and addiction. During Prohibition, the incidence of cirrhosis of the liver (generally associated with alcohol abuse) and the estimated number of deaths from alcoholism both declined. After Prohibition ended, both of these indicators rose again. A potential rise in drug abuse and addiction is one of the costs of legalization that must be considered.

One of the most frightening aspects of drug legalization is the prospect that children would also be more likely to use drugs. The thought of children using heroin, cocaine, or any of a variety of other psychoactives is enough to give any parent nightmares. The physical immaturity of children makes them more susceptible to physical and mental damage from drugs, and their emotional immaturity increases the risk of psychological damage, drug abuse, and worse. Indeed, the prospect of a widespread rise in drug consumption, abuse, and addiction among children is a compelling argument against legalization. Now, proponents of legalization are quick to point out that there would be no reason to legalize drugs for children, even though they were made legal for adults. Nevertheless, cigarettes are currently legal for adults but illegal for juveniles, yet children seem to have little difficulty obtaining them from vending machines, convenience stores, and so forth.

Protecting our children from drugs is clearly one of the critical elements that must be addressed in any discussion of a change in the drug laws. Our current laws against drugs have not prevented people from consuming drugs. Why should a law against the underage consumption of drugs prevent children from consuming drugs? Most proponents of legalization seem anxious to sidestep this question as quickly as possible.*

One of the principal tenets of most drug-legalization proponents is the importance of preserving individual choice. Thus, it is argued, what business is it of Mr. Smith if Ms. Jones wants to smoke a marijuana joint in the privacy of her own home? In a nation like America, where freedom has always been a prized possession, worth fighting and dying for, such an argument is compelling. But there is another side of the coin. If the federal government legalized drugs, such a move would *itself* deprive Americans of an important element of choice—the choice to live in a community that is, if not perfectly drug-free, at least an inhospitable environment for drug users and dealers.

Under today's laws, Americans cannot choose to live in an area of the country in which drugs are *legal*. If the federal government mandated the legalization of drugs, Americans would be unable to live in a community in which drugs were *illegal*. Clearly, people would still be free as individuals to choose not to consume drugs. Nevertheless, they would be deprived of freedom in other dimensions.

The consumption of psychoactives, particularly the abuse of such substances, carries with it the potential for adverse third-party effects. The classic example of this is found on our nation's highways, where drunk drivers kill over 20,000 people every year. Penalties targeted at third-party effects, such as jail time for drunk drivers, help reduce these effects. But laws against the consumption of drugs add an additional level of protection from these effects. With nationwide legalization, individuals would be deprived of the choice of living in communities in which that additional protection was available.

The lost freedom of choice implied by federal legalization would also add an additional burden on those parents wishing to raise their

---

*We return to this issue in the next chapter, in which we show that it *is* possible to protect our children from drugs—although not in ways available under current laws, and not (as the proponents of legalization would have it) by simply passing laws against underage consumption of drugs.

children to "just say no." Such parents would be compelled (short of leaving the country) to live in a jurisdiction in which the *government* said it was just fine to use drugs. Clearly, such a message would make it far more difficult for parents to convince their children of the hazards of drugs. This in turn would make it more likely that their children would choose to say "yes" to drugs.*

There is one final point: What happens if the federal government legalizes drugs, and we don't like the outcome? Although the general nature of the effects of legalization are reasonably well understood, the exact magnitude of the potential changes is uncertain. Drug use will rise if drugs are legalized, and the experience of the Harrison Act and Prohibition suggest that the rise would be modest. But no one can *guarantee* that drug use won't, say, triple. Drug abuse and addiction would likely rise far less than would drug use under legalization, but we can't be certain of that outcome. Violence and street crime will no doubt decline sharply if drugs are legalized, but will the drop be enough to offset the costs of added drug use, abuse, and addiction? The proponents of legalization think that the beneficial consequences of legalization would exceed the adverse effects, but their estimates are just that—estimates, which are surrounded by an enormous range of uncertainty.

Risk is no excuse for inaction if one judges that the expected outcome of action is positive. But the presence of risk means that contingency plans must be carefully considered. For most of the twentieth century, the federal government has been in the vanguard of government efforts against drugs. Time and again, federal politicians and bureaucrats have persuaded, cajoled, and even bludgeoned state and local officials to follow them into battle.† If the federal government now decided to "just say yes," and if the results were

---

*Social commentator Charles Murray has attempted to sidestep this problem by arguing that it could be overcome if we had an educational voucher system in which parents could send their children to whatever schools they deemed best. Under such a system, some schools would presumably offer a drug-free environment in which the parents' admonitions to say no would be supplemented by the same message at school.

Murray's suggestion has merit, but in point of fact, we currently do not now have a voucher system for schools, nor are we likely to get one in the near future. It seems to us to be wishful thinking to imagine that we could protect our children from drugs with the aid of a system that doesn't exist. As a practical matter, if drugs are legalized nationwide, parents who send their children to public schools simply won't have the option of sending their children to drug-free schools.

†And sometimes, as exemplified by the states that have decriminalized marijuana possession, not even the most determined federal efforts have been enough to get other levels of government to fully cooperate.

not what the proponents of legalization hope they will be, what would we do? Will we have opened a nationwide Pandora's box that cannot be closed? Will the federal government have any credibility left to close it? Will Congress ever again be able to bring itself to face the issues? These questions must be addressed by those who would propose nationwide legalization of drugs.

THE BENEFITS OF GETTING TOUGH

The most frequently discussed alternative to today's current drug policies is a true "get-tough" policy. Such a policy would involve more severe sentences for drug users and drug traffickers, more law enforcement, and more involvement by all levels of government—federal, state, and local—in a new all-out war against drugs.

What would an all-out war on drugs involve? Here are some suggestions that have been proposed by various government officials:

1. Casual drug users "ought to be taken out and shot" (suggested by Los Angeles Police Chief Daryl Gates in testimony before Congress).
2. Coca and marijuana fields should be destroyed with defoliants and nuclear fire (the suggestion of a Peruvian general).
3. The Amazon should be salted with Agent Orange (the suggestion of two Colombian officials).
4. Planes suspected of carrying drugs should be shot down (suggested by a former U.S. Customs Commissioner, by the former head of the President's Office of National Drug Control Policy, and by forty-eight U.S. Senators).
5. Boot camps should be established for the detention of all users of all illegal drugs, including marijuana (suggested by numerous U.S. officials).
6. The death penalty should be imposed on large-scale drug dealers (suggested by a former governor of Florida, and by a majority of the U.S. House of Representatives).
7. All of the necessary forces of the U.S. military should be used to stop the flow of drugs into the United States (the suggestion of numerous U.S. officials).

For the proponents of the get-tough policy, an all-out war means just that—no holds barred. Indeed, the logical conclusion of the true get-tough policy is "if you try, you die"; even drug *use* would be a capital offense, punishable by death. As we noted in chapter 3, the governments of Malaysia and Singapore have been executing small-time dealers (and even some users) for more than a decade.

Make no mistake: People do respond to incentives. Raising the cost of using and dealing drugs would reduce the number of users and dealers, and it would reduce the consumption of drugs. If casual users, who comprise perhaps 70 or 80 percent of all drug consumers, were in fact likely to be caught and penalized for use with long jail terms, the decision to use drugs would no longer be a casual one. The pool of users would shrink until it was comprised chiefly of addicts.

We could even expect a decline in the number of abusers and addicts, as well as a reduction in the amount of drugs they consumed. Since fewer people would be exposed to drugs, fewer would become abusers or addicts to begin with. Some current abusers and addicts would seek treatment, while others would switch to legal psycho-actives. Even among those who remained committed to their current drugs of choice, consumption would probably decline as they made do with less because of the radically higher costs of their habits.

We could also expect a reduction in many of the adverse third-party effects of drug use and abuse. If users faced death or even twenty years in prison if caught, their consumption would likely take place under circumstances in which contact with third parties was minimal. The level of drug-related violence might rise initially, as law-enforcement officials sought to establish the credibility of the new policy. Nevertheless, it is plausible that violence would actually decline in the long run. More people would be obeying the law, and most of those who did not obey it would either be behind bars or dead. Eventually, our streets and our neighborhoods would become safer.

Could we actually mount an effective all-out war against drugs? We have long had in place a policy of all-out war against murder, and historically, the police have been able to nab roughly 80 percent of all murderers, compared to the roughly 2 percent of all drug users who are presently arrested.* The all-out war on bank robbery has

---

*Although the success rate on murders has been declining in recent years, particularly in major cities. "Traditional" murderers typically know their victims fairly well, making the job of the police easier. Drug-related homicides (such as drive-by shootings) account for much of the recent rise in homicides; since the connection between killer and victim is either nonexistent or unknown to the police, such murders are much more difficult to solve.

been even more successful: Nearly 100 percent of all bank robbers are eventually arrested and convicted.

The federal government is currently spending more than $10 billion per year on the war on drugs. That sounds like a lot, and it is, amounting to about $40 per year for each citizen of the United States. But that sum is *one-fifth* of the amount that the federal government spent in the Persian Gulf war against Iraq.[3] The current so-called war on drugs hardly qualifies as a skirmish by military standards. The politicians and bureaucrats in Washington, D.C., make a lot of noise about the war on drugs, but the true commitment of resources—less than 1 percent of the federal budget—falls far short of an all-out commitment to rid the country of drugs.

THE COSTS OF GETTING TOUGH

The presumed benefits of a get-tough policy on drugs rest on two premises: An all-out war will substantially increase the expected costs of using and dealing in drugs, and this in turn will sharply cut drug consumption in America. But what would be involved in substantially raising the perceived costs of using and dealing drugs? What impact would this likely have on prospective buyers and sellers of drugs?

Nearly 40 million individuals have used illicit drugs in each of the last few years, and the number of Americans currently involved in supplying drugs almost certainly totals in the millions.* About 1.2 million people are arrested on drug charges each year, about three-quarters of them for possession of drugs. Thus, a bit over 2 percent of users, plus a somewhat higher proportion—perhaps 10 percent—of suppliers, are arrested each year.

If we truly wanted to have an impact on drug use, we would presumably have to arrest a significantly higher percentage of drug users than we now do. Suppose we decided to arrest one out of five current

---

*If the number of suppliers sounds high, consider the fact that domestic production of marijuana, which only accounts for 25 percent of U.S. consumption of pot, totals about 10 million pounds each year, and has a farm value of roughly $10 billion. If we suppose that each of these domestic growers earns $50,000 per year from his or her crop, this means that 200,000 Americans are involved just in *growing* domestically produced marijuana. Applying similar calculations to the rest of the drug trade suggests that at least two to three million Americans are directly involved in supplying illegal drugs.

users, and to double the number of dealers we are currently arresting. Now, simply arresting and releasing people is not likely to have much impact, so we would need to plan on putting these users and dealers in jail. Assume that we sentence users to an average jail term of, say, ninety days—certainly a modest penalty. Suppose also that dealers are sentenced to an average of two years in prison. If our arithmetic is correct, we would have to arrest better than seven million users, plus some 600,000 suppliers. This number would exceed by a large measure the total number of persons currently arrested for *all* of the nation's serious crimes, including aggravated assault, rape, robbery, auto theft, and murder. Simply building the prisons needed to house all of the additional drug users and suppliers would cost at least $100 billion. And, once they were in prison, it would cost us nearly $100 billion each year to keep them there.

Of course, these numbers assume we have managed to arrest and prosecute all of these people. How would the nation's police and prosecutors and courts handle the work load? One can easily imagine that we would have to double or even triple the number of police officers, judges, district attorneys, and support staff we now employ. How much would this cost? New York City alone spends about $120,000 to arrest and prosecute the average felon.[4] New York is an expensive place to conduct business, so we might suppose that it would cost the typical jurisdiction only half this sum—say, $60,000— to arrest and prosecute a felon.[5] Since dealers presumably would be brought up on felony charges, the cost of arresting and prosecuting the added 300,000 suppliers under a get-tough policy would be another $18 billion per year. Since users would likely be charged with misdemeanors, they would be cheaper to process, say, $5,000 to arrest and prosecute each of them. The cost of the additional arrests and prosecutions of users would still be about $35 billion each year.

The total annual bill for this hypothetical get-tough policy would be roughly $150 *billion*—some $2,400 per year for each family of four in America, many of whom will have a member in jail on drug charges. Now, this is just a hypothetical program, and perhaps we won't need to arrest this many people to be successful. But remember that none of our figures include any of the resources that the users and dealers will be devoting to defending themselves, nor do the cost estimates take into account the fact that most of the users who would be arrested are productive citizens. When we throw them in jail, we are throwing away the goods and services they would have produced, and the taxes they would have paid. And for many of them, we are probably destroying their careers as well.

What results could we anticipate from a get-tough policy such as this? Certainly we could expect a drastic reduction in the numbers of casual drug users. Even the rate of drug addiction would fall, because more addicts would seek treatment and because fewer individuals would be exposed to drugs in the first place.

Nevertheless, no one should expect a "drug-free America" to result from a get-tough policy. First we must contend with the balloon principle, encountered in chapter 2. Even if we somehow managed to seal our borders against imported drugs, all of them can be (and to varying degrees are) grown domestically. If we then managed to eradicate outdoor sources of American-grown drugs, all of them can be commercially cultivated indoors. And if we somehow eliminated all cultivation of naturally occurring drugs, near-perfect chemical substitutes for them either exist or would surely soon be invented. The suppliers of drugs are simply too ingenious and persistent for us to expect to eliminate them all.

Second, there is the phenomenon that we shall term the *principle of psychoactive substitution*. All users of psychoactives seem to have their own "drugs of choice," that is, drugs which they prefer above others when allowed to choose freely. Nevertheless, all drug consumers—even addicts—demonstrate a remarkable willingness to substitute other drugs when their drug of choice is unavailable. When heroin supplies are disrupted, addicts switch to a combination of alcohol and barbiturates to tide them over. Similarly, when marijuana supplies are disrupted, heavy pot smokers commonly substitute toward alcohol or black-market prescription tranquilizers. When cocaine or crack supplies dry up, users of these drugs often switch to black-market amphetamines or to crystal meth. In each case, they may not be terribly happy about it, but for most of them substitution beats the alternative of doing without.[6]

The implications of substitution for any get-tough policy are ominous. The willingness of users to switch drugs means that the authorities cannot simply focus on one or a small handful of illegal substances. Major successes in interdicting marijuana, for example, will lead former pot smokers to look elsewhere for psychoactive satisfaction. This in turn will create a major market for some other drug that previously had been considered a minor problem. Thus, a true get-tough policy will have to attack *all* of the illegal psychoactives simultaneously, which means that the costs of the policy will be higher and the chances of success lower.

We noted in chapter 7 that Americans have been drinking less alcohol and "lighter" alcohol over the past ten to fifteen years. Presumably, part of this trend has been due to an increasing awareness of the health hazards of alcohol. But this trend may have occurred partially because people who are prone to abusing psychoactives have switched from booze to other drugs as the supplies of those drugs have risen. If this is true, we can expect a get-tough policy against illegal drugs to yield a widespread return to alcohol. In effect, we may end up converting a substantial amount of our *drug* problem into an *alcohol* problem. Do we then resurrect Prohibition?

History also tells us that a get-tough policy will have to be a *permanent* policy. Prohibition reduced alcohol consumption, but as soon as Prohibition was ended, consumption quickly rose. World War II sharply reduced heroin consumption because it disrupted supplies of the drug; yet once the war was over, heroin addiction rose to (and even above) its prewar levels. If we want to *get* tough, we will have to *stay* tough. But getting tough will involve even more intrusion into our privacy than we currently endure. It will mean more informants and wiretaps and undercover operations. It will mean more asset seizures and less regard for our constitutional protections. Will getting tough mean giving up the Bill of Rights—forever? This question is one that must be addressed by anyone proposing a *real* war on drugs.

WHERE DO WE GO?

The current war on drugs is not working. Just as clearly, the principal alternatives—legalization or an all-out war—offer perils that seem almost worse than the current state of affairs, though both alternatives surely contain positive elements. Is there a way to shape policy so that the strengths of legalization are utilized at the same time that its weaknesses are minimized? Can we get tough where and when it is really needed and yet avoid the costly excesses that a true *war* on drugs would entail? Is there some middle course that blends the best, while recognizing the pitfalls that may be encountered? Would such a policy be viable? We think the answers are yes—and it is to this approach, the Constitutional Alternative, that we now turn.

CHAPTER II

································

The Constitutional Alternative

AT 3:32 P.M. (MOUNTAIN TIME) ON DECEMBER 5, 1933, THE RESULTS WERE announced: The people of Utah had voted in favor of the Twenty-first Amendment to the U.S. Constitution. Citizens across the land celebrated, for Utah was the thirty-sixth of the thirty-six states needed to ratify the Twenty-first Amendment, repealing Prohibition. After fourteen years of strife, pitting the government against its citizens and neighbors against friends, America's liquor wars were over. Within days, the bootleggers and rum-runners were out of business. The people of America had retaken control of their nation and their destinies.

The bold step taken by the American people in 1933 ended an era which produced more misery than any prior peacetime span in our nation's history. This chapter explains how the people of America can take similar action to end the misery of today's drug wars. Our proposal, the Constitutional Alternative, does *not* mean surrendering to drugs, nor does it subject us to the costly results of today's misguided policies. On the contrary, our proposed course of action would enable Americans to wage the war on drugs on *their* terms, on a playing field tilted in *their* favor. If we are to undo drugs and thus retake America, we must adopt the Constitutional Alternative.

PROLOGUE

The story of the Twenty-first Amendment really begins on January 16, 1920, when U.S. Secretary of State Bainbridge Colby certified that, effective at midnight, the Eighteenth Amendment to the Constitution was the law of the land. The Eighteenth Amendment prohibited "the manufacture, sale, transportation, importation, or exportation of intoxicating liquors for beverage purposes," thus beginning the era known as Prohibition.

Many people believe that Prohibition represented the first and only significant effort by government to control the drinking behavior of Americans. In fact, *state* governments have had the power to regulate liquor consumption since the inception of our country, and they exercised that power in a variety of ways prior to 1920. Beginning early in the nineteenth century, several states gave local jurisdictions the option of prohibiting alcohol within their boundaries. By the early twentieth century, some states had even prohibited alcohol statewide; by 1920, thirty-three of the forty-eight states were, to varying degrees, "dry" states. What was different about the Eighteenth Amendment (and thus "Prohibition" as we now think of it) is that it got the *federal* government involved in trying to control the drinking behavior of Americans. Previously, except for taxing alcohol as a source of revenue, the federal government had left decisions about drinking up to the people and their state and local governments.

The importance of this point lies in the fact that the Twenty-first Amendment—the repeal of Prohibition—simply repealed the *federal* prohibition of "the manufacture, sale, transportation, importation, or exportation of intoxicating liquors for beverage purposes." The Twenty-first Amendment did *not* mandate that alcohol be legal. Instead, it returned to the states the powers they originally held under the Constitution, but which had been taken from them by the Eighteenth Amendment. Simply stated, prohibition was not repealed in 1933; only *federal* prohibition was repealed. The states and their local jurisdictions were free to exercise whatever degree of regulation, control, or prohibition of alcohol they felt appropriate. Indeed, the Twenty-first Amendment went one step further to reaffirm and strengthen the states' power to control alcoholic beverages: Section 2 of the amendment expressly prohibits the transportation or importation of alcohol into any state whenever and wherever such actions violate state and local laws. Thus, under the terms of the Twenty-first Amendment, state and local governments can call upon the federal authorities to aid them in enforcing major components of their local liquor laws.

The Twenty-first Amendment, then, did not simply turn the booze barons loose on the country. Instead it returned to the states the rights that they had held since the inception of our country. In doing so, the Twenty-first Amendment returned to the citizens of America much more direct control over the course of their lives. The federal government retained the right to tax alcoholic beverages for revenue purposes, and it gained the explicit right to assist the states in enforcing their liquor laws whenever the interstate transportation or importation of liquor was involved. Otherwise, the Twenty-first Amendment simply removed bureaucrats and politicians in Washington, D.C., from the business of deciding whether or not Americans could have a cold beer on a hot Saturday afternoon. Viewed in this light, the Eighteenth Amendment (Prohibition) was a constitutional aberration, and the Twenty-first Amendment (Repeal) was the means of removing that anomaly. On December 5, 1933, the people of Utah reaffirmed the system of law envisioned by the framers of the Constitution and, in so doing, enabled American citizens to retake America.

THE POWERS OF THE STATES

The American system of government is an unusual one, even among Western democracies. Most nations have *unitary* systems of government, in which the central, or national, government occupies a singularly powerful position. Under the unitary system of government, the powers of subnational governments (such as states or provinces) derive explicitly and solely from the central government. The only powers belonging to subnational governments in unitary systems are those powers that have been *granted* them by the central government.

By contrast, we have a *federal* system of government in the United States. It is our Constitution that is the source of all government power in the United States: Both the national government and the subnational governments (the states) derive powers from that document only. The Constitution reserves some powers to the national government, reserves other powers to the states, and provides that some powers are to be enjoyed by both levels of government. Importantly, however, it is the states and the *people* of the United States, rather than the national government, which are accorded special status. In particular, the Tenth Amendment to the Constitution, a part of the original Bill of Rights, specifies that "The powers not delegated to the United States by the Constitution, nor prohibited by it to the States, are reserved to the States respectively, or to the people." This means that when the Constitution is silent about a particular power (as it quite often is), that power is *automatically* assigned to the state governments or to the people, not to the national government in Washington, D.C.*

Our founding fathers chose the federal form of government, buttressed by the Tenth Amendment, because they understood the dangers of an all-too-powerful central government. They had their fill of edicts issued by King George III and taxes levied by the British Parliament, and wanted to avoid creating a national government that would impose more of the same. Both the federal system of government and the Tenth Amendment were viewed by the founding fathers as essential to maintaining the freedoms they had fought so hard to achieve.[1]

The states have taken the Tenth Amendment to heart. They have, among other things, established fifty different legal systems, fifty different tax systems, and fifty different educational systems. Even for matters as elemental as birth, marriage, and death, there are fifty different systems for recording and certifying the occurrence of each. And within the fifty states, there are provisions for local governments to handle all sorts of matters in different ways, which is to say, in ways that most closely match the desires of the affected citizenry.

The United States was founded by individuals who cherished individual freedom. As much as the residents of, say, Virginia and Massachusetts may have liked and respected one another 200 years ago, they had little interest in having their lives run by the residents of the other state. The Tenth Amendment was thus incorporated into our Constitution to help ensure that, when government action was necessary, it would be undertaken at such a level and in such a manner as to conform as closely as possible to the preferences of the affected citizens. The role of the Tenth Amendment in ensuring that our government is "of the people, by the people and for the people" is evident in almost every aspect of our lives.

---

*This is why, for example, it took an amendment to the Constitution (the Eighteenth Amendment) to give the national government the power to impose Prohibition: The Constitution had not originally given this power to the national government.

The Regulation of Alcoholic Beverages

Prior to Prohibition, the various states each had their own systems for regulating the manufacture, distribution, and consumption of alcoholic beverages. And when Prohibition was repealed, each state chose its own method of exercising the freedom restored by the Twenty-first Amendment. Three states (Kansas, Mississippi, and Oklahoma) continued Prohibition. Seventeen others elected to permit the distribution of alcoholic beverages only through wholesale or retail outlets owned and operated by the state government. Over thirty states decided that local jurisdiction (such as counties) should be able to choose whether alcoholic beverages were to be legal or prohibited within their boundaries. Many states prohibited the sale of alcoholic beverages on Sundays, and most (but not all) limited the number of hours each day that liquor stores could be open. In Utah, the voters decided that liquor could be sold by the bottle but not by the drink. In neighboring Nevada, liquor by the drink or by the bottle was for sale 24 hours a day, 365 days a year. In South Carolina, beer and hard liquor could not be offered for sale in the same room; in Kentucky, numerous counties chose to remain dry, but at liquor stores in some of the "wet" counties, one could purchase alcohol at drive-up windows, saving the buyer from the inconvenience of leaving his automobile.

The diversity of regulatory schema chosen in the aftermath of Prohibition continues even today (although Kansas, Mississippi, and Oklahoma are no longer completely dry). In the bulk of the states, liquor is available for sale in all local jurisdictions, but there are still dry counties in ten states; indeed, in Arkansas and Kentucky, roughly 40 percent of the residents live in dry counties. In Nevada, liquor stores are open around the clock; in South Carolina, hard liquor by the bottle may be sold only from 9:00 A.M. to 7:00 P.M., Monday through Saturday. Until 1984 (when the federal government imposed a uniform age limit of twenty-one), the minimum age for purchasing alcoholic beverages varied from twenty-one to eighteen, with different ages applicable to different beverages in some states. In short, the states (and, in many cases, local jurisdictions) have responded to the differing preferences, attitudes, and beliefs of their citizenry by choosing a diverse set of rules and regulations governing alcoholic beverages. Indeed, this sort of diversity is found in virtually all of the decisions that the states make in response to the wishes of their citizens, which is exactly what our founding fathers expected.

Other Examples of Regulatory Diversity

Choose any matter in which a government might have an interest. The chances are high that, unless the federal government has imposed itself, the various states and their local jurisdictions have concocted an amazing variety of rules to deal with the matter. Alcohol, for example, is not the only psychoactive regulated by the states: Tobacco is subject to a host of differing state and local rules regarding minimum age to purchase, the rate at which it is taxed, how it may be sold, and even where it may be smoked (or chewed). Many medicines with psychoactive properties are also subject to state regulations regarding the methods by which they are dispensed, and even the hours during which they legally may be sold.

The acts of marriage and divorce are both regulated by all of the states, and no two states have chosen the same set of rules with regard to either of these activities. In the case of marriage, the various rules that differ across the states include minimum age (with and without parental consent), waiting period (before and after issuance of a license), premarital medical examinations (scope and duration of validity), and even the nature of legal marriages (common-law versus statutory). Divorce rules differ across the states not only with regard to minimum state residency requirements (which range from none to one year) but also the grounds for divorce (which may, depending on the state, include adultery, impotency, pregnancy at marriage, drug addiction, or any of half a dozen other factors).[2]

Taxation is also a means of regulation and control, and here again the states (and their local jurisdictions) exhibit enormous diversity. State sales taxes range from zero (in five states) to 7.5 percent (in Connecticut). Forty-three states tax the incomes of their residents, but seven do not. All fifty states have some minimum form of inheritance tax, but twenty-six have additional estate taxes above this minimum level, and seven even tax gifts. All of the states tax both liquor and cigarettes, but the tax rates vary across states by a factor of six for alcohol taxes, and by a factor of twenty for cigarette taxes.[3]

And layered upon or interspersed among these various state taxes are a host of local taxes that vary across counties, cities, townships, and even sewer and school districts.

The Vitality of Diversity

As this brief sampling suggests, the diversity of the matters on which the citizens of our fifty states (and thousands of local jurisdictions) choose to differ is staggering. And this is as it should be, for reasonable men and women are often prone to disagree. Indeed, the diversity we observe across states and localities is, for a variety of reasons, essential to the great strength and vitality of our nation.

Many of the nation's founders agreed with Thomas Jefferson when he remarked, "that government is best which governs least." Yet the framers of the Constitution—Jefferson included—also knew that some government interference with individual freedom was both inevitable and even necessary. The framers foresaw that by yielding some personal freedom to government interference, individuals could thereby gain *more* freedom in another dimension. By instructing our government to outlaw murder, for example, we give up the right to commit murder, but we obtain in return greater freedom from the fear of being murdered.

To obtain the greatest advantage from the tradeoff among freedoms inherent in government action, the founders knew that government decisions had to be made at a level that most closely corresponded to the wishes and circumstances of the affected citizens. Only in this way could the citizens ensure that the freedoms they *sacrificed* to government interference were more than offset by the freedoms they *gained* as a result. The Tenth Amendment reflects the conviction of the founders that decentralized government was essential to ensure this matching between the actions of government and the wishes of the governed.

The founding fathers also recognized the need to guard against the "tyranny of the majority." Even in a democratic society, when the interests and circumstances of different citizens differ markedly, it may be possible for one faction to obtain the support of "50 percent plus one" of the voters, and thereby impose its wishes upon the remaining minority. Indeed, the desire to escape such democratic tyranny (particularly regarding religion) led many of our original settlers to leave their homelands in the first place. The founding fathers knew all too well that *the least individual freedom occurs when the majority is a monopoly majority.*

By reserving powers to the states and the people, the Tenth Amendment helps ensure that people *within* our nation will have the greatest choice of the majorities to which they must subject themselves. If a resident of one state does not like the rules imposed by the majority there, he is free to move to a state whose laws better suit his preferences or circumstances. This forces the states to compete with one another in selecting rules that will benefit the greatest number of people, and it allows individuals a means of escape (moving to another state) should the process fail in their current state of residence. Members of an oppressed minority living under a unitary system of government have no choice but to submit or, if they are permitted, emigrate to another nation.

Another powerful protection accorded by decentralized decision making is that it promotes the greatest levels of innovation and adaptability to changing circumstances. No government is all-knowing. Governments, like human beings, fail to recognize problems when they develop, and fail to grasp the correct solutions to known problems. Under a unitary system of government, the citizenry get only one shot at having the government recognize and solve problems; and if the national government fails in either endeavor, the people are stuck. Under our federal system of government, there are fifty sets of eyes watching for problems, and just as many legislative bodies and executive branches searching for solutions. Purely in the abstract, there is no particular reason to suppose that state government bureaucrats per se will be more responsive to the citizenry than will federal government bureaucrats. Nevertheless, there is no doubt that *competing* bureaucrats are more responsive than are *monopoly* bureaucrats. In reserving the unenumerated powers to the people and the states, the Tenth Amendment was implemented to ensure the maximum degree of competition among our governments.

The Tenth Amendment also implicitly recognizes that the people of differing communities have different preferences and face differing circumstances, and so may wish to make different choices. Even if citizens in community x end up choosing something that is not suitable for those in community y, the process of making decisions in x and the ensuing experience with those choices produces valuable information for the citizenry of community *y*. Not every state will necessarily "get things right" the first time around, but citizens will have the opportunity to observe what their state is doing and what others are doing. In this way the citizens across the land can see for themselves what works and what doesn't, instead of being stuck with whatever the national government stumbles upon or, perhaps, stumbles over.

THE CONSTITUTIONAL ALTERNATIVE

Two hundred years of experience with the Tenth Amendment have revealed the advantages of allowing the American people to express their diversity of preferences and circumstances in their state systems of government. Fourteen years of experience under Prohibition demonstrated the costly consequences of interfering with this diversity. The current efforts to impose and enforce federal drug laws have resulted in even less effective control, and even more costly consequences, than witnessed with federal alcohol law under Prohibition. Taken together, these experiences lead us to a simple, yet powerful proposal that will enable us to retake America, just as Americans did sixty years ago.

Our proposal—*the Constitutional Alternative*—is that the power to control the manufacture, distribution, and consumption of all psychoactives revert to the states, under provisions *identical* to those of the Twenty-first Amendment. As with the repeal of Prohibition, the Constitutional Alternative would repeal only the *federal* prohibition of psychoactives. As was true with the repeal of Prohibition, the Constitutional Alternative would return to the states the powers that they held from the inception of our nation; thus, the states would regain full powers to control the manufacture, distribution, and consumption of psychoactives within their borders. As provided for under section 2 of the Twenty-first Amendment, the Constitutional Alternative would specify that the transportation or importation of any psychoactives in violation of state laws would also be a federal crime. Indeed, the Constitutional Alternative would differ from the repeal of Prohibition in only one significant dimension: It would *not* require a Constitutional amendment to implement it.

Implementing the Constitutional Alternative

National legislation explicitly intended to suppress the consumption of psychoactives dates back to the 1909 Smoking Opium Exclusion Act, which banned the importation of smoking opium. Subsequent legislation includes the Harrison Narcotics Act of 1914,[4] the Narcotic Drug Import and Export Act of 1924, the Marijuana Tax Act of 1937,[5] and the Opium Poppy Control Act of 1942.[6] These and other laws were ultimately superseded by the Controlled Substances Act of 1970,[7] which applies to all psychoactives considered dangerous by the government.* As amended in 1984, 1986, and 1988, the Controlled Substances Act of 1970 is the controlling national drug legislation of today. Moreover, although each of the fifty states technically has its own set of drug laws, whenever a conflict between state law and national law arises, the Controlled Substances Act always governs. Thus, the outward impression of independent state drug policies is a fiction.

Implementing the Constitutional Alternative would require simply that the Controlled Substances Act of 1970 be amended by Congress to eliminate the federal prohibition of psychoactives. Under such an amendment, the national government would retain the power to tax all psychoactives, as it currently taxes alcohol and tobacco products. In addition, this amendment to the Controlled Substances Act would include (as did section 2 of the Twenty-first Amendment) the specific provision that the importation or transportation of psychoactives in violation of state laws would also be a violation of federal law. In this way, the considerable resources of the federal government could be called upon by the states, much as they may call upon those resources today to enforce interstate violations of their alcohol laws. With one simple piece of legislation, Congress could accomplish with the other psychoactives what the repeal of Prohibition accomplished with alcoholic beverages—an end to the internal war wracking America.

The Flexibility of the Constitutional Alternative

At first blush, the alternative we are proposing may seem like little more than a disguised form of de facto legalization of drugs. It is not.

---

*The act excludes distilled liquor, wine, beer, tobacco products, and caffeine. It is also called the Comprehensive Drug Abuse, Prevention, and Control Act of 1970.

What it does do is permit the states to choose drug-control strategies more in tune with the preferences and circumstances of their citizens. For some states, this may (and probably will) mean a relaxation of legal strictures against some drugs. But there is nothing in our proposal that would prevent states from adopting as *state* law the current provisions of the Controlled Substances Act. Any state choosing this option would be able to apply as much (or more) pressure on drug dealers and users within its boundaries as it is able to under the current system. Moreover, the Constitutional Alternative will actually *enhance* political pressures for more stringent drug laws in states in which antidrug sentiment is greatest, at the same time that it permits a relaxation of drug laws in states in which the prevailing sentiment favors such a move.

Under current policies, the Controlled Substances Act applies nationwide. For a drug dealer who is deciding where to set up operations, there is no particular advantage to choosing one state over another—which is to say, there is no advantage in avoiding any particular state. Dealers face the same set of risks everywhere, namely, the risks imposed by the Controlled Substances Act. This holds true even for states that have "decriminalized" marijuana, since the decriminalization does not apply to dealers. Under the Constitutional Alternative, states in which there is particularly strong antidrug sentiment will be able to make themselves unatttractive to dealers (and users) in a way that they cannot effectively do now: All they need do is adopt and seriously enforce drug laws that are more stringent than those chosen by other states. For example, suppose that our proposal is implemented and Utah imposes the death penalty for selling drugs. There is little doubt that Salt Lake City dealers will soon depart for greener pastures, taking their drugs with them. Except for the death-penalty provision, this is exactly what Kansas, Oklahoma, and Mississippi did after the ratification of the Twenty-first Amendment in 1933, when they chose to remain "dry." During Prohibition, bootleggers and drinkers faced the same penalties wherever they conducted their activities. But after 1933, Kansas, Mississippi, and Oklahoma became singularly unappealing places to either buy or sell alcohol. This is not to say that no liquor was sold or consumed in these three states after 1933, only that less of those activities took place there.

It might be thought that states could achieve this same result under today's system, simply by adopting laws that are more stringent than the Controlled Substances Act. As a practical matter, however, this argument simply will not hold water. Given the existence of a national law and a national enforcement effort, state legislatures are able to "pass the buck" to the U.S. Congress, using the argument that the responsibility for drugs lies with the federal government.* Under the Constitutional Alternative, state legislators in states in which anti-drug sentiments run high will no longer be able to hide behind the Controlled Substances Act and the U.S. Congress. Instead, they will be forced to answer to their constituents for the drug laws that they have adopted, or failed to adopt.

Of course, voters in some states may respond to the Constitutional Alternative by demanding drug laws that are *less* stringent than the current Controlled Substances Act. Indeed, ten states have already chosen to decriminalize marijuana possession, despite the strictures of the act. Should the residents of a given state decide to reduce the penalties for possession of some drugs, or even legalize some drugs, they presumably will do so only after having taken into account both the costs and benefits of their action, given *their* preferences and *their* circumstances. The residents of Alaska, for example, may conclude that THC is no more harmful than ethyl alcohol as a means of relieving the tedium of long Arctic winters, and may decide some day to put marijuana on an equal footing with bourbon and beer.[8] There is little doubt that some residents of the "lower forty-eight" would disapprove of such a decision; yet even *they* would benefit from legalization in Alaska, for at least some dealers and users of marijuana would opt for frigid freedom over the legal hassles of balmier, smoke-free locales. And besides, one attractive advantage of the Constitutional Alternative is that it gives marijuana opponents the option of moving to Alaska and voting their conscience.

Naturally, not all of the residents of any given state may necessarily agree with the majority of their fellow state residents about drugs. As a result, the voters of some states may choose to permit local jurisdictions to have broad powers over psychoactives, subject to state oversight. Indeed, the diversity of alcoholic beverage regulations we currently observe *within* states suggests that some intrastate diversity might occur with drugs under the Constitutional Alternative. More than thirty of the states currently have provisions for local

---

*This sort of "buck-passing" is exactly what takes place, for example, with environmental matters covered by the U.S. Clean Air Act—which is why so many companies that are major polluters prefer having a national law, rather than fifty separate state laws.

authorities at the county or city level to decide regulations regarding the sale and use of alcoholic beverages. In all of these states, localities have taken advantage of these "local option" rules to varying degrees, including ten states in which the residents of some counties have opted to completely prohibit alcoholic beverages. Just as the Tenth Amendment permits the citizens of America the greatest possible freedom to regulate alcohol (and tobacco and caffeine) in accord with their wishes, so too would the Constitutional Alternative give Americans that freedom with other psychoactives.

PROSPECT

When change is proposed, the natural reaction is that "It sounds fine in theory, but won't work in practice." Indeed, this response comes instinctively simply because it is so often the correct reasoning; after all, today's policies (regarding drugs or anything else) were not developed in a vacuum, and did not survive this long because they were patently absurd on their face. We defer until the next chapter a complete discussion of precisely why the Constitutional Alternative will work; here we simply lay the groundwork for that discussion, by noting briefly the features of our proposal that illustrate its great advantages over present policy.

As we saw in chapter 10, Americans seem able to agree on only one aspect of today's policies: They don't like them. Some people feel that all psychoactives should be legalized *en masse*, while others feel that drug users and dealers should be dealt with far more harshly than they are now. Some even feel that the well-established evidence of the dangers of alcohol and tobacco mean that these two psychoactives should be treated on a par with cocaine and heroin. Many individuals are convinced that harsher penalties are the only way to deal with drugs; others reason that drug abuse and addiction are fundamentally medical issues, to be dealt with using education and treatment. At times it seems as though there are more opinions on the subject of drugs than there are people to espouse them.

The enormous disagreement over "what to do about drugs" points the way precisely toward the Constitutional Alternative. On three separate fronts, our proposed solution—and only ours—offers a means of resolving the fundamental conflicts that exist within our nation regarding the course of drug policy.

First, the Constitutional Alternative offers Americans the opportunities to choose drug policies that conform more closely to their disparate preferences and circumstances. Some may choose the repression of all psychoactives; others may decide that, as with tobacco, the responsibility for choice lies with the individual. But all will have the opportunity to express their opinions at the ballot box, in a setting that greatly enhances the possibility that the outcomes will conform to what *they* want.

Second, the Constitutional Alternative offers us freedom from the tyranny of the majority. Under today's policies, each of us is forced to accept the hodgepodge of political and bureaucratic decisions that emanate from Washington, D.C. Often those decisions are unfathomable; usually, they are not what we would have chosen. But if we are to remain Americans, we are forced to accept the nationwide decisions that are made by the federal government—a government that too often has too little sense of the circumstances relevant to the piece of the country in which we reside. Under the Constitutional Alternative, we will have the freedom—even if we chose not to exercise it—to live with individuals whose preferences and circumstances lead them to prefer drug policies that conform more closely to our own wishes.

Finally, the Constitutional Alternative recognizes and takes advantage of the simple, inescapable fact that no government is perfect, nor immune to ignorance or error. When the federal government "gets it right," it gets it right for all of us. But when the bureaucrats and politicians in Washington get it wrong, we all suffer.

One reason that the debate over drug policy is confounded by so many different opinions is that there is much we do not know about drugs—the physical and psychological damage they cause (or don't cause), the proper methods of treating addiction, and even the possible *beneficial* effects that seemingly dangerous drugs may have. The list of unknowns is almost endless, and is likely to remain that way as long as the politicians and bureaucrats in Washington, D.C., have a monopoly on making decisions. The Constitutional Alternative eliminates this monopoly, replacing it with competition among alternative governments, each seeking to do what is best for its citizens. In so doing, our proposal enhances the prospects that we will broaden our understanding of psychoactives, and thus ultimately enhance the value of our decisions, for ourselves, and for our children.

DRUGS AND CHILDREN

It is indeed our children who present perhaps the greatest concern when we contemplate the course of drug policy. If the Constitutional Alternative is implemented, and the state in which we live chooses to, say, legalize marijuana, what will happen to our children? Will they be able to buy drugs on every street corner? Will they become addicted, their lives ruined? What will happen to our children if our state or a neighboring one legalizes cocaine? These are legitimate questions—questions that the Constitutional Alternative is designed to deal with far more effectively than current policy.

We urge readers who have teenage children to think about the following three questions:

1. Has my child ever used illegal drugs?
2. Does my child have the opportunity to use illegal drugs?
3. Do my child's schoolmates use illegal drugs?

The truthful answer to at least one of these questions will almost certainly be yes. The simple fact is this: In virtually every high school (and many junior high schools) across the country, illegal drugs are routinely and readily available today, under current policy. In fact, in many schools, students report that illegal drugs are easier to obtain than alcohol. Today's policies have not protected our children from psychoactives; if anything, our current policies have *increased* the chances that our children are exposed to drugs. This is a striking conclusion, so it is best to be clear as to exactly why it is correct.

Under current national policy, sales of psychoactives such as marijuana, cocaine, and heroin are illegal whether the drugs are sold to adults or to children. There is no reason for a drug dealer to prefer selling to adults rather than children: The penalties are the *same* either way. As long as the kids have cash, there is no incentive *not* to sell to them, so the dealers nurture contacts with children just as intensively as they cultivate deals with adults. Indeed, kids are even more attractive as customers, because if they get hooked, they'll be drug users that much longer.

It's true that the 1986 amendments to the Controlled Substances Act[9] created harsher penalties for selling drugs on or near school campuses, but as a practical matter, these penalties are virtually meaningless. Most of the dealers who operate on or around schools are students themselves, and therefore juveniles. Due to the kinder, gentler provisions of juvenile law, children caught selling drugs typically receive punishments that amount to no more than a slap on the wrist—a warning perhaps, or at worst, probation. The supposedly tougher penalties of the 1986 amendments to the Controlled Substances Act don't apply to them. Besides, dealer and user can "come to an understanding" on campus, and then leave the school grounds for the actual exchange of drugs for money, thereby circumventing the tougher campus-dealing provisions of the amended Controlled Substances Act. The higher penalties for on-campus dealing do almost nothing to keep drugs away from kids. When added to the fact that dealers face no tougher penalties for selling to children rather than adults, it's little wonder that parents worry about drugs.

How would the Constitutional Alternative help change the current situation? In states that choose a tougher stance against drugs, the imposition of harsher penalties would be much more effective than uniform national penalties in drying up drug supplies to users of all age brackets, kids included. Penalties would likely be tougher in states where antidrug sentiment is greatest, because state legislators would feel the heat from parents who were serious about keeping drugs away from their children. Separate, tougher penalties for selling to persons under the age of twenty-one could be imposed, including, perhaps, the death penalty. Voters in some states might even decide they wanted a "drug exception" to the more lenient laws relating to juvenile crimes; for example, underage illegal dealers might be subject to the full force of the state's drug laws *unless* they fingered their adult suppliers. Across the board, then, a variety of tough measures could be implemented in order to make children distinctly unattractive as customers for drug dealers.

But what about states which might contemplate a relaxation of their drug laws under the Constitutional Alternative? Surely, this is every parent's nightmare. It shouldn't be, however, because a carefully crafted decriminalization or legalization of drugs can—and almost certainly will—*reduce* the availability of drugs for children. Since this conclusion seems so contrary to common sense, it clearly merits special attention. Let's see what we can learn from liquor.

Item 1: Under the laws of all fifty states, the right to sell alcoholic beverages is controlled by the state governments. The states grant liquor licenses and the states can take them away. Moreover, the numbers of these licenses are limited to varying degrees in all of the states. As a result of these limitations, the right to sell alcohol is a valuable economic right, one typically worth tens of thousands of dollars—money that the license-holder forfeits if his license is revoked.

Item 2: Under the laws of all fifty states, sales of alcoholic beverages to minors are illegal and are grounds for revocation of a liquor license. The owner of a liquor license can thus openly and legally make a handsome profit by selling to adults; but if the dealer makes even one sale to a minor, he faces the loss of an asset, the liquor license, which may represent his entire livelihood.

Item 3: Eighty percent of all alcohol is consumed by "heavy drinkers"—the abusers and alcoholics. The overwhelming majority of these people are above the age of twenty-one, and virtually all of them are over the age of eighteen. As long as these heavy drinkers have access to a reliable, legal source of supply, they have no reason to turn to illegal sources, such as bootleggers and moonshiners. And without the enormous volume of business accounted for by the heavy drinkers, there is simply no opportunity for any sort of organized, illegal sources of supply to develop.

In effect, the abusers and alcoholics exist in a peculiar symbiotic partnership with the purveyors of booze. The heavy drinkers patronize (and thus make profitable) the legal sources of supply. The licensed suppliers wish to avoid selling to minors, because doing so would jeopardize the profits they earn from sales to heavy drinkers. And without the profits from abusers and alcoholics, potential illegal suppliers—who would gladly sell to minors—never get off the ground. The result is that most minors have more difficulty obtaining legal alcohol than illegal drugs.

To be sure, there are unscrupulous liquor license owners who are casual about checking the identification cards of their younger clientele, and minors can sometimes find adults who will buy alcohol on their behalf. But notice the distinction. Crack houses don't check identification cards at the door. Drug dealers don't even *ask* their customers how old they are. With alcohol, we need worry only about the unscrupulous or irresponsible few; with marijuana and cocaine, every user and every dealer is a potential supplier to our children.

States wishing to liberalize their drug laws under the Constitutional Alternative clearly would do so in a way that would help keep drugs away from kids, and kids away from drugs. The critical elements are twofold. First, a mechanism would have to be established (such as state-owned stores or limited private licenses) that would service the abusers and addicts; this would run the illegal suppliers out of business. Second, penalties for sales to minors (including loss of license) would have to be established that would eliminate the legal dealer's profits from selling to underage customers. Both elements have been established for alcohol, and could be established for the other psychoactives. To be sure, the creation of a strictly controlled, legal distribution system for some psychoactives would have a cost; people who are *already* addicts would be able to feed their habits more easily. But this is a trivial price to pay for keeping drugs away from our children.

Do not misunderstand. The Constitutional Alternative will not eliminate all drug use by children. No matter how tough a state gets, some drugs are bound to slip through the enforcement net and into the hands of children. In states that liberalize their laws, there are bound to be some suppliers who, despite the costs, will be foolish or desperate enough to sell to underage consumers, as well as some irresponsible adults who will buy on behalf of children. It is all too easy—and incorrect—to dismiss a program such as the Constitutional Alternative by arguing that it would not yield the perfect outcome. Doing so, however, is a commission of the "grass is greener" fallacy, because no policy is perfect. What is relevant and important is that the Constitutional Alternative would *reduce* the consumption of drugs by children, which makes it a major improvement over current policy.

If it is possible to reduce our children's exposure to drugs by either cracking down hard, or by regulating rather than prohibiting drugs, why hasn't this happened already? At the state level, the answer is twofold. In states where antidrug sentiment is greatest, the existence of a supposedly "tough" federal policy on drugs removes the heat from state legislators who would rather not raise the taxes needed to pay for even tougher state laws and law enforcement. In states where less stringent drug laws are preferred, federal law effectively eliminates the regulation route, because such a path is illegal under the current form of the Controlled Substances Act.

At the national level, we haven't taken the steps necessary to effectively protect our children from drugs precisely because national policy is an ineffective and unsatisfactory blend of Americans' conflicting attitudes about drugs. Current federal policy is a fatally flawed compromise between the wishes of those people who want tougher laws and those who want more lenient laws. This results in laws that are onerous enough to generate enormous costs to society, but not tough enough to do the job—including the job of protecting our children. Current drug policy is the worst of both worlds. To be sure, compromises will take place at the state and local level. Yet it will represent *less* compromise, because there will be greater commonality of beliefs within each state than there is across all states. By adopting the Constitutional Alternative, we could thus reduce the costs we are incurring, enhance the effectiveness of policy, and along the way, help our children just say no.

FLEXIBILITY AND FREEDOM

The founding fathers had no knowledge of the place we now call Alaska, nor of the Mormon religion (so prominent in Utah), whose followers shun all psychoactives. Yet the founders knew that it was freedom—of speech, religion, and thought—that attracted people to this land. The founding fathers knew also that, despite the unifying beliefs common to many Americans, the residents of the various states differed fundamentally in their individual preferences, and in the circumstances in which they conducted their lives. Both the federal system of government and the Tenth Amendment were intended to allow the maximum flexibility in the expression of these differences. The Constitutional Alternative offers precisely this flexibility and this freedom.

Our proposal for returning drug policy to the states may seem radical, but it was just such a move—embodied in the repeal of Prohibition—that ended America's liquor wars. It is an approach that is solidly embedded in our Constitution, and one that has been used with great success in virtually every aspect of everyday life. The only truly radical aspect of the Constitutional Alternative is that the history of our nation clearly and convincingly demonstrates that it will accomplish the objective—undoing drugs.

....

CHAPTER 12

Toward a More Perfect Union

DRUGS ARE AN ISSUE THROUGHOUT THE NATION. THAT FACT DOES NOT mean that drugs should be dealt with in the same manner throughout the nation. Indeed, a fundamental flaw in current drug policy lies in the reality that as a *national* policy, it is born of the forces of compromise needed to forge national legislation.

It sits squarely in the middle of the spectrum of different policies favored by different Americans. It is a political compromise that is onerous enough to impose substantial costs upon us, but not tough enough to get the job done. For some Americans, current drug policy goes too far; for others, not far enough; for almost none of us is it the correct policy.

Returning to the states their constitutional right to regulate psychoactives will not lead to perfection. Indeed, no policy will. Instead, the Constitutional Alternative will yield a *better* set of drug policies, as the states adjust their policies to correspond to the differing preferences and circumstances of their citizens. Some states will choose harsher measures toward drugs; others will embrace more lenient policies. Yet however they choose, as long as those choices reflect the wishes of their citizens, *all* states will improve the welfare of the people—which is, after all, the role for government envisioned in our Constitution.

As we explore the improvements that will be possible under the Constitutional Alternative, it is essential to keep one thought in mind. If one were to *randomly* impose get-tough policies on some states and legalization on others, the result would be arguably no better than today's mess. The Constitutional Alternative will work because it allows the people for whom policy x is best to choose x, while the people for whom policy y is best are free to choose y. It is the *self-selection* possible under the Constitutional Alternative that makes diversity of policies such a powerful force for improvement.

ORGANIZED DRUG GANGS

Current drug policy has provided the perfect environment for the growth of nationwide drug gangs such as the Jamaican posses. The federal government's approach to the drug wars, for example, has created the economic incentive to develop higher-potency drugs. Crack is one of these drugs, and it has provided the profits to fuel the expansion of organized gangs throughout the United States. Moreover, the increase in penalties for drug trafficking, relative to the penalties for the violent acts committed in association with trafficking, has effectively given the gangs carte blanche to engage in indiscriminate violence and terror. The result has been the spread of gang violence unknown since the days of Prohibition. Finally, of course, the uniformity of national policy has fostered the nationwide character of these gangs, for it has given them an enormous competitive advantage over petty individual dealers, and even over small-time, local gangs.

Under the Constitutional Alternative, the backbone of the organized drug gangs will be crushed. The diversity that will flourish as states bring their drug policies into agreement with the wishes of their citizens will, for different reasons in different states, largely eliminate the profitability of drug gangs. Moreover, national gangs such as the Jamaican posses likely will be destroyed altogether, and there will be a major nationwide decline in gang violence, terror, and intimidation. Let's see why these conclusions are correct.

Under the Constitutional Alternative, some states undoubtedly will liberalize their drug laws. The illegal market for drugs in such states will simply dry up, for few people will choose to buy substances of uncertain purity and potency from violent thugs, when they can legally cultivate their own, or purchase reliable goods from a reputable, legal dealer. The drug gangs thrive on the risk premium currently built into drug prices, because they are willing and able to engage in the lawless, violent behavior needed to successfully deal drugs. If a drug or class of drugs is legalized or decriminalized in a state, this risk premium will disappear because the risk will disappear. The only profits left in drugs will be those currently present for other goods—profits that are far too low to warrant the risks of violence, intimidation, and terror.

Progress against gangs will also be made in states that toughen their laws, enforcement, and penalties, because tougher measures will increase the costs of dealing and using drugs, thereby lowering the profits that motivate the gangs in the first place. We currently don't observe tougher national policy because many Americans aren't willing to bear the costs. But in states in which the citizens feel strongly about stopping drugs, these measures will pass, and the drug gangs will pay the price. Tougher laws will produce higher costs for the gangs, higher costs that mean lower profits—and profits are the reason for the existence of the gangs.

Whatever route states choose to take in response to the Constitutional Alternative, they will be induced to engage in more cost-effective targeting of their law-enforcement resources than the federal government does. For example, when President Bush announced an expansion in the drug wars in the fall of 1989, a key element of the plan was to devote more resources toward punishing *users* of drugs, to "make them pay the price" for their drug use. Bush's initiative led to a rise in "reverse-sting" operations, in which drug agents posed as sellers of drugs in the hopes of catching unsuspecting users. This type of policy makes for good public relations but lousy law enforcement.

One of the reasons law-enforcement agencies generally target the suppliers of illegal goods is that each seller typically deals with many buyers, often hundreds. Not only are there fewer sellers to contend with, but catching each one disrupts supplies of the good for many would-be buyers. Thus, seller-targeting is much more effective. Focusing on buyers (and some 40 million Americans buy illegal drugs each year) is an incredibly expensive way to try to conduct law enforcement; it simply spreads the police too thin.

Reverse sting operations such as those pushed by the federal authorities also enhance the competitive position of organized drug gangs. When cops are posing as sellers, buyers want to be sure they are buying from someone they know is not a cop. Since the gangs are careful to prevent infiltration by drug agents, gang membership of a seller becomes a critical assurance to potential buyers that the dealer is not a narc. Independent sellers are put at a competitive disadvantage, because they don't have any way of guaranteeing to buyers that their interest lies in selling them drugs instead of a trip to prison.

The *diversity* of policy responses across states under the Constitutional Alternative will present special problems for the national gangs, who are the most violent and lawless of all. Under current policy, the national gangs know that what works in Los Angeles will work in Seattle and Kansas City too, because their opponents are fundamentally the same everywhere. Once the states begin adopting differing policies and tactics, the knowledge of what works in one location will be useless in attempting to set up shop elsewhere. The enormous advantage currently enjoyed by nationwide gangs will disappear, largely eliminating the reason for their existence.

This scenario regarding organized crime is exactly what happened in the aftermath of Prohibition. Three states and hundreds of counties throughout more than two dozen additional states remained dry after the ratification of the Twenty-first Amendment. Even among those states that legalized alcohol, many retained severe curbs on its distribution. Other states, of course, legalized alcohol immediately.* The impact of this diversity on organized crime was devastating. To be sure, some individual citizens or even small groups of individuals smuggled booze from wet states or counties to dry ones, or continued to manufacture illegal moonshine in isolated mountain stills. Nevertheless, the involvement of organized crime in the alcohol industry effectively disappeared almost overnight.

Don't get us wrong. Gangs per se will never disappear completely from American life—they have simply been with us too long. As long as there are profits to be made from illegal activity, individual criminals will attempt to organize in ways that facilitate the capture of those profits. Nevertheless, the twin blades of diversity will wreak havoc with the organizing efforts of criminals. In states that liberalize their drug laws, the reduction in the demand for illegal drugs will slash potential profits. In states that get tough, the higher costs imposed on dealers and users will also drive illegal drug profits down. And across the country, the diverse responses of fifty different states will sow confusion among those who would seek to monopolize the

---

*In Virginia, for example, even ten years after the end of Prohibition, there was still only one liquor store for every 50,000 residents of the state. In Utah, many citizens had to drive more than 100 miles to buy alcoholic beverages. And throughout the South, even in those states that did not continue to prohibit alcohol, a majority of the citizens lived in counties where liquor was prohibited.

trade. In these ways, the Constitutional Alternative will reduce the profitability of illegal drugs, and so diminish the size, influence, and extent of the gangs who live off those profits.

CRIME

Crime menaces the very fabric of American society. Serious crimes are on the rise, and there is no end in sight under the current national approach to the drug wars. The Constitutional Alternative will enable us to sharply reduce crime, both in states that liberalize their drug laws, and in those that decide to get tough. States that decide to crack down on drugs will have to remember that drug users and drug dealers respond to real incentives, not to the claims of politicians or to supposed get-tough laws that have no real teeth in them. At the national level, Congress hasn't committed the resources needed to make tougher sentencing laws effective, because there is no real national consensus that the effort is worth it. The result is that more cases are plea-bargained (for sharply reduced sentences), and people sent to prison are more likely to get out early because the prisons are full. State legislators have been able to hide behind the veil of federal leadership, so that even in states like New York, where supposedly tough mandatory drug sentences are in place, the government hasn't committed the resources—cops, courts, prisons, and prosecutors— needed to translate the tougher laws into a harsher reality.* The authorities say they're tough on drugs, but the users and dealers know different. Harsher tactics against users and dealers will work, but only if adequate resources are committed to do the job.

Organized drug gangs are the principal source of violent crimes associated with drugs. In fact, law-enforcement agencies across the country are the first to note that the rise in urban murder rates we have observed over the past decade is due almost solely to drug dealers murdering each other and killing innocent bystanders along the way. The most important perpetrators of these murders are the drug gangs. As we have already seen, implementation of the Constitutional

*In New York City, fully 97 percent of the felony drug cases are plea-bargained for drastically reduced sentences, and virtually all misdemeanor drug cases are plea-bargained, producing "wrist slaps" compared to what the law says will happen to those who are guilty.

Alternative will have a major impact on these groups, which in turn will help reduce the violent crimes now perpetrated by gangs.

Harsher drug laws in get-tough states will also have an important indirect effect on crime by inducing casual users to leave the picture. Although casual users generally are not directly responsible for crime, the arrest and prosecution of these individuals use up an enormous amount of police, court, and prison resources. Tougher laws will be most effective in discouraging these individuals from using drugs, because casual users have the least commitment to drugs. Truly tougher policy will prevent many of these people from using drugs, and thus prevent them from clogging up the criminal justice system. States will therefore be able to target their law-enforcement resources on abusers, addicts, and dealers.

States that get tough will also be able to reduce the crimes caused by addicts, who steal to feed their habits. More than one-third of the nation's heroin addicts live in New York City. They don't live there because it's *difficult* to get heroin in New York; they live there because New York is the *easiest* place in the country to obtain heroin. Addicts are addicted to the drug, not to the location in which it is consumed. Any state that wants to seriously reduce the addict population within its borders, and thus the crimes committed to finance addiction, can do so under the Constitutional Alternative simply by making their state an extremely inhospitable location for addicts.

What will occur in states that liberalize their drug laws? Clearly, such states will immediately free up the law-enforcement resources previously devoted to enforcing current drug laws. Casual users will no longer clog the courts and jails, and the police will no longer spend their time busting pot smokers instead of car thieves and murderers. Thus, at no additional cost, the authorities in these states will be able to redirect law-enforcement resources toward the criminal activities that concern their citizens the most. Moreover, since organized drug gangs will no longer find such states to be profitable places of operation, they will die out there, reducing crime rates directly and freeing-up even more law-enforcement resources for targeting on other criminals.

One concern that arises regarding states that legalize or decriminalize drugs is the prospect that drug use will rise, and that crime will somehow rise as a result. Drug use will rise in states that legalize or decriminalize drugs, but we must remember the two principal sources of the link between drugs and crime: violent, lawless behavior by the purveyors of illegal drugs, and property crimes committed by persons addicted to illegal (and therefore expensive) drugs. If certain drugs are legalized in a state, there will be no drug gangs committing mayhem to protect their profits in those drugs, just as liquor store owners do not today engage in drive-by shootings to protect their "booze territories." Similarly, addicts will not have to engage in criminal behavior to finance their addictions to legal drugs, just as the 15 million or so alcoholics in America today don't have to steal cars and burgle houses to finance their addiction. When drugs are cheap, the cheapest way to obtain them is through legal means.

Do not misunderstand. Crime will not disappear under the Constitutional Alternative. Nevertheless, communities across the country will be able to *reduce* crime far more effectively than is possible under today's drug policies. The drastic declines in assaults and murders and corruption that occurred in the aftermath of Prohibition are just one indication of what is possible.

Reductions in crime will not come magically. In states that get tough, citizens will have to spend the money needed to transform tough words into tough action. In states that liberalize drug laws, some of the law-enforcement resources saved will have to be redirected toward making sure that drug abuse doesn't create other adverse effects. Thus, such states will want to prevent pot smokers from joining in the highway mayhem currently being perpetrated by drunk drivers. Nevertheless, by taking control of their own destiny and shaping their laws to fit their own preferences and circumstances, the citizens of all fifty states will be able to do what today's drug warriors cannot accomplish—make our streets and our neighborhoods safe once again.

LIFE IN THE INNER CITY

Inner cities are the basement of life in America: There is nowhere to go but up. Yet under our current drug policies, inner-city residents will never even make it to the ground floor. Current drug policy has created the drug-law lottery—the visions of Mercedes and Rolex watches—that drives the life of inner-city youngsters. Current drug policy has transformed law enforcement in the ghetto into *drug*-law enforcement. Current drug policy has helped destroy an entire generation of inner-city youngsters, and unless that policy is changed it will surely destroy another.

The Constitutional Alternative offers the greatest prospect for the improvement of inner cities in those states that choose to liberalize their drug policies. As the illegal drug market opportunities dry up in those jurisdictions, inner-city residents will return to legal endeavors. Moreover, since gang life will no longer offer the lure of huge profits, youngsters will turn to education, not to the drug bosses, as a path to long-term achievement. After all, it is only the "example effect" of successful drug lords that induces youngsters to lead a life of crime in the illegal drug trade.

Nowhere in America are drugs cheaper or more readily available than in our inner cities. Any current inner-city resident who wants to use drugs has used drugs. And for those over the age of eighteen or so, if they *will* become addicted to drugs, they generally already *are* addicted.[1] Thus, the risk of additional drug use and addiction will be at a minimum in inner cities if drug policies are liberalized under the Constitutional Alternative. The death rate and spread of AIDS and syphilis among users and addicts will also decline sharply: Drug consumers will switch to less intensive drug forms and delivery systems, drug purity and potency will no longer be subject to uncertainty, and intravenous drug users will no longer be forced to share contaminated needles. Moreover, the millions of dollars now spent in these jurisdictions every year on drug interdiction efforts can be used for drug-treatment programs, drug-prevention programs in the inner-city schools, increased social welfare services, expanded educational opportunities, and so on. The inner cities will be served best of all by the "peace dividend" occurring in those jurisdictions which choose to cease fire in the war on drugs.

Some jurisdictions will, of course, choose to get tougher on drugs. We have already seen that organized drug gangs will suffer under tougher enforcement, and because these gangs are a major source of violence in the inner cities, their diminished role will make life there safer and less terrifying. Redirecting the interest of inner-city residents away from the drug trade will also, however, require additional targeting of the enforcement activities in get-tough jurisdictions.

The attractiveness of the drug-law lottery lies in the unevenness of the outcomes: It is the chance, however small, of striking it rich that provides the allure of the drug trade. The elimination of this allure thus requires that get-tough jurisdictions focus on making sure that "equal opportunity" pervades the industry. Achieving this will no doubt require different tactics in different jurisdictions. In some areas, it may mean ensuring that every supplier in the chain of distribution knows with virtual certainty that he will spend some time in jail every year he is in business. In other jurisdictions, the best policy may be to ignore small-time dealers completely, and focus all of the drug-enforcement resources on the "big fish," so that even the hint of success brings immediate legal retribution. Other approaches are no doubt possible. One of the advantages of the Constitutional Alternative is that it will induce innovation among state and local authorities, as they are forced to focus on the specific tactics that will work best in their jurisdictions.

Heroin plagues many large inner cities and, because there are so few casual users, is particularly difficult to deal with. Whether they liberalize or get tough, all jurisdictions may want to consider the model used so successfully in Britain for more than forty years: Legalize the drug for existing addicts, but engage in tough efforts to prevent illegal distribution of heroin. Given legitimate access to maintenance doses of, say, forty to sixty milligrams of cheap heroin each day, addicts would have little reason to engage in crime to pay for the drug, and equally little reason to turn to illegal suppliers. Dealers would lose 90 percent or more of their current business, and would have no incentive to recruit new addicts, knowing that once those individuals were hooked, they would have ready access to cheap supplies of the drug. There are risks to this approach, including the possibility that unscrupulous doctors or corrupt clinic employees could divert heroin to illegal channels. Yet it's hard to imagine any outcome for such an approach that would be worse than the horror that stalks many of the streets of New York City every day under current policy.

Not even the Constitutional Alternative can transform our inner cities into the tree-lined streets of suburbia. But there can be little doubt that the approach of the federal government has failed—abysmally. There is a downside risk with experimentation at the state and local level, but the far greater risk is staying the course of current policies. Unless we are prepared to simply throw away our inner cities and the lives of the human beings who live there, the Constitutional Alternative may be our *only* alternative.

U.S. "POLICE ACTION" IN SOUTH AMERICA

The United States is no stranger to military "police actions" throughout the world. Vietnam was one of them. We started small—just a few "military advisers"—and we ended up with half a million troops mired in a far-off jungle. Fifty-eight thousand of those troops came home in body bags. Today there is a very real possibility that the same type of "police action" could occur in South America. We have already sent millions of dollars worth of helicopters, jeeps, assault rifles, and other assorted military hardware to South American governments for use against drug growers and traffickers. There are even American troops serving as "advisers" in South America, all as part of the federal government's futile attempts to stop cocaine at its source.[2]

Despite the dismal chances of eradicating the world's supply of coca bushes, the fall of the Iron Curtain in 1989 raised the prospects of sending even more military advisers to South America. The principals in these discussions included members of Congress and senior military officers, all of whom were worried about what *glasnost* would do to military budgets. The war with Iraq put these talks to an end— for the time being. Nevertheless, as peace returns, the military and its Congressional supporters will look for some way to prevent military budget cutbacks. If we are still pursuing the current federal war on drugs, sending American troops to South American mountains and jungles will become a very real possibility again. Implementation of the Constitutional Alternative would put an end to such discussions for good, for it would largely remove any federal incentive to commit troops to a futile police action against drugs in foreign lands.

DRUG-TREATMENT PROGRAMS

The least talked about, the least financed, and the least explored tools in the war on drugs are drug-treatment and drug-maintenance programs. Virtually all of the innovation and improvement in drug-treatment programs in this country have been the result of private-sector efforts.[3] The overwhelming majority of all public funds spent on the drug problem in America has been for law enforcement, not treatment or preventive education. At the federal level, the funding for drug-treatment programs has always been at best an afterthought.

When Washington, D.C., was made a showcase for a new get-tough federal drug policy in 1989, less than 10 percent of the total amount of money allocated to the program was earmarked for drug treatment and preventive drug education *combined*. Nationwide, federal funding for drug-treatment research currently amounts to only $380 million per year—about $1.50 per capita. And according to the U.S. General Accounting Office, much of this money is wasted due to obsolete priorities, inadequate methods, lack of accountability, and inadequate direction.[4] Many states simply ignore the importance of engaging in and improving upon drug-treatment programs—which is not surprising given that the mandate from the federal level is to "arrest more people, seize more drugs."

The treatment of psychoactive addiction is not easy. As recently as sixty years ago, recovery from alcoholism was deemed by most medical experts to be nearly impossible; even the most "successful" treatment efforts yielded sustained recovery in less than 5 percent of the cases. By the mid-1950s, treatment approaches, including Alcoholics Anonymous, had brought long-term recovery rates up substantially. Today's programs (which generally include some elements of the Alcoholics Anonymous approach) are capable of yielding long-term recovery rates of 60 percent or more among middle-aged men and women—the individuals in which the effects of the disease are most pronounced.[5]

Current recovery rates from cocaine (including crack) and heroin addiction are much lower—about 20 percent, which are comparable to the chances that a long-term, heavy smoker will successfully quit cigarettes. Cocaine addiction rates were relatively low until recently, and so treatment experts have less experience with the drug; on this margin, many experts believe that experience will help breed better success. Recovery from cocaine addiction is also hampered by the fact that most addicts originally enter treatment only because they have spent all of their money on the drug, or because they have been threatened with incarceration if they do not participate in a treatment program. On both counts, they frequently enter treatment unconvinced that they really have a lifetime problem that requires a lifetime approach to solve. Consequently, once the short-term crisis that drove them into treatment is over, they resume using the drug, believing that their "problem" is lack of money or a vindictive judicial system rather than addiction. Almost invariably, resumption of use brings another plunge into the abyss of practicing addiction, and so the cycle continues. Sometimes three or four attempts at recovery are required before it finally sticks, while some addicts never recover.[6]

The low recovery rates from heroin addiction stem in part from the fact that the drug itself is remarkably benign, its only established, long-term side effect being constipation. Morphine, the active ingredient in heroin, is closely related to endorphins, the painkiller/euphoriants naturally produced by the human body. Perhaps because heroin so closely mimics our own biochemical processes, the drug has few adverse physical effects on those who consume it, other than producing physical dependence. Of course, since heroin is a central nervous system depressant, a massive overdose of the drug can cause death—although addicts are apparently able to survive doses up to 100 times greater than the typical ten- to fifteen-milligram street dose.[7] Most heroin addicts thus enter treatment only because they are tired of legal hassles; fear the diseases, such as AIDS and hepatitis, that are transmitted by contaminated needles; or they have run out of money, perhaps because a recent drug bust has driven up the price of heroin. Absent these factors, many heroin addicts feel that there is little to gain from recovery, except perhaps for the fact of no longer being addicted.[8]

For heroin, there is already an alternative—methadone maintenance programs. Consider New York City's Beth Israel Medical Center, the largest heroin treatment center in the nation. At Beth Israel's methadone clinic, Dr. Robert Newman has to turn away 100 addicts each month because of federal limits on counselor-client ratios. These people apply knowing that there isn't space available, and that there is a three- to four-month waiting list, and yet knowing that they need help.

Some criticize methadone treatment for heroin addiction because it substitutes one drug for another. Yet not all addicts remain on methadone for life. Methadone also gets heroin addicts out of the crime cycle, for they no longer must steal to finance their habits. Moreover, it at least starts them on the road to full, drug-free recovery. The statistics from Beth Israel's methadone program are revelatory: Fifty percent of its clients remain actively enrolled after three years. At any point in time, fully half of the clients have full-time jobs (compared to less than 15 percent when they enrolled in the program) and still others have part-time jobs or have gone back to school. In addition, other drug addictions abate while individuals are in a methadone program. As Dr. Newman points out, "Once people see that they don't have to use heroin several times a day, then for the first time they can entertain the thought of trying to do something about the other drugs they use."[9]

With government drug policy where it should be—in the hands of state and local governments—jurisdictions will be forced to develop the most cost-effective methods for dealing with drugs, in part because of the scrutiny of taxpaying constituents who want the most for their money. Preventive education and drug treatment will become major components of this effective drug policy, since these are generally recognized as the only realistic long-term solutions to addiction. The mere threat of government sanctions—including death— has never eliminated addiction to any drug in any country in recorded history.

Even for states that choose to get tough, education and treatment must be part of the package of tools used to reduce the potentially harmful effects of psychoactives. An additional million dollars for cops, courts, and prisons can help get some addicts off the streets and into jail. But that same million dollars can also be used in treatment programs to get them off drugs, out of jail, and into jobs. Spent on education, that money may well keep them off drugs from the outset.

What is the most efficient mix of all these options for dealing with drugs? We do not know, and indeed, no one knows—least of all the federal government. Innovation and experimentation are the hallmarks of America. But it is competition that has been the great spur to innovation in this country, not monopoly, and certainly not government monopoly. Yet today's federal drug policy is effectively a monopoly—and the dismal results we observe are the unsurprising outcome. Returning drug policy to the states will bring taxpayers into closer proximity with the expenditure of their tax dollars, a fact that will force government officials to make choices more in line with what makes sense, instead of what makes news. The result can only be a better mix of prevention, eradication, and treatment.

CIVIL LIBERTIES

Implementation of the Constitutional Alternative is likely to lead to some divergence in the civil liberties enjoyed by the citizens of different states. Clearly, civil liberties will improve in states that liberalize their drug laws, for the police will be breaking down far fewer doors in the middle of the night. Domestic espionage, the use of drug courier profiles, and visits by drug agents intrigued by orchid-growing equipment will also diminish in these states. Citizens also will no longer have to worry about forfeitures and seizures because of the drug consumption habits of friends who borrow their cars or boats, or the occupations of the previous owner of their house or the current tenant in their basement apartment. In short, the Bill of Rights will again mean what the founding fathers intended it to mean.

The Constitution is, of course, a bit of a nuisance when one is trying to enforce the law. Citizens in states where getting tough is the order of the day may face further erosion of their civil liberties, though there are several factors that will tend to mitigate and possibly even reverse this loss of civil liberties.

States and local governments have never been averse to bending the civil rights of their citizens in the name of suitable causes. This is, after all, why we have the Fourteenth Amendment to the Constitution, which ensures that *state* laws must meet the tests imposed by the Bill of Rights. Nevertheless, when it comes to the drug laws, the federal government has been in the forefront of the assault on our civil liberties. It was the U.S. Customs Service, for example, that first proposed that "if you fly, you die." It was the U.S. Customs Service that was successful in gaining the right to force "suspicious" immigrants to defecate to prove that they were not carrying drugs. And it was the U.S. Customs Service that posted toll-free telephone numbers urging "concerned citizens" to report their suspicions about strangers. When it comes to the war on drugs, the federal government has taken the lead in devising new ways to intrude on our civil liberties. Absent the federal government's leadership role in this dimension, it is possible that even get-tough states will proceed more cautiously in any further assault on freedom.

The Constitutional Alternative will also mitigate the conflict of interest that currently hampers the federal enforcement of our civil liberties in drug cases. The Drug Enforcement Administration is an arm of the U.S. Department of Justice, the agency charged with upholding the Constitution. Under current policy, when a drug bust creates a possible violation of our Constitutional rights, a Justice Department attorney must decide whether to prosecute a DEA agent (whose office may be just down the hall). No doubt there exist Justice Department procedures to help ensure that such decisions will be made in a proper manner. It is equally certain that federal prosecutors will have fewer second thoughts when they are prosecuting state government officials, rather than their federal colleagues, for civil rights violations in drug cases.

An additional civil liberties protection embedded in the Constitutional Alternative lies in *competition* among the states. Citizens in get-tough states will be able to observe events at home and in other jurisdictions. They will be able to decide for themselves if the reduction in drug use at home (relative to more liberal states) is worth the decline in their privacy and freedom that may take place. If it is not, they can act through the ballot box to change things, and if this fails, they have the option of "voting with their feet"—moving to another state and taking their tax dollars with them. Thus, competition under the Constitutional Alternative will force state and local governments to proceed with care regarding the rights of their residents. The forces of competition clearly are far weaker under the current federal monopoly. Not only are fewer civil liberties protected in most alternative nations, but the cost of moving from one country to another is clearly greater than simply moving across state lines.

The final point is that casual drug use—the type of consumption engaged in by the largest number of drug consumers—will decline the most in get-tough states. The chance that an innocent person will be mistaken for one who is guilty rises sharply when there are many guilty people (in this case, casual users). Because so many fewer people will be using drugs in get-tough states, the police will have less occasion to intrude upon the rights of any given person. Thus, if civil liberties are reduced in get-tough states, the brunt of the burden will be borne by the relatively small numbers of addicts and their dealers who remain, not by the average citizen. We are not arguing that addicts and dealers are undeserving of protection by the Bill of Rights, but that the social damage done by violations of our rights is greater the greater are the number of people whose rights are violated. There will be fewer of these people in get-tough states than there are presently, and thus less total damage to civil liberties.

DISEASE AND DEATH

Under current policy, drugs have brought disease and death to America. This is true today more than ever before, because of the spread of AIDS through contaminated needles, the spread of syphilis and other STDs in crack houses, and the accidental overdoses suffered by unsuspecting users like the late basketball star Len Bias. These tragedies, and the deaths produced by allergic reactions to cutting agents and by drug-switching (such as between heroin and barbiturates), are chiefly the result of the *illegal* nature of the drugs involved. But disease and death also can result from the use of *legal* drugs as well— the diseases of addiction and cirrhosis and emphysema, as well as the deaths on the highways or in the cancer wards. However the various states respond to the Constitutional Alternative, care must be used to avoid destroying more lives than are saved.

Consider states that get tough. Fewer people will use drugs in these states, but for those who continue using them, the drugs will be just as lethal as today, if not more so. Crack houses and contaminated needles will continue to exist, people will still be encouraged to use intensive drug forms and delivery systems, and the illegal drugs on the street will continue to be of uncertain purity and potency. But some addicts will seek treatment to avoid the threat of harsher enforcement, while others will simply move to jurisdictions where their habits are cheaper and easier to feed. The reduction in the number of people who use drugs to begin with will also mean fewer new addicts entering the at-risk population. On both counts, the incidence of death and disease due to illegal drug use will decline in get-tough states. On the other hand, harsher penalties and tougher enforcement will foster still more intensive drug forms and delivery systems among the reduced user population. Overall, we would expect at best a modest decline in drug-related death and disease in states that get tough.

Such states could improve matters markedly by taking steps that the federal government has steadfastly eschewed. First, they could permit or even sponsor needle-exchange programs for addicts, thereby reducing the spread of AIDS and other diseases. Some cities in the United States have already begun such programs despite the vigorous opposition of the federal government, which argues that needle-exchange programs encourage drug addiction. Though there is merit to the federal government's logic, hundreds (and soon thousands) of innocent young children will die of AIDS each year because one of their parents contracted the disease from a contaminated needle. Somehow we think that state and local officials, even some of the toughest ones, are likely to allow humanity to override logic.

States that choose to liberalize their drug laws stand to enjoy the biggest health benefits while facing the greatest health risks. For each drug that is decriminalized, the health hazards associated with illegal use will be reduced; for each drug legalized, they will be eliminated. Thousands of lives would be saved each year; given the growing threat of AIDS, this number would mount into the tens of thousands.

Yet there is another side of the coin: Liberalized drug laws mean more drug use, abuse, and addiction. These raise the specter of the kinds of consequences we now see emanating from the abuse of, and addiction to, nicotine and alcohol. States that liberalize their drug laws will have to invest their law-enforcement peace dividend in preventive education and drug treatment, and focus their law enforcement against third-party effects—such as driving under the influence—if they are to avoid creating more adverse public health effects than they cure. Yet modest first steps, such as decriminalization of marijuana and needle-exchange programs, would create immediate net public health benefits and free substantial amounts of law-enforcement resources that could be directed toward education and treatment. Whether these are the best first steps, we do not know. A great advantage of the Constitutional Alternative, however, is that the diversity of the American people will no doubt produce a diverse range of first steps. Some will work and thus be adopted elsewhere; others will fail and be discarded. And along the way, we shall learn better the proper balance between the adverse effects and beneficial consequences of our policies toward psychoactives. The Constitutional Alternative is no "magic bullet," offering an instant cure for disease and death. It promises progress, not perfection. And in judging it, we must always remember to make the comparison not with the ideal, but instead with the awful reality we face with today's policies. In our view, progress is an improvement.

THE CORRUPTION OF OUR LEGAL SYSTEM

Hardly a day goes by without another report of corruption among the people who are supposed to enforce the drug laws. Law-enforcement personnel are not inherently immoral; they are merely human. The money is too big and the crimes too easy to conceal. Illegal drugs today, like illegal booze sixty years ago, are the perfect breeding ground for corruption.

The most obvious impact of the Constitutional Alternative on corruption will be at the federal level, for federal agencies largely will be removed from the drug wars. Corruption will also diminish in those states that liberalize their drug laws. Bribes are offered only when there are large profits to be made; but illegal drug profits will be reduced where drugs are decriminalized, and nonexistent where they are legalized.

Even in jurisdictions where drug laws are made harsher, corruption may well diminish. Citizens who vote for harsher potential penalties upon *themselves* for using drugs will surely insist on harsher penalties for those who violate the public trust of enforcing those laws. More importantly, the process of self-selection in law enforcement will reduce corruption. Just as persons with the greatest personal commitment to drug law enforcement are today drawn to the U.S. Drug Enforcement Administration, state and local law-enforcement personnel who feel the greatest personal commitment to enforcing the drug laws will be drawn to states that decide to get tough under the Constitutional Alternative. Moreover, just as DEA personnel are remarkably (albeit not perfectly) resistant to the lure of corruption today, the law-enforcement personnel in get-tough states will show similar resistance. Though "everyone has a price," personal values can make that price too high even for the best-heeled drug dealer. Under the Constitutional Alternative, it is likely that the most "expensive" police, prosecutors, and judges will be found in those states that have decided to "just say no" to drugs in reality, not just in words.

FDS BABIES AND DRUG TESTING

Drug-related issues are nationwide in scope, and they are also intensely personal. Within the last five years, two drug-related issues have emerged which rival any others in their simultaneous national and personal scope: fetal drug syndrome (FDS) babies and drug testing.* The thought of an unborn child who is irreparably and terribly

---

*Strictly for compactness, in this section we divert from standard usage by using the term "FDS babies" for all babies who are damaged by their mother's consumption of psychoactives while pregnant. Thus, crack babies, children suffering from fetal alcohol syndrome (FAS), fetuses damaged by their mothers' cigarette smoking during pregnancy, and so forth, are all referred to as FDS babies.

damaged by its mother's consumption of crack or alcohol during pregnancy is horrifying. The thought that the pilot of the commercial jet on which we are a passenger may be under the influence of alcohol or marijuana is also terrifying. All of us agree that the world would be a better place if such events never took place. But they do occur, and many of us disagree over exactly how to prevent them. The issues involved come precisely to the core of the fundamental question of privacy: What right do we have to the privacy of our own minds and bodies?

Drug Testing

Most of us feel that we have the right to sober airline pilots, and thus the right to require that they be subject to drug testing.[10] To what other occupations does this right of assurance extend? Probably to nuclear-plant operators, but how about teachers? How about business executives, whose decisions under the influence might cost shareholders millions of dollars? Even if we decide on the occupations that warrant inspection, we must still decide on whether off-the-job testing is to be included. Should we require that people be tested for drugs *before* they are allowed to drive their cars, rather than wait until they have killed somebody on the road?* Should we, as part of a get-tough enforcement program, be required to wear blood or urine monitoring devices twenty-four hours a day to make sure that we are not violating the drug laws?

Should the tests cover only the presence of drugs, or should they look for the *effects* of drugs? A pilot with a bad hangover may have no alcohol in his blood, yet his hazy mental state may be a threat to his passengers. On the other hand, drug-testing equipment is now sufficiently sophisticated that if you eat a poppyseed roll, you will test positive for opiate consumption because of trace amounts of morphine in poppyseeds, despite the absence of any detectable psychoactive effects.[11]

At what intervals should testing be conducted? Every day, or week, or month? Or should we have random drug testing? What methods

---

*Repeat DUI offenders in some jurisdictions are required to undergo such testing as a condition for having their driving privileges restored. Their motor vehicles are equipped (at their expense) with breathalyzers linked to an ignition interlock system. Unless they pass a breath test when they get behind the wheel, their cars will not start.

should be used for testing—urinalyses, blood tests, hair samples, or eye-hand coordination? What drugs should be included? Until recently, most people would not have included alcohol in the list, and yet alcohol produces more adverse third-party effects than any other psychoactive. Would you have tested positive for alcohol in your bloodstream after lunch last Friday? Should you be fired if the answer to that question is yes?

Questions such as these could be extended for pages. Deciding on the appropriate role for drug testing in society is an extremely difficult problem, yet it will shape the way we and our children will live our lives for years to come. We do not know the answers, but we do know that a nationwide, federal policy with respect to drug testing will not be the correct policy. Why? Because as a national policy it will be born of the forces necessary to produce a national compromise. It will be the wrong policy for almost everyone, and yet it will be the agreed-upon policy because it is exactly in the middle of a host of widely differing and strongly held opinions. It will rob us of choice, and it will stifle innovation. And most importantly, it will leave unanswered some of the most fundamental and troubling personal questions that we must face if we are to approach the issue in the best manner.

FDS Babies

Crack babies are a problem. Children suffering from fetal alcohol syndrome are a problem. Even babies born to mothers who smoke cigarettes during pregnancy are a problem. What do we do? Once again, we don't know the answer, but we do know that it is tied to many other difficult, soul-searching questions.[12]

Physicians know that a woman's consumption of psychoactives during pregnancy can harm her fetus. Physicians do not know how much consumption is required to produce measurable injury, nor do they understand why the same amount of consumption by two otherwise comparable women can produce horrible damage to the child of one, yet leave the other's unscathed. Physicians do not even know how much of the damage that appears to be due to psychoactive consumption is in fact due to the poor prenatal care that often accompanies drug and alcohol abuse by pregnant women.

Even if these and other medical questions were answered, the moral, philosophical, and legal questions that remain are both profound and troubling. Does a human being have an absolute right to his or her body? If the bodies of two human beings are inextricably linked, whose rights take precedence? What is a human being?

Some jurisdictions have chosen to prosecute pregnant drug-using women for reckless endangerment of the lives of their unborn children. Are pregnant women who do not wear their seatbelts in automobiles culpable of such endangerment? Since secondhand smoke is believed to cause adverse health effects in bystanders—particularly infants and small children—should fathers be prohibited from smoking in the presence of their children? If the consumption of psychoactives causes chromosome damage, should prospective fathers have their sperm tested before they are permitted to impregnate a woman?

Even this small sampling of questions suggests the intensely personal nature of the issues involved, issues that strike at the very nature of our identities as human beings and the fundamental distinction between self and society. The danger we face in continuing with our current federal policy toward drugs is this: Expedient "solutions" to narrowly defined drug-law enforcement questions will seriously alter the ultimate resolution of far more profound questions that may even yet be unasked. As we decide on the future course of our lives and those of our descendants, the broadest range of thinking and problem solving must be brought to bear on these issues. Retaining the current federal monopoly on law and policy endangers this process and the shape of our destiny. This dangerous monopoly must be replaced with an alternative that broadens the scope of the decision making, and ensures that the rights of individuals are not buried beneath an avalanche of expediency. The Constitutional Alternative is such an option.

ACTION AND PURPOSE

Any government action represents an intrusion upon individual freedom. Yet government action is sometimes required to preserve that freedom. This fundamental paradox has been a source of tension and a focus of debate regarding the proper role of government for as long as humans have governed themselves. When our founding fathers grappled with this paradox, they did so while holding the conviction that the purpose of government was to serve the governed. With this thought in mind, they sought to create a union of peoples in which this purpose was reflected in the actions of government.

The evolution of national drug policy over the course of the last century represents a fundamental deviation from the principles upon which our nation was founded, much as was national alcohol policy during Prohibition. The Constitutional Alternative offers a means of returning the United States to the course charted by the founding fathers. Imperfect though it may be, the Constitutional Alternative will allow the people of America to adjust drug policy to fit their preferences and circumstances, to make the actions of government conform to its purpose as their servant, and so to make possible a more perfect union.

CHAPTER 13

····································

Challenges

NO POLICY IS WITHOUT ITS CHALLENGES. THE CONSTITUTIONAL ALTER-native does not promise perfection. It offers improvement. It will also produce innovation and experimentation as the states seek the drug policies most closely attuned to the wishes of their citizens. We already know that great harm has resulted from current drug policy. Can we be sure that the Constitutional Alternative will not lead to worse? In this chapter we show that even the worst-case scenarios under our proposal are better than current policy, because the Constitutional Alternative enables the people of America to adapt to changing circumstances in ways that are impossible under a federal monopoly.

PANDORA'S BOX?

Under the Constitutional Alternative, certain states will undoubtedly liberalize their drug policies. And some states may allow a degree of local control, as occurred with alcoholic beverages after Prohibition was repealed. In any event, decriminalization of certain drugs, especially marijuana, will probably spread beyond the states in which it now exists. Other states may fully legalize at least some psychoactives that are currently illegal. One of the principal challenges raised against legalizing drugs is that once done it could not be undone. As we saw in chapter 10, there are some merits to this fear in the case of a nationwide *federal* legalization of drugs. There are powerful reasons, however, why these arguments do not apply to the Constitutional Alternative.

First and foremost, there is little doubt that the changes occurring under the Constitutional Alternative will be carefully measured and paced. The rapid legalization of alcohol that occurred after the repeal of Prohibition took place because the people of America had recent prior experience with legal availability of that drug. Given their knowledge of methods that suited their preferences and circumstances, the citizens of the various states were both willing and able to move quickly to achieve their goals. By contrast, it has been more than fifty years since marijuana was legal in America, and nearly a century since cocaine and the opiates had that status. Voters will want to consider the range of alternatives available for different drugs, including the possibility of liberalizing the law for some and making life far harsher for the users and sellers of other drugs. It is one thing to propose radical change when most of the consequences will fall upon other people; it is quite another thing when it is your community's future that is under consideration.

Thus, it is unlikely that, say, State "Yes" will immediately legalize cocaine and opiates, just as it is improbable that State "No" will instantly impose the death penalty for dealers who sell drugs to minors. The changes initially occurring in both directions will be modest at first, as the citizens of each state move toward the mix of policies that best suit them. Residents of each jurisdiction will thus be able to observe the effects of their decisions as they proceed, and alter— or even reverse—course as conditions warrant.

Of course, citizens in other states will be observing too, noting the advantages and disadvantages of the different paths of progress. Some states, where current policy is furthest from voter preferences, will become leaders in change—although naturally the changes may be very different in different states. These states will become the controlled experimental laboratories that citizens in other states will be watching. Success or failure will send valuable information elsewhere—information not readily available with our current federal monopoly on policy. If, say, more liberal drug policy in one state results in unacceptable increases in drug use and addiction, the damage will be limited to that locale. If a get-tough state begins jailing huge numbers of its citizens, those who live elsewhere will see for themselves the downside of such policy. Thus, within each state, as well as across states, the people of America will not stray far from what is known, and so need not fear the unknown. As trial and error proceed and more is learned, change will proceed apace until all of the states have settled into the legal frameworks that suit their citizens the best.

The quiltlike pattern of laws likely to emerge under the Constitutional Alternative provides an additional safeguard against the prospect of "irreversible" change. Citizens who liberalize their drug laws and are unhappy with the result will be able to point to one or more other states where drug laws are different from theirs and more successful than theirs. Not only will such states provide the political impetus for reversal ("If they can control drugs, why can't we?") but they will provide the practical guides for policies that work.

One of the beauties of the Constitutional Alternative thus lies in its incremental nature. At no point will we have to venture too far off the beaten path, risking loss of our way. Yet change will continue to be possible, for experimentation and innovation will be extending the path, clearing the way into territory that now seems foreign and threatening. No one will be forced into the realm of the unknown, yet all will have the opportunity to expand the frontiers of government policies toward psychoactives.

WILL THE DRUG LORDS
OVERWHELM THE STATES?

Once the federal government is seemingly "out of the picture," some may wonder whether the drug lords will somehow "pick off" the states, one by one, turning them into their private realms of drug terror. After all, in the absence of uniform federal legislation, won't the jurisdictions that wish to keep drugs out be unable to cope with organized gangs armed with their Uzis and AK-47s?

Quite the contrary. In those jurisdictions where an altered drug policy leads to some type of government-monitored or government-controlled free market in certain psychoactives, the profits from the illegal drug trade will dry up. People only deal with Uzi-toting thugs when they have no alternatives. Hence, states that liberalize their drug laws will have nothing to fear from the gangs, which will simply go out of business.

The diversity of policy choices will help protect jurisdictions where get-tough policies are the preferred choice. No longer will the nationwide gangs be able to clone their operations from one state to another, which will remove their chief competitive advantage under current law.

Even more importantly, consider the likely characteristics of states where the citizens decide to pursue a true get-tough policy against drugs. On average, voters will be individuals who are willing to commit the resources needed to get the job done, so that officials will know that if they fail to hire the police and build the prisons that are needed, they'll soon be *former* officials. Moreover, these states are likely to be populated with people who have less than the average interest in consuming drugs. After all, people who grow marijuana or line up to snort coke at parties aren't likely to vote for get-tough drug policies! Thus, prospective dealers will face a double problem in such states: consumers who are, on average, not interested in buying their product, and a well-financed legal system that *is* interested in throwing them in jail. Carrying coals to Newcastle would likely be more profitable. At least there the police aren't arresting the coal merchants. After all, many people in America might consider Utah's extensive restrictions on alcohol sales to be "repressive." And indeed, if those restrictions were *imposed* on the citizens of wide-open Nevada, they would be repressive—and would also create a lucrative market for those who would evade the law. But remember that many of the residents of Utah are Mormons, who generally have little interest in consuming alcohol. Being unable to find an open liquor store is about as repressive for them as it is for a nonsmoker to be unable to find an open tobacconist.

Reinforcing the efforts of state and local officials will be the same help from the federal government that has been available in the alcohol business since the repeal of Prohibition. Under the Constitutional Alternative, the national government would retain the power to tax all psychoactives just as it currently taxes tobacco and alcohol products. Our proposal would also include a specific provision stating that the importation or transportation of psychoactives in violation of state laws would simultaneously be a violation of federal law. The federal government's resources could be called upon by any of the states that choose to maintain current drug policies or to intensify them. The big difference is that these federal resources will be targeted at the states that get tough, because no federal resources will be needed in states that liberalize their drug laws. Thus, the drug gangs trying to do business in get-tough states will face not only tougher state laws but also a more concentrated dose of federal law enforcement.*

THE POSSIBILITY OF INTERSTATE
DRUG SHIPMENTS

One seeming challenge to the Constitutional Alternative is the possibility that any given state could be inundated with drugs from other states where those drugs had been decriminalized or even legalized. Some interstate transfer of drugs will no doubt occur, just as there is today interstate movement of drugs. Nevertheless, there will be strong forces operating against such transfers.

Our alternative includes a provision for banning interstate activities—including drug shipments—in violation of state laws. Indeed, federal law-enforcement activities toward drugs will be devoted strictly toward enforcing this provision. Instead of being spread thinly across all fifty states and all conceivable forms of activities, federal resources will be targeted on one function—illegal interstate drug shipments—and on only a subset of the fifty states—those that decide to get tough. This targeting of federal resources, in conjunction with the added law-enforcement resources utilized in get-tough states, will be a formidable barrier to illegal interstate drug shipments. Ultimately, however, the most important protection for get-tough states may well come from states that *liberalize* their drug laws—a point to which we now turn.

TAXATION AND CONTRABAND

It may seem as if any states choosing legalization of drugs under the Constitutional Alternative could reap enormous tax revenues—large enough, perhaps, to induce them to act irresponsibly when deciding whether to get tough or liberalize their laws. Consider the arithmetic: It costs less than $1 to manufacture an amount of cocaine that carries a street price of $50. Thus, a state could legalize the drug, impose a

---

*You might wonder, What will happen to states that are caught in the middle between liberal states and get-tough states? The operative but misleading word here is "caught," because unlike today they won't be caught anywhere—all states will have the freedom to choose where they want to be on the spectrum of policy options.

tax of $49, and smile all the way to the bank. For large states, such as California or New York, arithmetic like this could seemingly produce tax revenues of several billion dollars a year. As it turns out, such taxation works fine in arithmetic, but not in practice.

To be sure, states that choose to legalize drugs would be able to use them as a source of tax revenue (as would the federal government). Nevertheless, although the potential tax revenues from legal drugs are substantial, they are not nearly as large as simple arithmetic would suggest. States hoping to tax currently illegal psychoactives will face three main constraints.

The first constraint on the tax rate will be the taxes levied in any other states that choose to legalize the drug in question. This is the same constraint faced by states when they tax cigarettes and alcohol today. When, say, the state of New York decides on the tax to be applied to a pack of cigarettes (currently thirty-three cents), it must take into account the fact that the state of North Carolina only imposes a tax of two cents on each pack of cigarettes. Given the differential in taxes between the states, it may pay tourists traveling north to load their station wagons or minivans with cheap cigarettes in North Carolina for (illegal) resale in New York. And if it pays tourists, it may pay bigger operators to load tractor-trailer trucks with low-tax cigarettes and sell them in high-tax states. Thus, although New York can successfully levy a tax of thirty-three cents a pack, it couldn't get away with a tax of, say, a dollar a pack.

The second constraint faced by states is the possibility of "home production" of untaxed units of the good. For example, a state that legalized marijuana and then tried to impose a tax of, say, $400 per ounce on it would likely find many consumers simply growing their own. This is not a realistic constraint in the case of tobacco taxation, because the process of curing tobacco is so cumbersome that, given the rate of taxation, it doesn't pay anyone to bother. This constraint is more relevant for alcohol taxation, however, since home production of beer and wine is relatively easy and inexpensive.

The third constraint on the taxing powers of states that legalize drugs is the existence of states that *don't* legalize drugs. Suppose one state decides to legalize marijuana, hoping to use the proceeds of the tax to fund more drug-treatment programs. Also assume that a neighboring state decides to get tough on marijuana, and manages to drive the price of marijuana to $300 per ounce. If the first state attempts to levy a tax of $400 per ounce on its legal marijuana, it faces the risk that the illegal suppliers selling pot next door will actually begin moving marijuana into the state where it is legal, simply because the tax in that state is so high.

Now, if we can figure this out, there is no doubt that officials in State "Yes" (the legal state) can too; thus, they will not attempt to levy a tax this high. But there is a more important point here for the officials in get-tough states worrying about marijuana being smuggled in from states where the drug is legal. The taxes being levied in legal states will make it less profitable to ship drugs from legal states to get-tough states. Moreover, the efforts of the legalizing state officials to make sure no one evades their taxes will help prevent the leakage of drug supplies from legal states to get-tough states. In effect, the incentive to collect taxes in legal states will reduce the enforcement costs of officials in get-tough states, thereby making their efforts to reduce consumption of the drug more successful!

WILL DRUG USE SKYROCKET?

One challenge that states wishing to liberalize drug laws face is the possibility of increased drug use. In states that decriminalize or legalize one or more drugs, the effective price (including legal risks) of using those drugs will decline. As with any good, when the price of a psychoactive falls, the quantity of it demanded by consumers will increase. Thus, we can expect higher total drug consumption in those jurisdictions that relax their drug laws.

The evidence from Prohibition suggests that we can expect two broad patterns of response in states that liberalize their drug laws. First, there will be a small rise in consumption, which will take place to some extent across the spectrum of consumers. People who had not used drugs will choose to use them, and those who already used them will consume more of them. Second, there will be a change in the nature of the drugs used and in the way in which they will be used. Specifically, there will be a move toward less intensive drug forms and less abusive patterns of use.

We also have evidence on this point from the Netherlands, as well as from ten states in the United States where marijuana has been decriminalized.[1] In the Netherlands, the consumption of marijuana, and particularly hashish, actually fell after these drugs were decriminalized.[2] In those states in the United States where there has been some form of decriminalization of marijuana, the evidence suggests little, if any, increase in total consumption of the drug.

Amsterdam, the capital of the Netherlands, is particularly instructive. Since the Dutch made Amsterdam a wide-open city for marijuana and hashish, the consumption of so-called "hard" drugs, such as heroin, appears to have declined. According to the *Los Angeles Times* foreign correspondent Rone Tempest, "In all the world, Amsterdam is one of the very few success stories in the struggle against hard drugs. Ridiculed for years as being too permissive, the Dutch experiment is getting a second look from other European countries these days largely because of its impressive reduction of addiction rates and extremely low incidence of AIDS among intravenous drug users."[3] Dutch authorities show a one-third reduction in heroin addiction as well as a slight decline in marijuana use. It is worth noting that these statistics are far more reliable than in other countries because heroin addicts are encouraged to surface in so-called "tolerance zones" in Holland, where their addiction is treated as a health problem rather than a criminal one. By at least one measure, the Dutch approach is paying some dividends. On a per-capita basis the Dutch drink as much alcohol as we do, and die about as often due to their consumption of tobacco. Yet the per capita incidence of death by drug overdose in that country is less than *half* of what it is in the United States.[4]

The evidence thus suggests that states choosing to liberalize their drug laws can expect at most a modest rise in drug consumption, as well as a significant switch from more intensive drugs to less intensive drugs. In some respects, however, this conclusion is beside the point. Under the Constitutional Alternative, there may well be jurisdictions in which drug use will increase. But it will increase only in those states where the citizens choose to let it rise through their selection of policies. It will not be forced on any state. Indeed, that is the key: Under the Constitutional Alternative, the citizens of every state will have the right to decide which set of policies best suits their preferences and circumstances.*

*It would be ironic—as well as distasteful to most of us—if the Constitutional Alternative had the effect of feathering the caps of the Colombian drug cartels. Fortunately, this is not something we need worry about. If any states decide to legalize cocaine or other coca-based products, there are 2.5 million square miles of land in South America on which coca bushes can be grown. The techniques for growing it are well known and simple, as is the manufacturing process. Indeed the pharmaceutical industry in the United States already manufactures cocaine legally, for use by physicians as a

ADDICT MIGRATION

One of the consequences—indeed, advantages—of the Constitutional Alternative is that the resulting diversity in state policies will produce self-selection among individuals. People who have an aversion to psychoactives and favor get-tough policies will tend to move to states where drug policies are harsh and drug consumption is costly. Conversely, people who wish to have the freedom to use drugs, or who oppose harsh penalties for persons who use drugs, will tend to move to those states that liberalize their drug laws. This process is fundamentally no different from the self-selection we see today regarding the other dimensions in which states and local jurisdictions differ. People who love city life move to urban areas, while those who prefer bucolic scenery tend to live in rural areas. Individuals who like to consume government-provided services and are willing to pay the high taxes needed to finance them tend to live in those states offering such a package. Other people have little interest in government services and are unwilling to pay the tax-price needed to support them; they thus tend to live in jurisdictions offering a selection of lower taxes and spending.

This process of self-selection leads to the concern that states that liberalize their drug laws will immediately become inundated with drug addicts who will send crime rates soaring and threaten the remaining citizenry. But, as we have noted before, radical and rapid liberalization—for example, the blanket legalization of all psychoactives—is unlikely in any state.* Initial steps are likely to be modest. As such, they are likely to produce benefits for the state, with little to fear in the way of costs. For example, consider a state that began a needle-exchange program for addicts. This would immediately confer substantial benefits by curtailing the spread of AIDS and other diseases among existing addicts. Of course, such a program could possibly encourage some addicts to immigrate. Yet it borders on the inconceivable that substantial numbers of heroin addicts would give up their regular sources of drug supply and move, say, halfway across

---

local anesthetic. In short, if a legal market for cocaine develops anywhere in the United States, there are ample supplies of the raw materials and the know-how to make the final product, without dealing with the Colombian cartels.

*And of course, if it *did* occur, it would only be because the citizens of that state had weighed the beneficial effects and adverse consequences and decided that they *wanted* such a change.

the country, simply to participate in a needle-exchange program. Hence the downside of such a program would be extremely minor, and in the meantime, the citizens of the state would have the opportunity to assess for themselves how well the program was working.

In the longer run, states will sort themselves along the spectrum of policies, adjusting those policies to fit the preferences of their citizens and to reflect the experience they have gained over time. Some states might well choose to aggressively expand methadone treatment programs as a way of combating heroin addiction. Some might even adopt the original British model that views addiction as a disease, which worked so well for so long. Some states might even choose to make all of the currently illegal psychoactives available by prescription, just as barbiturates, tranquilizers, and amphetamines are currently available.

Such schemes would surely attract users and even addicts from other states. Would this result in a surge in crime and an outbreak of drive-by shootings and gang warfare? The answer, unequivocally, is no. The link between addiction and addict crime is produced by the inordinate expense of the illegal drugs and the inordinate profits that accrue to the successful illegal suppliers of them. Once the drugs are available at something resembling the pharmaceutical cost of production, addicts will no longer have to commit crimes to finance their addictions, just as alcoholics, Valium addicts, and nicotine addicts generally do not have to commit crimes to finance their addictions. Moreover, once the addicts have access to inexpensive, legal supplies of their drugs, they no longer have to turn to the danger and expense of dealing with criminal suppliers. There will be no gangs supplying the drugs, because there will be no market for their wares. Moreover, there will be no incentive for would-be dealers to try to push their drugs on nonusers, because they can never match the prices of legal suppliers. In short, most of the principal adverse third-party effects of addiction would either be eliminated or sharply mitigated as a result of policies such as these.

There is no doubt that such policies would have to be developed and monitored carefully to minimize the "leakage" of drugs from legal channels to illegal channels. This, of course, is no different from what must be done today to reduce the diversion of prescription psychoactives into illegal uses. Legal addicts are still addicts, and as such are unlikely ever to become pillars of the community or leading business executives as long as they continue consuming their drug of choice. Nevertheless, as both the British experience and the history of methadone programs demonstrate, many addicts can become productive, law-abiding members of society when given access to the proper programs. Conceivably, many jurisdictions may choose to accept somewhat larger numbers of addicts in return for less of the crime, disease, and death that characterize today's federal drug policies.

WHAT ABOUT CRACK?

Some may worry that any liberalization of state laws under the Constitutional Alternative will lead to an increase in the use of hard drugs such as crack and heroin. In fact, the opposite will occur. Recall, from chapter 7, the Bad-Drug Theorem: When drugs are illegal, more damaging drugs drive out less damaging drugs. In jurisdictions that liberalize their drug laws, this process will reverse itself: There will be a move toward lower-intensity and less potent psychoactives. The evidence on this from Prohibition is unequivocal: As soon as Repeal occurred, the consumption of hard liquor dropped by more than *two-thirds*. In addition, there was a massive shift from the higher-potency "moonshine" liquor toward the lower-proof varieties of hard liquor. And as consumers switched back to beer, their alcohol of choice before Prohibition, even wine consumption dropped sharply.[5]

The vast majority of all people, addicts and alcoholics included, do not consume psychoactives as a means of destroying their lives. Nor do they consume them intending to become addicted to them. Abuse and addiction are the adverse consequences that sometimes occur when psychoactives are consumed, just as broken bones are the adverse consequences that sometimes occur when people go skiing. They are the survival-threatening features of the behavior in question, not the functional or pleasurable features that fundamentally motivate the behavior. The most important reason for the spread of crack and of the injection of heroin is that when opiates and cocaine are illegal, low-potency versions of these drugs become extremely expensive. Thus, consumers are induced—by the law—to switch to more intensive and more harmful drug forms and delivery systems. Absent the incentives created by current policy, consumers will revert to the modes of consumption that are less damaging.

There is nothing—except the law—that is intrinsic to opiates, or cocaine, or marijuana, that makes them particularly suitable for consumption in high-potency forms using highly efficient delivery systems. Caffeine, nicotine, and ethyl alcohol all can be injected intravenously to produce extremely potent psychoactive effects with very small doses. The legal nature of nicotine, caffeine, and alcohol enables people to take lower-potency drugs using less intensive delivery systems. Relaxing the laws against currently illegal psychoactives would induce consumers of these drugs to modify their usage in the same way.

Neither the smoking of crack nor the injection of heroin will disappear in states that liberalize their drug laws. After all, despite the availability of low-tar, low-nicotine cigarettes, some people continue to consume high-potency, unfiltered cigarettes. And despite the availability of beer, some people continue to drink hard liquor. The overwhelming majority of individuals, however, do not want the "big bang" from their psychoactives; they want the pleasurable effects at the least possible cost. In states that liberalize their drug laws, individuals will find that high-intensity drug forms and delivery systems no longer satisfy this condition. Crack will go the way of 150-proof "white lightning"—a relic of another time and another law.

STILL WORRIED ABOUT CRACK?

Heroin addicts can be maintained on regular daily doses of heroin or its synthetic substitute methadone, and can thereby lead productive lives. But crack, in the minds of many, is different. Addicts binge on it, smoking more and more until they either fall unconscious or simply run out of money. Users of crack do not so much consume the drug as they are consumed by it; partly for this reason, it is the drug that the most vicious gangs choose to sell, hoping their customers will become addicted to it.

Crack is among the most harmful and dangerous drugs ever devised by man, a fact that is coming to be recognized by a growing number of drug consumers. A similar pattern happened with PCP (angel dust), which enjoyed a sharp rise in popularity during the 1970s. As knowledge of the harmful effects of PCP spread, consumers and potential customers began staying away from it in droves. In the parlance of the street, crack is beginning to "tame" users, inducing would-be consumers to shy away from it, and compelling more of those addicted to it to seek treatment.

Moreover, and just as important, the flexibility of the Constitutional Alternative is ideally suited to deal with singularly dangerous drugs like crack. In states that liberalize their drug laws, considerable law-enforcement resources will be freed up from their duties in the war against less damaging psychoactives. These resources can then be targeted toward drugs such as crack, enhancing the effectiveness of efforts to reduce the consumption of these drugs. Just as citizens will be able to choose get-tough policies in general, citizens will be able to choose which drugs to hit the hardest.

THE COST OF GETTING TOUGH

Getting tough on drugs won't be easy or cheap. After all, the federal government is already spending more than $10 billion a year on a policy of not getting tough. Nevertheless, state and local governments would have some great advantages over the federal government in implementing a tough, cost-effective policy against drugs.

Without a doubt, the actual taxpayer cost of a get-tough policy would be far lower under the control of state and local officials than under federal control. State and local governments are much more closely scrutinized by their taxpayers than is the federal government, and won't be able to engage in counterproductive ploys such as buyer-oriented enforcement. State and local officials will be forced to focus on cost-effective enforcement, rather than public relations gimmicks. This will produce more enforcement for the money, thus reducing the costs of getting tough.

The greater scrutiny to which state and local officials are subjected is nowhere better illustrated than in the case of budget deficits. Year after year, the federal government runs huge budget deficits. Congressmen make speeches about the deficit, and raise our taxes—supposedly to reduce the deficit—but the federal debt just keeps on rising. By contrast, state and local governments only rarely spend more than their receipts, and when they do, the politicians who are responsible either fix things quickly or find themselves out of a job. In 1988 the governor of Massachusetts, Michael Dukakis, was the toast of his state and the nation as the Democratic Party's nominee for president. Less than a year later, he was forced to announce that he wouldn't even be running for reelection as governor. Why? Because he had been unable to get Massachusetts' budget crisis under control, and the voters of the state had turned against him. When drug policy is actually in the hands of state and local officials, those officials will be forced to do things right, or they too will face the prospect of political unemployment. This in turn can only mean more efficient, more effective drug law enforcement.

There is a second element of the Constitutional Alternative that will reduce the taxpayer cost in states that get tough. Under the current federal monopoly on drug policy, the uniformity in policy across the nation means that drug users have no particular incentive to avoid any specific state. When there is diversity of policies across states, drug users will tend to gravitate toward states where drug policies are liberal and avoid—like the plague—states that impose harsh penalties on users. Fundamentally, such a process is no different than the current tendency of people who like sunshine and warm weather to move to states that have warm, sunny climates. The diversity brought about through the Constitutional Alternative will act much like a pressure-relief valve; over time, users will tend to self-select themselves to states where the cost of their consumption is lowest. This in turn will reduce the pressure on, and costs of, drug enforcement in states that decide to get tough. Again, more efficient and more effective policy will be the ultimate result.

THE PROBLEM OF THIRD-PARTY EFFECTS

The Constitutional Alternative does not in any way eliminate the possibility that those who use certain psychoactives will act in ways that harm others. We currently face a serious problem on the nation's highways because of individuals who operate motor vehicles under the influence of alcohol. How do we avoid adding to the carnage by putting a bunch of pot smokers and cocaine users out on the highways, or in the cockpits of airplanes, or at the helms of oil tankers?

The Constitutional Alternative could not in itself handle this problem. Rather, problems such as aggressive, antisocial behavior, or driving under the influence of drugs, must be dealt with by the penalties that are imposed on such behavior. We currently have laws that punish those who drink and drive. Making those penalties harsher would reduce the number of people who persist in such behavior. There is no reason we shouldn't have the same laws (or even stricter ones) that apply to individuals' behavior while under the influence of other drugs. Clearly, people cannot drive drunk if they do not first drink. Nevertheless, people can, and most often do, drink without then driving. Irresponsible behavior has always been, and will always be, a problem in any society. The central issue is the strength of the signal that society wants to send to these irresponsible individuals. Harsher penalties, meted out more consistently, will reduce the incidence of driving under the influence of alcohol or any other psychoactive.

There is no reason that a state that legalizes drug x, for example, could not mandate a presumption of guilt if there is even the slightest trace of drug x in the bloodstream of a motor vehicle (or oil tanker) operator. There is no commandment, for example, that says that we must accept a substantial concentration of a drug in someone's blood (as most states do with alcohol) before we can declare that person guilty of "operating under the influence." If specific behavior—such as the creation of adverse third-party effects—is the concern, then the appropriate policy is to target penalties on that behavior, not on some other behavior.

DRUG ADVERTISING

Some concerned citizens fear that any jurisdiction which decriminalizes or legalizes any currently illegal psychoactives would be inundated with advertising. Advertising presumably would induce more people, including children, to try psychoactives, resulting in additional use, abuse, and addiction.

There are two areas of concern here. First, there is the matter of advertising on television and radio, whose transmission crosses state lines. Clearly, states that wish to get tough on drugs will object strenuously to national advertising of drugs that are illegal in their states. This is one of those rare instances in which, for technological reasons, the monopoly power of the federal government might have to be exercised. Just as cigarette advertising is now banned on the airwaves, the federal government could ban advertising of other psychoactives.

The second issue concerns print advertising, such as billboards and newspapers, which are chiefly intrastate. Many states currently impose restrictions on advertising by distributors of alcohol (retailers and wholesalers) within their boundaries, and similar restrictions could be imposed on distributors of other psychoactives. Whether all advertising of newly legalized psychoactives could be banned is a considerably thornier legal question that ultimately might have to be decided in the courts. The important point to keep in mind, however, is this: Under the Constitutional Alternative, the states retain the ultimate weapon. They can simply ban the psychoactive in question, leaving them no worse off than presently. This weapon is precisely the feature of the Constitutional Alternative that gives the citizens of every state the power to control their own destiny, rather than having it controlled from the corridors of Washington, D.C.

A NO VOTE FOR THE STATUS QUO

There are, no doubt, other conceivable challenges to the Constitutional Alternative besides the ones we have mentioned here. Indeed, the Constitutional Alternative would undoubtedly be vigorously challenged by the bureaucrats and politicians in charge of current policy in Washington, D.C. After all, no monopoly likes competition, even when it is a government monopoly. But remember this essential point: Every public policy carries with it costs and benefits, including the status quo. Rational observers of the current policy know that its costs far exceed its benefits. The Constitutional Alternative has costs associated with it as well, but this alone is no reason to blindly opt for the status quo. Only by examining the *net* benefits of all possibilities can we reach a policy that allows us to undo drugs and thus retake America. The balance-sheet results favor the Constitutional Alternative.

CHAPTER 14

····························

We, the People

OUR GOVERNMENT WAS FORMED TO SERVE THE PEOPLE, NOT TO MAS-
ter them—to enhance our liberty, not to diminish it. In setting drug
policy, the government as servant has two tasks. First, it must protect
our liberties from those who would infringe upon them by consuming
psychoactives irresponsibly; as normally conceived, individual freedom does not include the right to inflict harm on innocent third
parties. Second, if individuals inflict harm on themselves or diminish
their own freedom by their consumption of psychoactives—if they
abuse drugs or become addicted—any action by the government
should reduce the damage, not exacerbate it. Whether or not one
believes that the government has a role in protecting self from self,
there is surely no justification for government actions that add to
self-inflicted damage.

Our current policies have things exactly backwards, and we the
people have failed to accept the responsibility for the resulting mal-
aise. Today's policies do not protect the responsible from the irresponsible. They do not even *distinguish* between them. People who
do not use drugs are forced to accept the higher taxes, loss of civil
liberties, fear of crime, and other adverse consequences of policies
directed against those who do use drugs. Yet today's policies are
directed against *any* use of drugs, rather than against *irresponsible*
use, so those who use drugs have no incentive to use them responsibly.
Moreover, these same policies encourage users to consume drug forms
and use drug delivery systems that produce more harm to self, and
increase the risk of freedom-destroying addiction. In every dimension,

current policies deprive us of liberty, without freeing us from the adverse consequences of psychoactives. The government has become our master, reversing what was intended by the founding fathers and upending the hopes of today's citizens. We the people must take control of our lives and our destinies, by taking control of our drug policy.

THE NUMBERS GAME

The blurring between form and substance that pervades all of government is nowhere more apparent than in the federal government's war on drugs. The drug wars have become a numbers game. We are barraged by drug-war numbers every day: billions in expenditures, thousands of arrests, millions of dollars in drugs seized, hundreds of millions in assets forfeited. The federal war of numbers is an attempt to mask the reality of failure with the appearance of success. Rising arrests and drug seizures don't mean we are winning the war on drugs, but that there are more users out there to be arrested and more drugs to be seized. Rising expenditures and asset seizures don't mean that the drug crisis is lessening; they mean that it is getting worse. Nevertheless, federal bureaucrats and politicians continue to bombard us with claims that if we just "tweak" federal drug laws, by spending more money and passing more laws, we are going to find the right solution, as if this "tweaking" resembled the manipulations performed by a TV technician to adjust the color on a slightly out-of-whack television set. Nothing could be further from the truth. No amount of tweaking of current federal drug policy will make the slightest bit of difference in the long run. The federal technicians have been tweaking for eighty years, and the picture just keeps getting worse.

As long as there is a federal monopoly on drug policy, the politicians in smaller jurisdictions—states, counties, and municipalities— can hide behind the veil of federal legislation. But when policy is truly in the hands of state and local officials, they have nowhere to hide. Local chiefs of police, mayors, and even governors who claim that they are solving their jurisdiction's problems won't last very long if their "proof" consists simply of numbers. Individual voters care little about the rhetoric of politicians when the subject matter affects them directly and importantly. No local politician can stay in office long by playing the numbers game that national politicians do.

The voter on the home front is unconcerned with political claims about inputs. Output is desired, and output is judged on rational, tangible criteria. The local voter cares not a whit how many cubic yards of garbage the city carted off last year; he cares that *his* garbage was picked up. Speeches about the gleaming fleet of snow plows purchased by the county or state don't garner votes; winter streets that are clear of snow and ice do.

When the drug policy buck stops at the state and local level, voters will gauge its success or failure by how their lives have been affected. How many break-ins have occurred in my neighborhood over the last year? Do I hear gunfire and police sirens at night? Is my child hooked on drugs? The answers to questions like these reflect the true output of government drug policy, not reams of numbers.

People want action from their state and local officials, not speeches, and action is what we will get with the Constitutional Alternative.

WHY THE FEDERAL MONOPOLY MUST END

The continuation of a federally mandated policy on drugs cannot work today any more than it worked with alcohol sixty years ago. There are simply too many conflicting preferences and circumstances to produce a national compromise that will achieve our goals and retain our liberty. Only action at the state and local level, unfettered yet supported by federal resources, can accomplish what we all seek— freedom from the adverse effects of psychoactives and from the failed policies that promise what they cannot deliver.

The federal government has taken control of and guides the direction of all drug policy in the United States, and it is the federal monopoly on drug policy that is the root of our drug policy failures. We have laws against monopolies for good reason—they do not serve the interests of the people. We also know the beneficial consequences that arise when monopolies are broken up. These same beneficial consequences would occur if the stranglehold of the federal monopoly over drug policy were lifted by implementing the Constitutional Alternative.

One way the failure of past government bans on psychoactives is sometimes interpreted is that government control of psychoactives is largely impossible. Following this view, one might conclude that the best role of government regarding psychoactives is no role at all. We would suggest an alternative view of past and present government efforts to deal with psychoactives.

In the course of 10,000 years of human use of psychoactives, individuals have developed an enormous capacity to both adapt themselves to their psychoactives, and to adapt their psychoactives to suit themselves. In doing so, people have been forced to confront the reality of psychoactives—their peculiar blend of beneficial effects and adverse consequences—in their dealings with them. Throughout much of this process, governments have left individuals in peace to make their choices. Governments have, in effect, played a remarkably minor role in the process of human adaptation to psychoactives, and as a consequence have assimilated almost none of the expertise accumulated by their citizens. Typically, governments have either ignored psychoactives (except as a source of tax revenue), or they have blindly prohibited their use. Rarely have they ventured to understand the psychoactives involved, or the relationship of their citizens with those psychoactives. Given this fact, governments have repeatedly placed themselves in the same box: either do nothing, or permit nothing.

In the course of the last century, government—most notably the *federal* government—has chosen to take an increasingly active role in making choices about psychoactives. Often, and particularly in America, the role chosen by the federal government has involved an abrupt about-face—from policies that permit complete freedom of choice to policies that permit no freedom of choice. The middle ground, where diversity, moderation, and balance hold sway, has been largely ignored, even though it is this middle ground that has characterized human adaptation to psychoactives. Until and unless government begins to learn what people already know, drug policy will degrade rather than improve the psychoactive choices made by its citizens. Blanket attempts at the national level to eliminate the use of psychoactives failed with alcohol in America 60 years ago, just as they failed with caffeine in Arabia 1,000 years ago. Today's federal policies toward psychoactives are nothing more than a repeat performance of the failed policies of the past. Unless the American people change the way drug policy is *made* in our land, the adverse consequences of that policy will continue to outweigh its beneficial effects, and we, the people, shall be the losers.

THE ONLY ALTERNATIVE IS THE CONSTITUTIONAL ALTERNATIVE

The Constitutional Alternative provides the vehicle the American people have been seeking to solve the drug crisis, but we must act now to take control. Our founding fathers reserved the unenumerated powers to the states and to the people because they understood the dangers of powerful central government. Yet many of these same powers have been usurped by the federal government in the war on drugs, producing exactly the damage that the founders of our nation feared.

Government action inherently encroaches on individual freedom. Yet there are instances in which encroachment in one area can produce an enhancement of our freedom in others. The tragedy of the federal monopoly on drug policy is that it has intruded upon our freedom in many areas, without enhancing it elsewhere. Only when the power over drug policy is returned to state and local governments will competition among governments produce outcomes in accord with our aspirations rather than the whims of bureaucrats and politicians in Washington, D.C.

The tyranny of the majority so feared by our founding fathers has become, in federal drug policy, the tyranny of compromise. We are an enormously diverse nation of peoples, united in our desire to balance the beneficial effects of drugs against their adverse consequences, yet divided in our beliefs about the proper role of government in promoting that balance. The federal monopoly on drug policy has destroyed this balance we seek, by forging a political compromise which suits no one, yet is forced upon everyone. No government as large and as distant as the federal government can hope to produce the adaptability and innovation which has helped make America great, and which is desperately needed now to formulate beneficial drug policies. No one—including us—knows what *the* correct drug policy is, because there is almost certainly no single drug policy best for all Americans. Only by determining these policies at the level of government that most closely responds to the diverse preferences and circumstances of Americans shall we discover what truly works.

WHAT YOU CAN DO

If you believe, as we do, that the monopoly stranglehold of the federal government on drug policy is not what is right for America, you can do something. The Constitutional Alternative is not a pie-in-the-sky political concept, but a constitutionally permissible policy. Unlike the case of alcohol, which had been subjected to a constitutionally based prohibition, no repeal amendment would need consideration, nor would Congress even have to repeal the Controlled Substances Act of 1970. The 1970 act is founded on the power given Congress under the Commerce Clause of the U.S. Constitution. Congress may choose to exercise that power by *concurrently* sharing it with the states or by *delegating* the power to the states. All that we need is an amendment to the 1970 act that expressly indicates a policy of delegation. (See Appendix B for a detailed legal analysis.)

What you can do is write to your senators, your members of the House of Representatives, and your governor, indicating your desire to end the federal government monopoly on drug policy in the United States. Don't buy the argument that altering the Controlled Substances Act of 1970 would lead to uncontrolled drug use in the United States. Presently, the states already have concurrent power with the federal government to control drug use. The existing state laws which regulate drug use would be unaffected by a change in federal legislation.

NOW THE FUTURE CAN BE BRIGHTER

When we throw off the shackles of uniform national drug control, our world will not be miraculously transformed overnight. The drug crises we face will not disappear the day we adopt the Constitutional Alternative. The entire generation of inner-city residents that has been criminalized will not immediately turn to legal endeavors. Crime will not plummet instantly when the Constitutional Alternative is implemented, and the spread of AIDS will not halt. All gangs will not immediately disband, nor will all crack houses miraculously disappear. The changes will be gradual, but they will commence, as the peoples of our fifty states begin the process of reformulating drug policies to suit their preferences and circumstances. These changes will be in the right direction, in the direction of a better America, an America that will reflect the diversity of our population. But these changes can only come about if we the people accept our responsibility and implement the Constitutional Alternative.

The time is now to undo drugs. The time is now to retake America.

PART FOUR

APPENDICES

APPENDIX A

Psychohistory

PSYCHOACTIVES ARE CHEMICALS THAT AFFECT THE BRAIN, YIELDING changes in emotions, perceptions, and behavior.[1] The most widely used psychoactives—caffeine, nicotine, and alcohol—are an integral part of the lives of many Americans. All of the psychoactives can produce beneficial effects, ranging from enhanced stamina to pain relief; yet all are potential sources of adverse consequences, including death. It is the prospect of the positive that induces humans to use them, and the existence of the negative that engenders government's interest in controlling that use.

NATURE'S FINEST

We do not know exactly when man first began using psychoactives, nor which proved to be his first drug of choice. Archaeological evidence and historical accounts suggest that either alcohol or opium are the most likely candidates, and that both were first used more than 10,000 years ago.

When a mixture of barley and water is left exposed to airborne yeasts for a week or more, the ensuing fermentation produces what we now call beer. If raw fruit or fruit juice stands long enough, fermentation yields wine. Eventually, some combination of hunger, thirst, and curiosity drove Neolithic agriculturists to sample these frothy, foul-smelling concoctions, and so alcohol entered man's culture. By the time of the Egyptian invention of the calendar in 4241 B.C., beer and wine had become permanent fixtures of society. When distilled spirits (hard liquor) made their first appearance some 5,000 years later, public drunkenness and the ravages of alcoholism were already well-known phenomena. Distilled spirits proved to be a far more efficient means of delivering the psychoactive punch of alcohol, and so amplified both the pleasant and unpleasant consequences of its consumption. The gradual growth in the popularity of spirits, which accelerated rapidly in the eighteenth and nineteenth centuries, also spread public awareness about the potential dangers associated with acute and chronic alcohol abuse.

The opium poppy probably began its role in man's life as a food source, for the 30,000 or so tiny black seeds in each seed capsule are both tasty and nutritious. The seeds contain small amounts of morphine (the active alkaloid in opium), but the poppy did not achieve psychoactive prominence until man learned that, during a critical ten- to fourteen-day period in the flower's growing cycle, the capsule walls become laden with a morphine-rich juice called opium. The consumption of opium soon spread throughout the civilized world, and by at least 3,500 years ago, opium was widely recognized as a tranquilizer, a soporific, a painkiller without peer, and as a source of considerable recreational pleasure. Among its attributes, opium had the great advantage that it could be eaten as a solid, dissolved (for example, in alcohol) and drunk as a potion, or heated to the point that its vapors could be inhaled. This not only provided a variety of convenient means of ingestion but also allowed fairly precise regulation of dosage size.

By the nineteenth century, opium was viewed in Europe and the United States as a veritable panacea, effective in treating everything from teething pains to tuberculosis, as well as a potential source of recreational pleasure. Morphine was first isolated from raw opium early in the century, and the subsequent perfection of the hypodermic syringe resulted in morphine's widespread use as a painkiller on the battlefields of the Civil War. Tens of thousands of veterans returned home addicted to the drug, and while many were able to satisfy their craving with morphine pills or potions, some found that only the needle would do. By the time heroin was refined from morphine late in the nineteenth century, there was widespread awareness that regular use of opiates could lead to addiction, and both physicians and the general public were approaching their use with increasing care.

While alcohol and opiates derived from plants that had prior roles as foodstuffs, caffeine and cocaine both originally came prepackaged as food. Caffeine from coffee is thought to have first been used by humans about 1,000 years ago in Arabia and Ethiopia. The stimulating effects of coffee were soon appreciated by Mohammedans as an aid to staying awake in lengthy religious ceremonies, and the use of coffee spread rapidly throughout the Middle East. Early European explorers and traders who pursued land routes to the East brought coffee home with them, as well as tea from China, and caffeine was soon established as a regular element in the psychoactive diet of many Europeans.

Although coffee flourishes in many South American climes, it was the coca shrub that provided New World inhabitants with their chief psychoactive stimulant. Indeed, the leaves of the coca bush had been chewed by Andean peasants for at least 4,000 years before the early Spanish explorers arrived in South America. Coca leaves have nutritional value as food, and the cocaine alkaloid in them acts as a powerful appetite suppressant, an effective antidote for altitude sickness, a potent local anesthetic, and a central-nervous-system stimulant. It is little wonder that the Incas revered coca leaves as a gift of the gods. The Spaniards eschewed the use of coca, perhaps because the shrub's leaves played a central role in the pagan religious ceremonies of the Incas, though they quickly learned the usefulness of coca in exploiting the indigenous population: The shrub's leaves not only suppressed the appetites of hungry slaves but also stimulated them to work more.

The chewing of coca leaves never became popular in Europe or America, and it was not until after cocaine was chemically extracted from the coca leaf in 1844 that the drug achieved popularity outside of South America. A host of late-nineteenth-century patent medicines eventually incorporated cocaine (often dissolved in alcohol) as the principal active ingredient, and the drug was even contained in the original formulation of Coca-Cola. Reportedly, Coca-Cola initially contained roughly sixty milligrams of cocaine per eight-ounce serving, about the same as found in a modern intranasal dose.* In the 1880s, Sigmund Freud published lavish praise of cocaine's ability to relieve both depression and fatigue, but he and other physicians soon realized that some of the drug's users became hopelessly addicted to it. The already growing public concern over opiate addiction meant

*In 1903 the Coca-Cola Company started using caffeine instead as the chief psychoactive in its product.

that once the words "cocaine" and "addiction" came together in the same sentence, most consumers began to look elsewhere for stimulation. Cocaine continued to be used on a small scale as a work-enhancing stimulant and as a recreational psychoactive, but by the turn of the century, it largely had been discarded by mainstream America.

The other principal psychoactives in human life have little or no connection with food, and (with the exception of marijuana) the plants which contain them have little role in our existence except as sources of psychoactives. Nicotine, for example, has been used as a psychoactive by the native peoples of the Americas for perhaps 8,000 years, despite the fact that the drug's toxicity makes the tobacco plant largely inedible. Christopher Columbus introduced tobacco to the Old World, after watching the Indians set fire to rolls of tobacco leaf and "drink" the smoke. The inedible nature of the plant proved no impediment to its rapid acceptance by Europeans, as they quickly learned that nicotine is perhaps the most addictive psychoactive known to man. They chewed it, they snorted it, and they smoked it; they carried it without fail on their voyages of exploration; they used it as a principal trade good; and they planted it in every colony in which it would grow. Mostly they found that if they could overcome the initial nausea and dizziness produced by its use, they simply could not get along without it. Within short order, nicotine had joined alcohol and caffeine as one of civilization's principal psychoactives of choice.

Marijuana parallels tobacco in that smoking is the principal means of extracting the main psychoactive, delta-9-tetrahydrocannabinol (THC), but marijuana users also eat the plant and drink tealike potions made from it. Marijuana is not only a source of a popular, potent psychoactive, but of a strong fiber used in making linen, canvas, and rope. The psychoactive properties of marijuana (and its potent derivative, hashish) have been enjoyed in India and China for at least 4,000 years and were appreciated in the Middle and Near East well before the time of Christ. The plant has been cultivated in Europe for more than 2,500 years, chiefly as a source of fiber, and has been used as a recreational psychoactive there for at least five centuries.

Spanish explorers introduced marijuana to South America in the sixteenth century. The Jamestown settlers brought its seeds to Virginia in 1611. The plant was an economically important source of fiber throughout the American colonies, and its cultivation was strongly encouraged by King George III. By the nineteenth century, the medicinal value of marijuana was widely recognized in Europe and America, and physicians recommended it as a remedy for insomnia and anxiety, as a pain reliever, an antidepressant, and as a treatment for the delirium tremens produced by alcohol withdrawal.

Marijuana and hashish were modestly popular as recreational psychoactives in Europe during the nineteenth century, but Americans preferred the effects of alcohol—at least until 1920, when Prohibition reduced alcohol's availability and raised its price. Marijuana continued to be grown as a source of fiber in the United States through the end of World War II, and as a result, it has established itself as a hardy weed that thrives throughout the country. In 1969 it was estimated that in Nebraska alone, some 156,000 acres of land were infested with "weed" marijuana—enough, in principle, to yield 600 joints a year for every man, woman, and child in America.[2]

Hallucinations are among the psychoactive effects produced by marijuana, but individuals whose principal interest lies in such effects are more likely to turn to the peyote cactus, or to any of several varieties of mushrooms. There is archaeological evidence that hallucinogenic mushrooms were used in Central America more than 5,000 years ago, and both psilocybin-containing mushrooms and peyote appear to have been used by the Aztecs long before Columbus's first voyage. A host of North and Central American Indian tribes incorporated peyote into their religious ceremonies, and many members of the Native American Church of North America use it for religious purposes even today. By and large, however, hallucinogens were ignored by Europeans and by most Americans until well into the twentieth century, when potent and readily available hallucinogens became some of the fruits born of modern chemistry.

HUMAN REFINEMENTS

Man's desire to improve on nature knows no bounds, and his approach to psychoactives has been no exception. The process of distillation first enhanced the potency of naturally fermented beer and wine more than 1,000 years ago. The invention of the hypodermic syringe and the isolation of morphine, heroin, and cocaine in the eighteenth century heightened the psychoactive punch of both the opium poppy and the coca bush. But it has really been only in the twentieth century that man's laboratories have proven to be in the same league with nature.

Anxiety and insomnia are two of the afflictions for which humans have most often sought relief, and it is fitting that the first psychoactives born of twentieth-century chemistry were the barbiturates, introduced in 1903. Like the opiates and alcohol, the barbiturates are central-nervous-system depressants. In small doses, they act to relieve anxiety; in moderate doses, they induce sleep. The popularity of the barbiturates grew rapidly after World War I, and by the late 1930s, literally billions of doses of them were being prescribed by physicians in America every year.

The barbiturates were joined after World War II by the tranquilizers and the hypnotics. Although the basic chemical formulation of these two psychoactives differ from that of barbiturates (and from each other), they too are central-nervous-system depressants, useful in relieving anxiety and inducing sleep. The most widely used class of these drugs comprises the benzodiazepams, which include Valium, Librium, and Xanax. During the 1970s, Valium was the single most widely prescribed drug of any type in the world. Methadone, a synthetic opiate developed during World War II, is also properly classed as a central-nervous-system depressant. Best known for its use in treating heroin addicts, methadone not only relieves the post-withdrawal syndrome—anxiety, depression, and craving—experienced by addicts for months or years after giving up heroin but also blocks the euphoric effects of heroin.

The similarities between the man-made depressants and the naturally occurring depressants extend beyond the fact that all are useful in relieving anxiety and inducing sleep. For example, all of them have been used both medicinally and recreationally, and all can be administered in small doses over extended periods of time without producing either physical damage or addiction. Despite this, millions of people are in fact addicted to both naturally occurring and man-made depressants, and abrupt cessation of their use by an addict produces acute physical symptoms—which can even result in death. All of the depressants are capable of producing death due to acute overdose, although only alcohol is known to cause death due to chronic (long-term) abuse.

If "downers" are most people's preferred psychoactives, "uppers" run a close second. The most important and widely used man-made stimulants are the various amphetamines, first marketed in 1932.

Like caffeine and cocaine, amphetamines produce euphoria, enhanced mental alertness, and increased physical stamina—which helps explain why they were distributed to both Allied and Axis combat forces during World War II. The effects of amphetamines are relatively prolonged, lasting six to eight hours or more, compared to the effects of cocaine, which are largely dissipated after thirty to sixty minutes. As with caffeine and cocaine, the amphetamines are used recreationally, and some users become addicted to them. And as with all psychoactives, injecting or smoking amphetamines—methods of administration that have become more common in recent years—raises the risk of addiction.

The final broad category of test-tube psychoactives are the hallucinogens, the best known of which is d-lysergic acid diethylamide, or LSD, discovered in 1938 and first used by a human in 1943. The chief effect of LSD is much like that of naturally occurring hallucinogens: extreme distortion of visual perceptions, ranging from the appearance of multicolored geometric shapes which do not exist to fantastic changes in the shapes and colors of objects that do exist. Although LSD has found some use in treating psychiatric patients, and has even been considered for use as a chemical weapon in time of war, it has achieved its fame as a recreational drug. LSD has no appreciable adverse physiological effects, although it sometimes produces psychological trauma, particularly if administered to individuals without their prior knowledge. Typically, users of LSD ingest it only at intervals of a week or more, and discontinue all usage after a matter of months or a few years with the result that there are apparently no known instances of addiction to it.

Phencyclidine, or PCP, is another man-made psychoactive which produces hallucinations, although it, like nicotine, also produces some effects that mimic stimulants and some that mimic depressants. PCP was originally developed as a surgical anesthetic, but its medical use in humans was stopped after it was found to produce severe psychological trauma in patients. Now used by some veterinarians to sedate large animals, PCP has a small recreational following among humans, despite the fact that, in the words of one pharmacologist, it "produces negative effects in 100 percent of the intoxications and positive effects only 60 percent of the time."[3]

THE ROLE OF GOVERNMENT

Although humans have demonstrated an unerring interest in using psychoactives, our governments have, until recently, displayed a remarkably uneven interest in our patterns of use. One of the first psychoactives which drew the government's attention was caffeine. Not long after coffee was initially used in Arabia, it was declared to be an "intoxicating" beverage, whose consumption was prohibited under Islamic law. The sale of coffee was forbidden, supplies of it were burned, and those who violated the law were punished. When coffee was subsequently introduced to Egypt, another round of "caffeine wars" broke out, with supplies of coffee again subject to seizure and immolation. In neither country did the efforts at prohibition work to quell demand; indeed, the use of coffee spread even more rapidly after the ill-fated attempts to prohibit it were imposed. Caffeine became, and remains today, the most widely consumed psychoactive in the Middle East.

Nicotine has also been the object of prohibition efforts by governments. In the century after Columbus returned from the New World with tobacco, the use of, and addiction to, nicotine spread rapidly around the world. There followed numerous efforts to quash the "evil weed." In 1603 the Japanese prohibited the use of tobacco, and repeatedly increased the penalties for violating the ban. Nevertheless, smoking continued to grow in popularity, and by 1625 the Japanese government abandoned its prohibition efforts. By the middle of the seventeenth century, bans on the use of tobacco were in place in Bavaria, Saxony, Zurich, Turkey, and Russia. Despite punishments that ranged from confiscation of property to death, the use of tobacco continued to spread in these lands, and so the bans were rescinded. Early in the twentieth century, the use of cigarettes spread rapidly, and several state governments in the United States attempted (without success) to ban them. The bans ultimately ended, and state and local governments in the United States now confine themselves to restrictions on the minimum age at which tobacco may be purchased, and the locations where tobacco may be smoked.

Government efforts to prohibit the consumption of alcohol, opiates, marijuana and hashish, and hallucinogens—psychoactives now portrayed as the most insidious and debilitating—did not begin systematically until well into the nineteenth century, although sporadic instances of bans on these drugs can be found scattered throughout history. In the fourteenth century, for example, the Emir of Joneima in Arabia tried, without success, to eliminate the use of marijuana and hashish. Beginning late in the eighteenth century, the government of China attempted to prevent British merchants from selling Indian opium in China; the British victory in the resulting Opium Wars (1839–42) enabled Britain to force China to accept imports of opium from India. There have also been assorted religious proscriptions against the use of alcohol, marijuana, opiates, and even caffeine and nicotine. Except for using alcohol as a source of tax revenue, however, governments largely have taken a "hands off" stance toward psychoactives until the last century or so.

In this country, state governments passed measures to restrict smoking opium and alcohol consumption during the last quarter of the nineteenth century.* These laws were followed by early-twentieth-century state-level legislation that restricted the sale of cocaine and opiates (and, in some states, peyote) to doctor-ordered prescriptions. By the late 1920s, more than twenty states had added marijuana to the list of psychoactives that could be obtained by prescription only.

These state-level measures varied greatly across the states (with some enacting no controls), and typically were aimed not at the complete elimination of the affected psychoactives, but rather at the control of their use. For example, state-level restrictions on smoking opium were directed at opium dens, rather than the drug itself, because the dens were viewed as sources of prostitution and gambling, and perhaps more importantly (given the racial attitudes of the day), were frequented by Chinese immigrants. Subsequent state-level restrictions on other opiates, cocaine, and eventually marijuana generally insisted only that they be dispensed by prescription. Even state-level proscriptions against alcohol were chiefly directed at moderating alcohol consumption and minimizing the disruptive social consequences of its use, rather than eliminating its use per se. In the South, for example, where many states nominally prohibited alcohol prior to the 1920 imposition of nationwide Prohibition, it was commonplace for the citizens to "vote dry and drink wet." Although sa-

---

*Smoking opium was specially selected and refined low-potency opium that had a morphine content of less than 10 percent. It was ingested by heating the opium in a pipe and inhaling the resulting vapors.

loons and retail liquor stores were outlawed, the manufacture of alcohol remained legal, and consumption continued apace in the privacy of homes and clubs.*

At the national level, the approach was different. Prohibition in the United States started in 1909 with a ban on the importation of smoking opium. This was followed in 1914 by the Harrison Act, which effectively banned opium, morphine, heroin, and cocaine, and in 1920 by the Eighteenth Amendment, which prohibited alcohol. In European nations, attempts to control opiates and cocaine flowed chiefly from the Hague Convention of 1912, an international treaty calling for restrictions on these drugs which was adopted at the insistence of the U.S. government. The treaty itself urged only that the distribution of opiates and cocaine be limited to medical and other legitimate purposes, which was the course that many nations took. The U.S. government, however, implemented the treaty by prohibiting the use of these drugs, just as it subsequently prohibited marijuana and the hallucinogens. Britain, by contrast, followed the spirit (and letter) of the Hague Convention by leaving the distribution of these drugs largely up to the discretion of physicians.

Over the ensuing decades, many of the efforts made in other nations to prohibit the cultivation, distribution, or consumption of the principal psychoactives have been undertaken at the insistence of the United States government. Indeed, it is the United States government, above all others, which has championed the outright elimination of use as the principal means of dealing with psychoactives.† The United States pressed for the principal international drug treaties—both the original Hague Convention of 1912 and the Single Convention on Narcotic Drugs of 1961, currently in effect. The U.S. government took the lead in banning smoking opium, other opiates, and cocaine, as well as pressuring state governments to prohibit (rather than regulate) marijuana before it prohibited pot under federal law. Finally, it has been the U.S. government that has coerced so many nations throughout the Far East, the Middle East, and South America to alter their domestic policies and drug laws to suit the prohibitionist desires of the U.S. government.

*Some historians have argued that Southern proscriptions on alcohol prior to Prohibition were importantly directed at reducing the ability of blacks to obtain it.
†The Communist Chinese government, though, has independently waged a brutal, repressive, and seemingly effective war against the opiates over the last forty years. Similarly, earlier this century, Russia, Norway, and Finland independently tried (without success) to prohibit the consumption of alcohol.

APPENDIX B

....

Legal Perspectives

THOUGH THE CURRENT DRUG PROBLEM IS A NATIONAL PROBLEM, IT IS not axiomatic that the problem requires a national government solution. An alternative scheme is to focus the initiative at the state level, much like the current scheme regarding another dangerous drug—alcohol.

Several legal issues arise with such a refocusing of policy, not the least of which concerns the United States' obligation as a signatory of the 1961 Single Convention on Narcotic Drugs. Another significant issue concerns the legal mechanism for achieving a state-level policy.

Under the current scheme, the federal and state governments have concurrent power in the field of drug control. At the state level, a majority of states have enacted the Uniform Controlled Substances Act.[1] At the federal level, the Comprehensive Drug Abuse Prevention and Control Act of 1970,[2] as amended, remains the pertinent legislation.

Subchapter I of 21 U.S.C.A. §§801 et seq. is the portion of the federal legislation which is most pertinent to the illicit drug trade. Part B, §§811-13, sets out the federal government's authority to control dangerous drugs and gives a detailed schedule of specific substances which are to be controlled, along with a regulatory mechanism for amending the schedule. Part D, §§841-52, delineates specific offenses and establishes a set of penalties for each offense.

As originally enacted, the 1970 Comprehensive Act did not contain a rigid penalty system. Rather, the law established only upper bounds for the fines and/or prison terms to be imposed for each offense. As amended, particularly with legislation passed in 1984 and 1986, current federal law does contain a complex range of penalties for each offense. For example, §844 imposes a series of staggered penalties for "simple possession," the severity of which depends on the nature of the substance involved, the quantity, and the number of prior offenses. The minimum penalty is a $1,000 fine, without a prison term. The maximum penalty is twenty years with or without a fine. A recent addition to the federal law, §844a, establishes a civil, rather than criminal, penalty for simple possession, the maximum fine being $10,000 per violation.

Under Article VI of the U.S. Constitution, valid federal statutes and treaties are declared to be "the supreme Law of the Land; and the Judges in every State shall be bound thereby, any Thing in the Constitution or Laws of any State to the Contrary notwithstanding." Because many of the powers delegated to the federal government are shared concurrently by the states, federal regulatory legislation within the scope of such delegated powers will often preempt and supersede state power to regulate the subject matter. It is, however, well established in the case law that the Comprehensive Act was not intended to preempt completely the states' role in controlling drugs[3]; neither did the signing of the Single Convention on Narcotic Drugs under the federal government's treaty-making power abrogate state narcotics laws.[4]

State law is limited only in §903 of the Comprehensive Act:

§903. APPLICATION OF STATE LAW

No provision of this subchapter shall be construed as indicating an intent on the part of the Congress to occupy the field in which that provision operates, including criminal penalties, to the exclusion of any State law on the same subject matter which would otherwise be within the authority of the State, unless there is a positive conflict between that provision of this subchapter and that State law so that the two cannot consistently stand together. (Pub. L. 91-513, title II, s 708, Oct. 27, 1970, 84 Stat. 1284).

The relevant clause is the last one, which contains the phrase "positive conflict" and establishes the preeminence of federal law. Any state laws, however, which do "not authorize what the [Comprehensive Act] prohibits" or which impose limits "consistent with the purpose of [the Act]" are not invalidated by §903.[5]

Most states have adopted the Uniform Controlled Substances Act approved by the National Conference of Commissioners on Uniform

State Laws in 1970. The Uniform Act was designed to supplant the Uniform Narcotic Drug Act and the Model State Drug Abuse Control Act. The Uniform Act was drafted to achieve uniformity among the states, to complement the federal government, and to provide an "interlocking trellis" of federal and state laws so as to more effectively control drug use.[6] Notwithstanding these efforts, conflicts with the federal laws occasionally arise and variances among the states' laws persist. For example, Minnesota treats marijuana possession and its sale in small amounts for no remuneration as a "petty misdemeanor"; the offender is subject to a maximum fine of only $200 and, unless the court deems it "inappropriate," participation in a drug education program.[7] In contrast, Florida law makes marijuana possession or delivery without consideration a first-degree misdemeanor.[8] For offenses involving up to twenty grams, an offender faces a possible fine of up to $1,000,[9] and/or a prison term of up to one year.[10]

Despite the preeminence of federal law under §903 and the continued discrepancies which exist among the states, the existing scheme has left intact, and at least "on the books," the state system of drug control. Indeed, the states' power to control drugs exists independently from *any* federal legislation, including the absence of such legislation. Moreover, case law firmly establishes that because of the dangerous nature and injurious effect of unregulated drug use, the states are afforded the maximum power permissible to combat drug abuse.[11] Although marijuana is generally considered to be the least noxious of substances currently regulated, state laws proscribing even minor possession have withstood due process, equal protection, and other federal constitutional law challenges.[12]

Absent preemptive federal legislation, state drug laws are independent of any federal scheme. State law is founded upon the general police powers which inhere in the state as a natural, sovereign power.[13] As mentioned earlier, even marijuana is controlled at the state level because courts afford wide latitude to states' legislative policy decisions in the areas of health, safety, and welfare.[14] Constitutional restrictions establish the outer parameters within which the states may exercise their police powers, but absent a fundamental rights issue, the U.S. Supreme Court will never second-guess a policy decision of the state in the exercise of its police powers; the merits, pro or con, are never at issue if a fundamental right is not at stake.[15]

Conversely, the federal branch is a government of limited powers;[16] only those initiatives enacted pursuant to the enumerated powers, or taken as necessary to effect those powers, are valid.[17] The federal role in drug policy is founded on the implied foreign affairs power, the express taxing power, and most importantly, the power granted under the commerce clause. Under the commerce clause, Congress is granted "plenary power." Dating back to the New Deal era,[18] almost any connection to interstate commerce, no matter how attenuated, has been sufficient to invoke Congress' power under the Commerce Clause. Though Congress' purpose may be to advance some policy other than interstate or international commerce, any connection with commerce is sufficient, even if the court has to strain logic to find the connection.[19] As is the case of state legislation, the court never looks to the merits of the policy itself.[20] If the court can find a constitutional basis, policy itself is irrelevant.[21]

This brings us full circle to the question of how a state-level control policy for drugs could be implemented. First, unlike the case of alcohol, which had been subject to a constitutionally based prohibition, no repeal amendment would need be considered. Second, Congress would not even have to repeal the 1970 Comprehensive Act to initiate a state-level refocusing of policy. Recall that the act is founded on the power given Congress under the Commerce Clause. Under the Commerce Clause, Congress may choose to exercise that power by concurrently sharing it with the respective states or by delegating the power to the states. The most efficacious way to achieve state-level initiative would be to amend the Comprehensive Act so as to expressly enunciate a policy of delegation. Even without such a delegation amendment, the same policy aims could be achieved through a revision of §903. Simply rewording the "positive conflict" clause so as to give preeminence to the state law whenever conflicts arise would, de facto, return control to the states. In substance, the two approaches are equivalent.

Regardless of whether the state-level initiative is achieved under repeal, amendment, or revision of §903 of the Comprehensive Act, there remains one problem that must be addressed: the foreign affairs implication of the United States' signing the Single Convention on Narcotic Drugs.

A treaty is accorded the same deference that ordinary legislation receives: The court will not strike down a treaty on the basis of policy; only a constitutionally impermissible action will nullify the treaty.[22] Since ultimate power in foreign affairs is one of the powers granted exclusively to the federal government—albeit by implication rather than by express language[23]—all self-executing treaties prevail over conflicting state law.

Determining whether a treaty is self-executing is not an easy task, as there is no mechanical solution yielded by the language of a treaty. The most general decision-rule looks to whether the language itself establishes a rule of law.[24] In the case of the Single Convention on Narcotic Drugs of 1961, the express prohibition of certain specific substances seems to fit within the rule. Thus, as a self-executing treaty, it would preempt conflicting state law.

A *federal* law, however, which subsequently conflicts with a treaty supersedes that treaty.[25] A repeal of the 1970 Comprehensive Act might create a void in federal legislation, leaving the treaty as preeminent should a conflict with state law arise. Given that repeal would leave intact the present state law schemes, this scenario is unlikely, as only enactment of a state law which eliminated the outright prohibition on substances enumerated in the treaty would give rise to a conflict.

If, however, the Comprehensive Act were amended properly, it would be tantamount to federal legislation which, being later in time, would supersede the treaty. In any case, a federal initiative, clearly expressing its purpose to return drug control to the states, would not be affected by the present international treaty, no matter which policy any state chose to pursue.

ALTERNATIVE CHANGES IN FEDERAL LAW

Alternative I:

Repeal of 21 USCA §801 et seq.

"The Enhanced States' Control Over Drug Abuse Act"

Section 1. "§§801-904, 21 USCA are hereby repealed."
Section 2. "The transportation or importation into any state, territory, or possession of the United States for delivery or use therein of any controlled substance, in violation of the laws thereof, is hereby prohibited."

Alternative 2:

Amendment of 21 USCA §903

"THE RETURN TO THE STATES CONTROL OVER DRUG ABUSE AMEND-MENT"
§903, 21 USCA, shall be revised to read as follows:

No provision of this subchapter shall be construed as indicating an intent on the part of the Congress to occupy the field in which that provision operates to the exclusion of any state law on the same subject matter which would otherwise be within the authority of the state. Any conflict between that provision of this subchapter and that state law so that the two cannot stand together shall be resolved by construing the law so as to give full effect to the relevant state law.

POTENTIAL CHALLENGE TO REPLACING OR AMENDING SECTION 903

Would state regulation be affected by the United States' commitment under international antidrug treaties? The answer is no. The power to deal in matters concerning foreign affairs is an exclusively federal power. Under the supremacy clause, treaties are the law of the land; as such they are treated as ordinary federal legislation. In matters over which federal law dominates, a treaty—if it is self-executing— preempts state law if the latter conflicts with the former.

The present treaty is almost certainly self-executing: It expressly prohibits certain activities. The treaty and subsequent legislation would be construed so as to avoid conflict, but if a state chose to legalize activities prohibited by the treaty a conflict would be un-avoidable.

However, when *federal* legislation which conflicts with a treaty is enacted subsequent to a treaty, the federal legislation being latter in time supersedes the treaty. In the antidrug field, Congress' intent to return to the states control over drug use would be sufficient to supersede the treaty. Thus, the very act of Congress getting out of the drug field would empower the states to pursue a policy that might conflict with the treaty.

NOTES

....

Introduction: Crossfire

1. National Institute of Drug Abuse data, reported in Sam Meddis, "Whites, Not Blacks, at the Core of Drug Crisis," *USA Today*, December 20, 1989, p. 11A. See also David R. Gergen, "Drugs and White America," *U.S. News & World Report*, September 18, 1989, p. 79.
2. "The Health Consequences of Smoking," Surgeon General's Report, Washington, D.C., 1988. See also Larry Martz, "A Dirty Drug Secret," *Newsweek*, February 19, 1990, p. 74.
3. U.S. Bureau of Justice Statistics, *Sourcebook of Criminal Justice Statistics, 1989* (Washington, D.C.: U.S. Government Printing Office, 1990).
4. James Cook, "The Paradox of Antidrug Enforcement," *Forbes*, November 13, 1989, p. 105. See also Dean R. Gerstein, "Alcohol Use and Consequences," in *Alcohol and Public Policy: Beyond the Shadow of Prohibition*, ed. Mark H. Moore and Dean R. Gerstein (Washington, D.C.: National Academy Press, 1981).
5. Ethan Nadelmann, "Drug Prohibition in the United States: Costs, Consequences, and Alternatives," *Science* 245 (September 1, 1989): 939. See also Susan Hamilton Saavedra, "Dire Economics Drive Coca Production," *The Drug Policy Letter* 2, no. 3 (May/June 1990): 2.
6. Paul M. Barrett, "Federal War on Drugs Is a Scattershot Affair, with Dubious Progress," *Wall Street Journal*, August 10, 1989, p. 1.

Chapter 1: Roots

1. Don Terry, "Council, Seizing the Crime Issue, Seeks to Expand New York Police," *New York Times*, September 7, 1990, p. 1.

2. Edward M. Brecher, *Licit & Illicit Drugs* (Boston: Little, Brown, 1972). See also Ronald K. Siegal, *Intoxication: Life in Pursuit of Artificial Paradise* (New York: Dutton, 1989).

3. More detailed discussions can be found in the following: Charles E. Terry and Mildred Pellens, *The Opium Problem* (New York: American Social Health Association, 1928; Montclair, N.J.: Patterson Smith, 1970); David T. Courtwright, *Dark Paradise: Opiate Addiction in America Before 1940* (Cambridge, Mass.: Harvard University Press, 1982); David F. Musto, *The American Disease: Origins of Narcotic Control* (New Haven, Conn.: Yale University Press, 1973); and Brecher, *Licit & Illicit Drugs*.

4. For additional details, see the following: Andrew Sinclair, *Prohibition: The Era of Excess* (Boston: Little, Brown, 1962); John Kobler, *Ardent Spirits: The Rise and Fall of Prohibition* (New York: Putnam, 1973); and David Kyvig, *Repealing National Prohibition* (Chicago: University of Chicago Press, 1979).

5. The most comprehensive discussion of this episode is found in "Russia's Anti-Drink Campaign: Veni, Vidi, Vodka," *The Economist*, December 23, 1989, pp. 50–54.

6. U.S. Bureau of the Census, *Historical Statistics of the United States, Colonial Times to 1970*, bicentennial edition, pt. 1, Washington, D.C., 1975.

7. Clark Warburton, *The Economic Effects of Prohibition* (New York: Columbia University Press, 1932; AMS Press, 1968); E. M. Jellinek, "Recent Trends in Alcoholism and Alcohol Consumption," *Quarterly Journal of Studies on Alcohol* 8 (March 1947): 1; and Dean R. Gerstein, "Alcohol Use and Consequences," in *Alcohol and Public Policy: Beyond the Shadow of Prohibition*, ed. Mark H. Moore and Dean R. Gerstein (Washington, D.C.: National Academy Press, 1981).

8. Siegal, *Intoxication*, pp. 224, 269, 310.

9. James Ostrowski, "Thinking About Legalization," *Cato Institute Policy Analysis*, no. 121 (May 25, 1989).

10. "Russia's Anti-Drink Campaign," p. 53.

11. The most carefully constructed estimates of opiate addiction in America during the late nineteenth and early twentieth centuries are by Terry and Pellens, *The Opium Problem*, and Courtwright, *Dark Paradise*.

12. See Gordon Witkin, "The Return of a Deadly Drug Called Horse," *U.S. News and World Report*, August 14, 1989, p. 31.

Chapter 2: Scourge

1. USDA source, cited in Ethan Nadelmann, "Drug Prohibition in the United States: Costs, Consequences, and Alternatives," *Science* 245 (September 1, 1989): 939.

2. Lindsey Gruson, "Drug Trafficking and Poppy Growing a Lush Home in Guatemala," *New York Times*, October 1, 1989, p. 12.

3. Mark A. R. Kleiman, *Marijuana: Costs of Abuse, Costs of Control* (New York: Greenwood Press, 1989).

4. Nadelmann, "Drug Prohibition," p. 939, and Susan Hamilton Saavedra, "Dire Economics Drive Coca Production," *The Drug Policy Letter*, no. 3 (May/June 1990): 2.

5. Kleiman, *Marijuana*.

6. John Kaplan, *The Hardest Drug: Heroin and Public Policy* (Chicago: University of Chicago Press, 1983).

7. Ibid. See also Fred Zackon, *Heroin: The Street Narcotic* (New York: Chelsea House, 1986).

8. Kleiman, *Marijuana*.

9. Jack Kelley, "40% in County Said to Grow Weed," *USA Today*, July 11, 1989, p. 1.

10. Kleiman, *Marijuana*.

11. James Brooke, "Peruvian Farmers Razing Rain Forests to Sow Drug Crops," *New York Times*, August 13, 1989, p. 1.

12. *The World Almanac and Book of Facts: 1990* (New York: Pharos Books, 1990).

13. Saavedra, "Dire Economics." See also Elaine Shannon, "Attacking the Source," *Time*, August 28, 1989, p. 10.

14. "Drugs: It Doesn't Have to Be Like This," *The Economist*, September 2, 1989, p. 2ff. See also Stanley Penn, "U.S.-Made Chemicals Supply Narcotics Labs Across Latin America," *Wall Street Journal*, July 13, 1988, p. 1.

15. Andrea Gabor, "Cocaine Countries Try to Grow Straight," *U.S. News and World Report*, October 23, 1989, p. 57.

16. Saavedra, "Dire Economics."

17. R. W. Lee, *White Labyrinth: Cocaine and Political Power* (New Brunswick, N.J.: Transaction Books, 1990).

18. Ibid. See also Tina Rosenberg, "The Kingdom of Cocaine," *New Republic*, November 27, 1989, p. 26; and Michael Massing, "In the War on Drugs, the Jungle Is Winning," *New York Times Magazine*, March 4, 1990, p. 267.

19. Paul Eddy et al., *The Cocaine Wars* (New York: W. W. Norton, 1988). See also Jose de Cordoba, "In Colombia, the War on Drugs Is Producing Some Real-Life Heroes," *Wall Street Journal*, September 7, 1989, p. 1.

20. "Colombia's Cocaine Overdose," *The Economist*, August 26, 1989, p. 29.

21. Saavedra, "Dire Economics."

22. Richard Wallace, "Mexico Displaces S. Florida as Drug Smuggling Mecca," *Miami Herald*, November 3, 1990, p. 1.

23. Peter Passell, "Fighting Cocaine, Coffee, Flowers," *New York Times*, September 20, 1989, p. 28. See also Saavedra, "Dire Economics."

24. Paul M. Barrett, "Federal War on Drugs Is a Scattershot Affair, with Dubious Progress," *Wall Street Journal*, August 10, 1989, p. 1.

25. Ibid. See also Peter Reuter, "Can the Borders Be Sealed?" *Public Interest* 90 (Summer 1988): 51.

26. See also Joseph B. Treaster, "Bypassing Borders, More Drugs Flood Ports," *New York Times*, April 29, 1990, p. 1.

27. Frank Greve, "In Drug War, Crafty Smugglers Stay a Step Ahead," *Miami Herald*, December 18, 1989, p. 1.

28. Ibid.

29. Ibid.

30. Eddy et al., *The Cocaine Wars*, p. 83.

31. John J. Fialka, "The Military Enters the War on Drugs and Finds Elusive Foe," *Wall Street Journal*, August 31, 1989, p. 1.

32. Douglas Waller, "Risky Business," *Newsweek*, July 16, 1990, p. 17.

33. Wallace, "Mexico Displaces S. Florida," p. 1.

34. Treaster, "Bypassing Borders," p. 1.

35. Kleiman, *Marijuana*.

36. Michael A. Lerner, "The Fire of Ice," *Newsweek*, November 27, 1989, p. 37.

37. Katherine Bishop, "Fear Grows Over Effects of New Smokable Drug," *New York Times*, September 16, 1989, p. 1.

38. Malcolm W. Browne, "Problems Loom in Effort to Control Use of Chemicals for Illicit Drugs," *New York Times*, October 24, 1989, p. 17.

39. Ibid.

Chapter 3: Home Front

1. James Cook, "The Paradox of Antidrug Enforcement," *Forbes*, November 13, 1989, p. 105. See also Gordon Witkin, "The Return of a Deadly Drug Called Horse," *U.S. News and World Report*, August 14, 1989, p. 31.

2. Sam Meddis, "Drug Arrest Rate Higher for Blacks," *USA Today*, December 20, 1989, p. 1. See also David R. Gergen, "Drugs and White America," *U.S. News and World Report*, September 18, 1989, p. 79.

3. U.S. Bureau of the Census, *Statistical Abstract of the United States: 1990*, 110th edition (Washington, D.C.: U.S. Government Printing Office, 1989).

4. Joe Davidson, "How a 24-Year-Old Reigned as Local Hero Until His Drug Arrest," *Wall Street Journal*, November 13, 1989, p. 1.

5. William Raspberry, "Target Effort at Well-Off User," *Miami Herald*, September 17, 1989, p. 1.

6. Sam Meddis, "Whites, Not Blacks, at the Core of the Drug Crisis," *USA Today*, December 20, 1989, p. 11.

7. *New York Times*, February 27, 1990, p. 17.

8. Michael Massing, "Crack's Destructive Spring Across America," *New York Times Magazine*, October 1, 1989, p. 38. See also Jane Meyer, "In the War on Drugs, Toughest Foe May Be the Alienated Youth," *Wall Street Journal*, September 8, 1989, p. 1.

9. Katherine Bishop, "Fear Grows Over Effects of New Smokable Drug," *New York Times*, September 16, 1989, p. 1.

10. Jack Kelley, "40% in County Said to Grow Weed," *USA Today*, July 11, 1989, p. 1. See also Mark Thompson, "California's Unwinnable War Against Marijuana," *Wall Street Journal*, January 8, 1990, p. 1.

11. Jack Kelley, "Cocaine, Other Hard Drugs Invade Rural Areas," *USA Today*, December 20, 1989, p. 11. See also James J. Kilpatrick, "Drugs: Here, There, and Everywhere," *Miami Herald*, September 2, 1989, p. 31.

12. Andrew Malcolm, "Crack, Bane of Inner City, Is Now Gripping Suburbs," *New York Times*, October 1, 1989, p. 1.

13. Joseph Pereira, "Even a School That Is Leading the Drug War Grades Itself a Failure," *Wall Street Journal*, November 11, 1989, p. 1.

14. Malcolm, "Crack," p. 1.

15. The literature on this topic is enormous. For a small sampling from fields ranging from medicine to economics, we suggest the following: Frank H. Gavin, "Cocaine Addiction: Psychology and Neurophysiology," *Science*, March 29, 1991, p. 1580; Gary S. Becker and Kevin Murphy, "A Theory of Rational Addiction," *Journal of Political Economy* 96 (August 1988): 675; Robert Byck, "Cocaine, Marijuana, and the Meanings of Addiction," in *Dealing with Drugs*, ed. Ronald Hamowy (San Francisco: Pacific Research Institute for Public Policy, 1987); Michael S. Gazzaniga, "The Federal Drugstore," *National Review*, February 5, 1990, p. 34; Alan Schwartz, "Views of Addiction and the Duty to Warn," *Virginia Law Review* 79 (April 1989): 509; and John Wallace, *Writings* (Newport, R.I.: Edgehill Publications, 1989), especially chapters I.2 and III.2.

16. Clark Warburton, *The Economic Effects of Prohibition* (New York: Columbia University Press, 1932; AMS Press, 1968); E. M. Jellinek, "Recent Trends in Alcoholism and Alcohol Consumption," *Quarterly Journal of Studies on Alcohol* 8 (March 1947): 1; and Dean R. Gerstein, "Alcohol Use and Consequences," in *Alcohol and Public Policy: Beyond the Shadow of Prohibition*, ed. Mark H. Moore and Dean R. Gerstein (Washington, D.C.: National Academy Press, 1981).

17. David T. Courtwright, *Dark Paradise: Opiate Addiction in America Before 1940* (Cambridge, Mass.: Harvard University Press, 1982).

18. The classic statement of this conclusion is contained in E. M. Jellinek, *The Disease Concept of Alcoholism* (New Haven, Conn.: Hillhouse Press, 1960).

19. John Wallace, "Treatment," in *Sixth Annual Special Report to the U.S. Congress on Alcohol and Health* (Washington, D.C.: Department of Health

and Human Services, 1987). See also Leonard Saxe et al., *The Effectiveness and Costs of Alcoholism Treatment*, Health Technology Case Study no. 22 (Washington, D.C.: Office of Technology Assessment, 1983).

20. Gerstein, op. cit. See also G. L. Klerman, "Prevention of Alcoholism," in *Alcoholism and Clinical Psychiatry*, ed. J. Solomon (New York: Plenum, 1982).
21. Edward M. Brecher, *Licit & Illicit Drugs* (Boston: Little, Brown, 1972). See also Cook, "The Paradox."
22. Steven Erlanger, "In Malaysia and Singapore, a Mixed Drug Picture," *New York Times*, December 15, 1989, p. 6.
23. Ibid. See also Jeffrey Eisenach, "Fighting Drugs in Four Countries: Lessons for America?" *Backgrounder*, no. 790 (Washington, D.C.: The Heritage Foundation, 1990).
24. Richard Burke, "Drug Woes Persist Despite Bush Vow to Clean Up D.C.," *Miami Herald*, October 22, 1989, p. 1. See also Philip Shenon, "Bush Officials Say War on Drugs in the Nation's Capital Is a Failure," *New York Times*, April 5, 1990, p. 1; and Michael Massing, "D.C.'s War on Drugs: Why Bennett Is Losing," *New York Times Magazine*, September 23, 1990, p. 36.

Chapter 4: The Rape of the Inner City

1. John C. Ball and Carl D. Chambers, "Overview of the Problem," in *The Epidemiology of Opiate Addiction in the United States*, ed. John C. Ball and Carl D. Chambers (Springfield, Ill.: Charles C. Thomas Publishers, 1970). See also John Kaplan, *The Hardest Drug: Heroin and Public Policy* (Chicago: University of Chicago Press, 1983); and Michael Marriott, "Latest Drug of Choice for Abusers Brings New Generation to Heroin," *New York Times*, July 13, 1989, p. 1.
2. Ronald K. Siegal, *Intoxication: Life in Pursuit of Artificial Paradise* (New York: Dutton, 1989).
3. Michael Marriott, "After 3 Years, Crack Plague in New York Only Gets Worse," *New York Times*, February 20, 1989, p. 1, and Katherine Bishop, "Fear Grows Over Effects of New Smokable Drug," *New York Times*, September 16, 1989, p. 1. See also "A Disaster of Historic Proportions Still Growing," *New York Times*, May 28, 1989, editorial, p. 14.
4. U.S. Bureau of the Census, *Statistical Abstract of the United States*, annual; U.S. Bureau of the Census, *State and Metropolitan Area Data Book*, annual; U.S. Bureau of the Census, *Current Population Reports*, annual; U.S. National Center for Health Statistics, *Health, United States*, annual; U.S. National Center for Health Statistics, *Vital and Health Statistics*, annual.
5. U.S. Bureau of Labor Statistics, *Employment and Earnings*, monthly. See

also R. Miller et al., *The Economics of Public Issues* (New York: Harper & Row, 1990).

6. U.S. National Center for Health Statistics, *Vital and Health Statistics*, annual.

7. R. Miller et al., *The Economics of Public Issues*.

8. Steven Wisotsky, *Breaking the Impasse in the War on Drugs* (Westport, Conn.: Greenwood, 1986). See also Paul Eddy et al., *The Cocaine Wars* (New York: Bantam, 1989).

9. Andrew H. Malcolm, "More Americans Are Killing Each Other," *New York Times*, December 31, 1989, p. 14.

10. Michael Massing, "Crack's Destructive Spread Across America," *New York Times Magazine*, October 1, 1989, p. 38.

11. Ibid.

12. Jane Meyer, "In the War on Drugs, Toughest Foe May Be Alienated Youth," *Wall Street Journal*, September 8, 1989, p. 1.

13. Ibid.

14. Lawrence Sherman, "The Death of Euclid Leslie," *Wall Street Journal*, July 10, 1989, p. 1.

15. Sam Meddis, "Drug War's 'Unseen' Victims: Traumatized Inner-City Kids," *New York Times*, October 19, 1990, p. 1.

16. Ibid.

17. Paul M. Barrett, "Program to Prosecute the Casual Drug User Is Casting Wider Net," *Wall Street Journal*, January 31, 1990, p. 1.

Chapter 5: Blinding Justice

1. "Housing Shortage," *Fortune*, November 20, 1989, p. 238.

2. David Boaz, "The Consequences of Prohibition," in *The Crisis and Drug Prohibition*, ed. David Boaz (Washington, D.C.: CATO Institute, 1990), p. 5, updated by the authors.

3. U.S. Department of Justice, preliminary estimated data, from press release, December 10, 1989.

4. Richard B. Abell, "The Price of Tight-fisted Policy," *Wall Street Journal*, March 21, 1989, p. 19.

5. Ibid.

6. Stephen Wermiel, "Drug Cases Crowd Out Civil Federal-Court Trials as Judge Calls Business Litigation a 'Stepchild,' " *Wall Street Journal*, February 6, 1990, p. A20.

7. Telephone interview, Barry Lynch, Florida State Attorney General's Office, Tallahassee, Fla., May 5, 1991.

8. U.S. Sentencing Commission, *Supplementary Report on the Initial Sen-*

tencing Guidelines and Policy Statements (Washington, D.C.: U.S. Sentencing Commission, 1987), p. 72.

9. "A Disaster of Historic Proportions Still Growing," *New York Times*, May 28, 1989, editorial, p. 14.

10. Ibid.

11. Abell, "The Place of Tight-fisted Policy," p. 19.

12. Ibid.

13. Sarah Sun Beal, "Get Drug Cases Out of Federal Courts," *Wall Street Journal*, February 8, 1990, p. A16.

14. "The Koppel Report: Drugs, Crime, and Doing Time," ABC News Special, 1990.

15. Ibid.

16. Wermiel, "Drug Cases Crowd Out Civil Federal-Court Trials," p. A20.

17. Ibid.

18. Beal, "Get Drug Cases Out of Federal Courts," p. A16.

19. Wermiel, "Drug Cases Crowd Out Civil Federal-Court Trials," p. A20.

20. *Miami Herald*, January 1, 1990, p. A4.

21. *Source Book of Criminal Justice Statistics, 1989* (Washington, D.C.: Bureau of Justice Statistics, Department of Justice, 1990).

22. Robb London, "Volunteer Prosecutors and Backlog of Drug Cases," *New York Times*, August 24, 1990, p. B9.

23. The National Institute on Drug Abuse conducts an annual survey. It currently estimates that there are about 23 million Americans who have admitted to using illegal drugs in the month preceding the survey. Many experts believe that this number is suspiciously low, mainly because individuals are reluctant, even if they believe the survey is strictly anonymous and private, to admit to having used an illegal psychoactive. Moreover, the survey does not pick up individuals who may have used an illegal psychoactive at least once during the previous twelve months. The best estimate of the current annual number of Americans who violate our drug laws at least once during any given year is closer to 40 million.

Chapter 6: Organizing Crime

1. Michael Massing, "Crack's Destructive Sprint Across America," *New York Times Magazine*, October 1, 1989, p. 38.

2. Ibid.

3. Ibid. Murder estimate from the Bureau of Alcohol, Tobacco, and Firearms.

4. Alex Kotlowitz, "Chicago Street Gangs Treat Public Housing as Private Fortress," *Wall Street Journal*, September 30, 1988, p. 1.

5. Stephen J. Hedges, "When Drug Gangs Move to Nice Places," *U.S. News and World Report*, June 5, 1989, p. 42.

6. Massing, "Crack's Destructive Sprint," pp. 60–62.

7. Ibid.

8. Ibid., p. 60.

9. Joe Davidson, "How a 24-Year-Old Reigned as Local Hero Until His Drug Arrest," *Wall Street Journal*, November 13, 1989, p. A1. See also Nancy Lewis, "Drug Gang: A Family Affair," *Washington Post*, April 18, 1990, p. A1.

10. Edward M. Brecher, *Licit & Illicit Drugs* (Boston: Little, Brown, 1972), pp. 261–262. See also *Source Book of Criminal Justice Statistics, 1989* (Washington, D.C.: Bureau of Justice Statistics, Department of Justice, 1990).

Chapter 7: Bathtub Gin and AIDS

1. James Ostrowski, "Thinking About Legalization," *Cato Institute Policy Analysis*, no. 121 (May 25, 1989), p. 40.

2. D. Des Jarlais and S. Friedman, "HIV Infection Among Persons Who Inject Illicit Drugs: Problems and Prospects," *Journal of AIDS* 1, 3 (1988): 268; and Ostrowski, "Thinking," p. 12.

3. Edward M. Brecher, *Licit & Illicit Drugs* (Boston: Little, Brown, 1972), pp. 3–7. See also David Courtwright, *Dark Paradise: Opiate Addiction in America Before 1940* (Cambridge, Mass.: Harvard University Press, 1982), chapter 2.

4. Frances Caballero, *Droit de la Drogue* (Paris: Dalloz, 1990), pp. 639–40; and Brecher, *Licit & Illicit Drugs*, pp. 48–63. See also John A. O'Donnell and Judith P. Jones, "Diffusion of Intravenous Technique Among Narcotic User," in *The Epidemiology of Opiate Addiction in the United States*, ed. John C. Ball and Carl D. Chambers (Springfield, Ill.: Charles C. Thomas, 1970).

5. Roger LeRoy Miller et al., *The Economics of Public Issues* (New York: HarperCollins, 1990); and Brecher, *Licit & Illicit Drugs*, chapter 59. See also Mark A. R. Kleiman, *Marijuana: Costs of Abuse, Costs of Control* (New York: Greenwood Press, 1989).

6. Brecher, *Licit & Illicit Drugs*, chapter 37.

7. Ethan A. Nadelmann, "Drug Prohibition in the United States: Costs, Consequences, and Alternatives," *Science* 245 (September 1, 1989): 940. But see Gordon Witkin, "The Return of a Deadly Drug Called Horse," *U.S. News and World Report*, August 14, 1989, p. 31, for reports of heroin purity levels as high as 40 percent.

8. "Heroin-related Deaths: District of Columbia, 1980–1982," *Morbidity and*

Mortality Weekly Report, 32, no. 25, Centers for Disease Control, July 1, 1983; and J. Ruttenber and J. Luke, "Heroin-related Deaths: New Epidemiologic Insights," *Science* 22 (October 1984): 19.

9. D. Des Jarlais, "HIV Infection Among Intravenous Drug Users in Manhattan, New York City from 1977 to 1987," *Journal of the American Medical Association* 261, 7 (1989): 1008.

10. "Ten Years Later: The Changing Face of AIDS," *Greenville News*, June 2, 1991, p. E1.

11. James Ostrowski, "Thinking About Drug Legalization," in *The Crisis in Drug Prohibition*, ed. David Boaz (Washington, D.C.: Cato Institute, 1989), p. 40.

12. "More Unsafe Sex," *U.S. News and World Report*, October 1, 1990, p. 14.

13. Lourdes Fernandez, "Good Guys Get Chance to Stand Up to Anti-Drug . . ." *Miami Herald*, October 22, 1989, p. 5B.

14. Andrew Murr, "So Little Time, So Many Cases," *Newsweek*, September 25, 1989, p. 59.

15. *New York Times*, October 15, 1990, p. E7.

16. On this topic, see Jan Hoffman, "Pregnant, Addicted—And Guilty?" *New York Times Magazine*, August 10, 1990, p. 33; Cathy Trost, "As Drug Babies Grow Older, Schools Strive to Meet Their Needs," *Wall Street Journal*, December 27, 1989, p. 1; Stanton Peele, "The New Thalidomide," *Reason*, July 1990, p. 41; A. M. Rosenthal, "How Much Is A Baby Worth?" *New York Times*, June 17, 1990, p. G7; Jacob Sullum, "The Suffering of Innocents," *Reason*, December 1989, p. 6; Morris E. Chafetz, "Alcohol and Innocent Victims," *Wall Street Journal*, March 5, 1990, p. 50; and Dale Gieringer, "How Many Crack Babies?" *The Drug Letter*, March/April 1990, p. 4.

17. A. M. Rosenthal, "How Much Is a Baby Worth?" *New York Times*, June 17, 1990, p. G7.

18. The Senate Judiciary Committee survey estimate maintains that 2.2 million Americans are addicted to cocaine. *USA Today*, May 10, 1990, p. 1.

Chapter 8: Farewell to the Founding Fathers

1. Tony Mauro, "Some Worry Police 'Out of Control,' " *USA Today*, November 15, 1989, p. 2. See also Steven Wisotsky, *Breaking the Impact on the War on Drugs* (New York: Greenwood Press, 1986).

2. Tom Morganthau, "Uncivil Liberties," *Newsweek*, April 23, 1990, p. 19.

3. John Dentinger, "Narc, Narc," *Playboy*, April 1990, pp. 49–50.

4. Richard Lacayo, "A Threat to Freedom?" *Time*, September 18, 1989, p. 28.

5. See his dissent in *Skinner v. Railway Labor Executives Association*, 489 U.S. 602, 109 S.Ct. 1402 (1989), 103 L.Ed.2d 639.

6. Huberman's story has been reported in numerous articles, including Peter Gorman, "Marijuana McCarthyism," *New York Times*, April 5, 1990, p. G6.

7. *U.S. v. D. Hernandez*, 473 U.S. 531 (1985).

8. Arthur S. Hayes, "Searches for Drugs Roil Boaters," *Wall Street Journal*, April 30, 1990, p. B4.

9. Ibid.

10. Ibid.

11. Rodrigo Lazo, "County to Launch Assault Against Crack Dens," *Miami Herald*, September 9, 1989, p. 1B. See also "Crack Addicts Swiping Shopping Carts," *Miami Herald*, September 9, 1989, p. 2B.

12. Eric Weiner, "In the War on Drugs, Planes Are a Big Enemy," *New York Times*, October 8, 1989, p. E4.

13. Justin Gillis and J. Leen, "Launderers Disguised Drug Profits Through Electronic Transactions," *Miami Herald*, March 17, 1990, p. 1.

14. Ibid.

15. Mauro, "Some Worry," p. 2.

16. Stefan Herpel, "United States v. One Assortment of 89 Firearms," *Reason*, May 1990, p. 33.

17. *Calero-Toledo v. Pearson Yacht Leasing Company*, 416 U.S. 663, (1974).

18. Ibid.

19. Ibid.

20. Wade Lambert and J. S. Hirsch, "Tough Drug-Case Seizure Rules Upheld," *Wall Street Journal*, August 20, 1990, p. B6.

21. *U.S. v. West 141 St. Realty Corporation*, U.S. Second Circuit Court of Appeals, August 1990.

Chapter 9: Thinking Psychoactively

1. Ronald K. Siegal, *Intoxication: Life in Pursuit of Artificial Paradise* (New York: Dutton, 1989).

2. Amy Dockser Marcus, "Some States Lower Blood-Alcohol Limits for Drivers, Generating Controversy," *Wall Street Journal*, January 26, 1990, p. B1. See also U.S. Bureau of the Census, *Statistical Abstract of the United States*, annual.

3. Ibid. See also Dean R. Gerstein, "Alcohol Use and Consequences," in *Alcohol and Public Policy: Beyond the Shadow of Prohibition*, ed. Mark H. Moore and Dean R. Gerstein (Washington, D.C.: National Academy Press, 1981).

4. Roger LeRoy Miller et al., *The Economics of Public Issues* (New York: Harper & Row, 1990).

5. James Ostrowski, "Thinking About Legalization," *Cato Institute Policy Analysis*, no. 121 (May 25, 1989).

6. For a more extensive discussion, see Charles E. Terry and Mildred Pellens, *The Opium Problem* (New York: American Social Health Association, 1928; (Montclair, N.J.: Patterson Smith, 1970); David T. Courtwright, *Dark Paradise: Opiate Addiction in America Before 1940* (Cambridge, Mass.: Harvard University Press, 1982); David F. Musto, *The American Disease: Origins of Narcotic Control* (New Haven, Conn.: Yale University Press, 1973); and Edward M. Brecher, *Licit & Illicit Drugs* (Boston: Little, Brown, 1972).

7. Terry M. Parssinen, *Secret Passions, Secret Remedies: Narcotic Drugs in British Society 1820–1930* (Philadelphia: Institute for the Study of Human Issues, 1983); Brecher, *Licit & Illicit Drugs;* and John Kaplan, *The Hardest Drug: Heroin and Public Policy* (Chicago: University of Chicago Press, 1983).

8. Ostrowski, "Thinking."

9. Richard J. Bonnie and Charles H. Whitebread, *The Marijuana Conviction: A History of Marijuana Prohibition in the United States* (Charlottesville: University of Virginia Press, 1974); Jerome L. Himmelstein, *The Strange Career of Marijuana: Politics and Ideology of Drug Control in America* (Westport, Conn.: Greenwood Press, 1983); David Solomon, ed., *The Marijuana Papers* (New York: Bobbs-Merrill, 1966); and Brecher, *Licit & Illicit Drugs.*

10. Ostrowski, "Thinking."

11. Ethan Nadelmannn, "The Case for Legalization," in *The Crisis in Drug Prohibition*, ed. David Boaz (Washington, D.C.: Cato Institute, 1990).

12. Brecher, *Licit & Illicit Drugs.*

13. Ibid. See also Lester Grinspoon and James B. Bakalar, *Cocaine: A Drug and Its Social Evolution* (New York: Basic Books, 1976); Robert Byck, ed., *The Cocaine Papers* (New York: Stonehill, 1974); and Lester Grinspoon and Peter Hedblom, *The Speed Culture: Amphetamine Use and Abuse in America* (Cambridge, Mass.: Harvard University Press, 1975).

14. Brecher, *Licit & Illicit Drugs*, and Grinspoon and Hedblom, *The Speed Culture.*

15. Brecher, *Licit & Illicit Drugs*, and Paul Eddy et al., *The Cocaine Wars* (New York: Bantam, 1989).

Chapter 10: Perils and Prospects

1. In recent years, a large number of commentators have argued that drugs should be legalized. A small but useful sampling of these views is conveniently contained in David Boaz, *The Crisis in Drug Prohibition* (Washington, D.C.: Cato Institute, 1990).
2. For a selection of the arguments used to support a true get-tough policy, see William J. Bennett, "A Response to Milton Friedman," *Wall Street Journal*, September 19, 1989, p. 17; Rep. Charles B. Rangel (D-N.Y.), letter to the editor, *Wall Street Journal*, November 22, 1989, p. 19; editorial, "The Devil You Know," *Wall Street Journal*, December 29, 1989, p. 6; Mark H. Moore, "Prohibition DID Work—And Still Could for Drugs," *Miami Herald*, October 25, 1989, p. 15; Richard M. Rubinson, "Drug Legalization: A Quick Fix That Ignores Myriad Dangers," *Miami Herald*, September 20, 1989, p. E-23; and James Q. Wilson, "Against the Legalization of Drugs," *Commentary*, February 1990, p. 21.
3. James Walsh, "A Partnership to Remember," *Time*, March 11, 1991, pp. 49–50.
4. "The Koppel Report: Drugs, Crime and Doing Time," ABC News Special, 1990.
5. L. Gordon Crovitz, "Lawrence Walsh, Drug Case and the Costs of Selective Prosecution," *Wall Street Journal*, May 30, 1990, p. 13.
6. Edward M. Brecher, *Licit & Illicit Drugs* (Boston: Little, Brown, 1972).

Chapter 11: The Constitutional Alternative

1. Steffen Schmidt, et al., *American Government and Politics Today*, 1991–92 edition (St. Paul: West, 1991, chapter 3).
2. *The World Almanac 1990*, (New York: Pharos Books, 1990), pp. 824–25.
3. *The 1990 Information Please Almanac*, (New York: Houghton Mifflin, 1990), pp. 83–85.
4. 38 Stat. 785; the Constitutionality was upheld in *United States v. Doremus*, 249 U.S. 86, 1919.
5. 50 Stat. 551; federal jurisdiction over marijuana is upheld in *United States v. Sanchez*, 350 U.S. 42 (1950).
6. California farmers engaged in an "opium revolt" against federal authorities subsequent to the passage of this act. See Edward Brecher, *Licit & Illicit Drugs* (Boston: Little, Brown, 1972).
7. 65 Stat. 767.
8. For a number of years marijuana was decriminalized in Alaska. In November 1990 the voting populace recriminalized marijuana.
9. 100 Stat. 3207.

NOTES

Chapter 12: Toward a More Perfect Union

1. Almost two-thirds of the addicts admitted to methadone maintenance programs in New York City were using heroin on a daily basis by the time they were eighteen. See Robert G. Newman and Margot S. Cates, *Methadone Treatment in Narcotic Addiction* (New York: Academic Press, 1977).

2. Andres Oppenheimer, "To Wound Cartels, Aim for Their Pocketbooks," *Miami Herald*, September 4, 1989, p. 1. See also Herald Wire Services, "First U.S. Anti-Drug Planes Arrive in Colombia," *Miami Herald*, September 4, 1989, p. 8; Robert Brooke, "U.S. Will Arm Peru to Fight Leftists in New Drug Push," *New York Times*, April 22, 1990, p. 1; and Linda Robinson and Gordon Witkin, "America's Deadly War in the Jungle," *U.S. News and World Report*, April 30, 1990, p. 26.

3. For a recent example, see Ron Winslow, "Spending to Cut Mental Health Costs," *Wall Street Journal*, December 13, 1989, p. B1. More generally, see John Wallace, "Treatment," in *Sixth Annual Special Report to the U.S. Congress on Alcohol and Health* (Washington, D.C.: Department of Health and Human Services, 1987). See also Leonard Saxe et al., *The Effectiveness and Costs of Alcoholism Treatment*, Health Technology Case Study no. 22 (Washington, D.C.: Office of Technology Assessment, 1983).

4. "Drug Treatment Programs Criticized," *Greenville News*, October 11, 1990, p. 18.

5. John Wallace, *Writings* (Newport, R.I.: Edgehill Publications, 1989).

6. Gina Kolata, "Experts Finding New Hope on Treating Crack Addicts," *New York Times*, August 24, 1989, p. 1. See also Kenneth H. Bacon, "Curtis Eagle's Story Shows How an Addict Can Conquer Cocaine," *Wall Street Journal*, August 2, 1989, p. 1; and R. A. Zaldivar, "Treatment Reduces Drug Abuse Sharply, National Study Finds," *Miami Herald*, November 17, 1989, p. 1.

7. Edward M. Brecher, *Licit & Illicit Drugs* (Boston: Little, Brown, 1972), p. 104.

8. Ibid. See also Newman and Cates, *Methadone Treatment*.

9. Ellen Benoit, "Drugs: A Case for Legalization," *Financial World*, October 3, 1989, p. 35.

10. For a sampling of some of the issues involved, see Wayne E. Green, "Drug Testing Becomes Corporate Mine Field," *Wall Street Journal*, November 21, 1989, p. B-1; "Here Come the Specimen Jars," *Time*, January 29, 1990, p. 60; Jim Lynch, "Splitting Hairs: Experts Debate Methods of Testing for Drugs," *Miami Herald*, September 21, 1990, p. C1; and Eugene Carlson, "Small Companies Have to Increase Anti-Drug Programs," *Wall Street Journal*, November 6, 1990, p. B2.

11. Ronald K. Siegal, *Intoxication: Life in Pursuit of Artificial Paradise* (New York: Dutton, 1989), p. 291.

12. Jan Hoffman, "Pregnant, Addicted—And Guilty?" *New York Times Magazine,* August 10, 1990, p. 33; Cathy Trost, "As Drug Babies Grow Older, Schools Strive to Meet Their Needs," *Wall Street Journal,* December 27, 1989, p. 1; Stanton Peele, "The New Thalidomide," *Reason,* July, 1990, p. 41; and Jacob Sullum, "The Suffering of Innocents," *Reason,* December 1989, p. 6.

Chapter 13: Challenges

1. Until November, 1990, marijuana was decriminalized in Alaska, where Professor Bernard Segal of the University of Alaska found that overall marijuana use among minors rose only slightly between 1983 and 1988, and that during the same period cocaine use "declined dramatically" to well below national rates. As reported in Richard Mauer, " 'Just Say No' Bombards Legalized Pot," *The Miami Herald,* November 3, 1990, p. 21.

2. *The Economist,* September 2, 1989, p. 24; Robert Scheer, "Drugs: Another Wrong War," *Playboy,* October 1990, p. 52; and Ellen Benoit, "Drugs: A Case for Legalization," *Financial World,* October 3, 1989, p. 34.

3. Ibid.

4. Ibid. See also "War by Other Means," *The Economist,* February 10, 1990, p. 50.

5. Dean R. Gerstein, "Alcohol Use and Consequences," in *Alcohol and Public Policy: Beyond the Shadow of Prohibition,* ed. Mark H. Moore and Dean R. Gerstein (Washington, D.C.: National Academy Press, 1981). See also Joseph Earl Dabney, *Mountain Spirits* (Asheville, N.C.: Bright Mountain Books, 1974).

Appendix A: Psychohistory

1. Edward M. Brecher, *Licit & Illicit Drugs* (Boston: Little, Brown, 1972); and Ronald K. Siegal, *Intoxication: Life in Pursuit of Artificial Paradise* (New York: Dutton, 1989), contain the most comprehensive surveys of various drugs. For additional details on any given drug, the references cited in the preceding chapters should be consulted.

2. Brecher, *Licit & Illicit Drugs,* p. 404.

3. Siegal, *Intoxication,* p. 217.

Appendix B: Legal Perspectives

1. See 28 C.J.S. Drugs and Narcotics Supp. §100, p. 133, n. 94.
2. 21 U.S.C.A. §§801, et seq. Also called the Controlled Substances Act of 1970.
3. See, for example, *Nicholas v. Board of Pharmacy*, 657 P.2d 216 (Or. App. 1983).
4. *U.S. v. La Froscia*, 354 F. Supp. 1338 (D.N.Y. 1973) and *Graham v. State*, 255 N.E. 2d 652, 253 Ind. 525 (1970).
5. *Nichols v. Board of Pharmacy*, 657 P. 2d at 219.
6. Uniform Controlled Substances Act (U.L.A.), Commissioner's Prefatory Note.
7. M.S.A. §152.027 subdiv. 4.
8. F.S.A. §893.13.
9. F.S.A. §775.083.
10. F.S.A. §775-082.
11. See, for example, *State v. Lee*, 382 P. Ed. 491, 62 Wash. 2d 228 (1963); *City of Seattle v. Ross*, 344 p. 2d 216, 54 Wash. 2d 655 (1959). See also *Whalen v. Roe*, 97 S. Ct. 869, 429 U.S. 589, 51 L.Ed. 2d 64 (1977); *Robinson v. State of Calif.*, 82 S. Ct. 1417, 370 U.S. 660, 8 L. Ed. 2d 758 (1962).
12. See 96 A.L.R. 3d §3 re due process and equal protection, §6 re right to privacy challenges, §7 re First Amendment challenges, and §9 re Ninth Amendment challenges.
13. *Whalen v. Roe* 97 S. Ct. 869, 429 U.S. 589, 51 L. Ed. 2d 64 (1977); *Robinson v. State of Calif.*, 82 S. Ct. 1417, 370 U.S. 660, 8 L. Ed. 2d 758 (1962). See also *Windfaire, Inc. v. Busbee*, 523 F. Supp. 868 (N.D. Ga. 1981); *Franza v. Carey* 518 F. Supp. 324 (S.D.N.Y. 1981). The U.S. Constitution imposes the delegated powers doctrine on only the federal government. Under the Tenth Amendment, all powers not exclusively delegated to the federal government, or prohibited by the Constitution, are reserved to the states.
14. See cases cited in note 11, supra. The term "police power" has no particular constitutional significance. It merely describes state legislative power to enact statutes and ordinances, all of which in one way or another promote the welfare of the citizens of the state or community.
15. There are three broad categories of constitutional limitations on the states' general legislative authority: express limitations which forbid specific forms of legislation, such as the Due Process and Equal Protection Clauses of the Fourteenth Amendment; judicial interpretations of constitutional language delegating specific powers to the federal government in terms which expressly or impliedly make such delegation exclusive; and limitations based on the federal government's exercise of one or more of its delegated powers, thereby invoking the supremacy clause and thus preempting state legislation.

16. *McCulloch v. Maryland*, 17 U.S. (4 Wheat.) 316 (1819).

17. The constitutional basis is the "necessary and proper" clause of Article I, Section 8 of the U.S. Constitution. The phrase has long been construed as permitting any measures which are "appropriate," not merely those which are essential or indispensable. *McCulloch v. Maryland* 17 U.S.(4 Wheat.) 316, 421 (1819).

18. The precise demarcation of the modern era is the seminal case of *N.L.R.B. v. Jones and Laughlin Steel Corp.*, 301 U.S. 1, 57 S. Ct. 615, 81 L. Ed. 893 (1937). See also *U.S. v. Darby*, 312 U.S. 100, 61 S. Ct. 451, 85 L. Ed. 609 (1941), overruling *Hammer v. Dagenhart*, 247 U.S. 251 (1918). Brest & Levinson point out that two distinct phases of the New Deal era are recognizable: an earlier period of corporatism, in which legislation such as the N.R.A. delegated regulatory power to industrial organizations; and, a latter period of welfarism, exemplified by the Fair Labor Standards Act and the Social Security Act. *Jones & Laughlin*, in this sense, is the dividing line between the earlier and latter periods. Paul Brest and Sanford Levinson, *The Process of Constitutional Decision Making: Cases and Materials*, 2nd ed. (Boston: Little, Brown, 1983), p. 313n16.

19. The Court's extreme deference to the legislative branch under the Commerce Clause is tempered only by the twofold requirement that there is some rational basis for finding a connection between the regulation and commerce, and that the means utilized are reasonably adapted to the ends sought under a particular policy scheme. *Hodel v. Virginia Surface Min. & Recl. Ass'n*, 452 U.S. 264 (1981).

20. As with state legislation, the legislation must not violate a constitutional restriction or a fundamental right.

21. See, for example, *Katzenbach v. McClung*, 379 U.S. 294 (1964).

22. *Reid v. Covert*, 352 U.S. 1 (1957).

23. See note 17, supra.

24. See, for example, *Foster v. Neilson*, 27 U.S. (2Pet.) 253 (1829), and *Whitney v. Robertson*, 124 U.S. 190 (1888).

25. *Chae Chan Ping v. United States*, 130 U.S. 581 (1889).

INDEX